T0327963

"This collection of essays points to the heart of one of the most pressing issues in the church today—the nature and task of spiritual formation. For pastors, academics, and laity alike, there is much here to be pondered and put into practice. Think alongside these thoughtful chapters and consider how we may faithfully engage the question of spiritual formation for the church today."
Kyle Strobel, associate professor of spiritual theology, Talbot School of Theology, Biola University, author of *Formed for the Glory of God*, editor of *Embracing Contemplation*

"This marvelous collection of thoughtful, well-researched essays will prove a boon to pastors and others engaged in spiritual formation. Though deeply rooted in the details of theological anthropology and modern psychology, they offer practical advice for tending to the needs of the whole person in the context of the church. Many thanks to the up-and-coming Center for Pastor Theologians for leading the way in the promotion of profound and utterly relevant ecclesial theology."
Douglas A. Sweeney, dean and professor of divinity, Beeson Divinity School

"Here we have a wonderful and eclectic set of essays that respectfully challenge many of the assumptions of the contemporary spiritual formation movement. This type of careful work, which is informed by the realities of church life, aware of social science findings, and committed to fresh theological reflection on spiritual formation is so important today. While this volume challenges many of the current assumptions and ways of framing spiritual formation, it does so with a respectful and constructive tone. It is worth reading to help one move beyond slogans to the kind of theory building that will enrich our spiritual formation."
James C. Wilhoit, professor of core studies and Scripture Press Professor of Christian Education, Wheaton College

"In the church we have often failed to integrate our spiritual life with the rest of our humanity, resulting in a truncated vision of discipleship. We rightly emphasize evangelism, Bible reading, and prayer but are underprepared to help the mentally ill, the lonely, the addicted, or the traumatized. These helpful essays draw from multiple disciplines and address a wide array of topics to encourage a more holistic understanding of spiritual formation."
Gavin Ortlund, senior pastor of First Baptist Church of Ojai

"I can hardly imagine a book that speaks more fully and directly into the issues I am dealing with as a pastor than *Tending Soul, Mind, and Body*. In our Southern California church, we say that when people come to faith in Jesus and become a part of our church family, we will give attention to the growth and development of the whole of their lives until 'each one is complete in Christ' (Col 1:28). However, that statement means that we have to address issues related to people's emotional challenges, physical well-being, mental health, and spiritual nurture. I find I need help from scholars and practitioners, theologians and psychologists, as well as anthropologists and exegetes. This book brings together all these resources. It is a relevant, excellent, and much-needed volume that speaks to the most important issues of our human condition while being firmly rooted in the gospel. I recommend it without reservation."

Greg Waybright, senior pastor, Lake Avenue Church, Pasadena, California

TENDING SOUL, MIND, AND BODY

THE ART *and* SCIENCE *of* SPIRITUAL FORMATION

EDITED BY GERALD HIESTAND
& TODD WILSON

Academic
An imprint of InterVarsity Press
Downers Grove, Illinois

InterVarsity Press
P.O. Box 1400, Downers Grove, IL 60515-1426
ivpress.com
email@ivpress.com

InterVarsity Press® is the book-publishing division of InterVarsity Christian Fellowship/USA®, a movement of students and faculty active on campus at hundreds of universities, colleges, and schools of nursing in the United States of America, and a member movement of the International Fellowship of Evangelical Students. For information about local and regional activities, visit intervarsity.org.

All Scripture quotations, unless otherwise indicated, are taken from The Holy Bible, New International Version®, NIV®. Copyright © 1973, 1978, 1984, 2011 by Biblica, Inc.™ Used by permission of Zondervan. All rights reserved worldwide. www.zondervan.com. The "NIV" and "New International Version" are trademarks registered in the United States Patent and Trademark Office by Biblica, Inc.™

Cover design and image composite: David Fassett
Interior design: Beth McGill
Images: The Adoration of the Shepherds by Guido Reni at Pushkin Museum, Moscow, Russia/Bridgeman

ISBN 978-0-8308-5387-8 (print)
ISBN 978-0-8308-7050-9 (digital)

Printed in the United States of America ∞

InterVarsity Press is committed to ecological stewardship and to the conservation of natural resources in all our operations. This book was printed using sustainably sourced paper.

Library of Congress Cataloging-in-Publication Data

Names: Center for Pastor Theologians. Theology Conference (4th : 2018 : Chicago, Ill.), author. | Hiestand, Gerald, 1974- editor. | Wilson, Todd A., 1976- editor. | Center for Pastor Theologians, issuing body.

Title: Tending soul, mind, and body : the art and science of spiritual formation / edited by Gerald Hiestand & Todd Wilson.

Description: Downers Grove, Illinois : IVP Academic, an imprint of InterVarsity Press, [2019] | Includes bibliographical references and index.

Identifiers: LCCN 2019027276 (print) | LCCN 2019027277 (ebook) | ISBN 9780830853878 (paperback) | ISBN 9780830870509 (ebook)

Subjects: LCSH: Spiritual formation—Congresses. | Theological anthropology—Christianity—Congresses. | Psychology, Religious—Congresses.

Classification: LCC BV4511 .C454 2019 (print) | LCC BV4511 (ebook) | DDC 253.5—dc23

LC record available at https://lccn.loc.gov/2019027276

LC ebook record available at https://lccn.loc.gov/2019027277

| P | 22 | 21 | 20 | 19 | 18 | 17 | 16 | 15 | 14 | 13 | 12 | 11 | 10 | 9 | 8 | 7 | 6 | 5 | 4 | 3 | 2 | 1 |
| Y | 39 | 38 | 37 | 36 | 35 | 34 | 33 | 32 | 31 | 30 | 29 | 28 | 27 | 26 | 25 | 24 | 23 | 22 | 21 | 20 | 19 | |

To Jack Nicholson, Scott Gibson, and Elliott Grudem

Contents

Acknowledgments

WE ARE GRATEFUL TO THOSE who presented at the annual Center for Pastor Theologians conference and whose contributions are now gathered together in this present volume. These essays provide pastoral leaders and churches with much-needed wisdom, guidance, and insight. We are grateful to partner with such an excellent group of ecclesial theologians, academic theologians, scientists, cultural critics, and Christian leaders.

We likewise owe a debt of gratitude to the Center for Pastor Theologians, the organizer of the conference from which the papers of this book are drawn. The Center continues to serve as a catalyst for our work and has been a repository of wisdom and counsel on all things pastoral and theological. The board and staff of the Center deserve our warmest thanks.

Since its inception, Calvary Memorial Church in Oak Park, Illinois, has graciously hosted our annual conference. We are thankful to the elders, staff, and congregation for their continued support and encouragement.

We are also grateful for our partnership with IVP Academic and for their commitment to ecclesial theology and the Center's vision for the pastor theologian. We are especially thankful for our editor, Dr. David McNutt, whose enthusiastic participation in the production of this book has gone a long way toward making it a reality.

For our families, and most especially our wives, we remain ever grateful. Their gracious support of us in the midst of our already busy schedules is a gift that we do not take lightly.

Finally, we would like to dedicate this volume to three individuals who have helped us tend our own souls: Jack Nicholson of SageQuest Consulting, Scott Gibson of Compass Counseling, and Elliott Grudem of Leaders Collective. Their grace, wisdom, and insight have helped us become more integrated human beings.

Introduction

The Art and Science of Spiritual Formation

GERALD HIESTAND
AND TODD WILSON

Tʜᴇ Cᴇɴᴛᴇʀ ғᴏʀ Pᴀsᴛᴏʀ Tʜᴇᴏʟᴏɢɪᴀɴs has a mission, and it is very simple. We exist to help pastors be theologians for today's complex world. The Center's vision is to see pastors as theologians leading thriving congregations that nurture faithful Christians who cultivate renewed communities. This, in a nutshell, is why we exist.

Our annual theology conference, hosted each October at Calvary Memorial Church in Oak Park, Illinois, brings together some of today's most thoughtful pastors, theologians, nonprofit leaders, practitioners, and ordinary Christians, to wrestle with an area of pressing concern for Christian faithfulness in the late modern world.

This past October 2018 was our fourth conference, and our topic proved to be no less fascinating than years past. Our theme was the Art and Science of Spiritual Formation, and it drew together an outstanding group of presenters and participants from a variety of walks of life, academic disciplines, and fields of service. Many were pastors. But we also enjoyed the presence of scholars, scientists, counselors, and many faithful lay Christians—all of whom were there to grapple with the integration of spiritual formation, theological anthropology, modern psychology, and contemporary brain science.

Several themes emerged from the fascinating array of presentations that nicely reinforced the conference theme. First of all, there was a clear recognition that spiritual formation is indeed *an art*. Attaining Christlikeness isn't as simple as screwing in a light bulb. Nor is it as straightforward as tying your shoes. Spiritual formation is the process whereby fallen human beings respond to God's grace and grow in Christ's likeness. As much as we have learned from advances in the fields of psychology, psychiatry, and brain science over the last half-century, we will never fully comprehend how God uses sometimes very ordinary means to re-create us in the image of his Son. There is something wonderfully mysterious and irreducibly complex—even art-like—about how broken people become more like Jesus.

A second theme that emerged at the conference and is now reflected in these essays is that spiritual formation is also *a science*. Or at least there are helpful insights to be gained by approaching the process of spiritual formation with an awareness of the last fifty years of advances in psychology, psychiatry, and neuroscience. Human beings are embodied creatures, and our brains—with their millions of synapses and neural pathways—are vital to everything we think, do, and feel. And while the brain remains the most complex entity in our universe, those who study its workings have helped us appreciate that there are genuinely important insights here for Christians interested in the process of spiritual formation.

There is a third and final theme worth mentioning. It is also the most important—*the Spirit is the Lord of spiritual formation*. Ultimately, formation into Christlikeness is not the result of human effort or self-will. Nor is it simply the byproduct of more prayer, more therapy, more Bible study, more positive psychology, more of anything! Instead, it is a new creational reality brought about by the Sovereign Spirit who is the Lord and Giver of Life. In the words of the Apostle Paul, "we all, with unveiled face, beholding the glory of the Lord, are being transformed into the same image form one degree of glory to another. For this comes from the Lord who is the Spirit" (2 Cor 3:18 ESV).

As conveners of this conference, and now as editors of this volume of essays, we offer this collection of scholarly and pastoral contributions to you with both gratitude and hope—we are grateful for seasoned and substantive Christian reflection on a wide range of issues pertinent to growing in Christlikeness, and we are hopeful that both pastors and congregations will be, even in some small way, better equipped to engage today's complex world, bearing the image of Christ, all for the sake of Christ.

Soli Deo gloria!

Part One

BIBLICAL, THEOLOGICAL, *and* HISTORICAL REFLECTIONS

1

Socialization and the Sanctuary

The Arrangement of 1 Corinthians
as a Strategy for Spiritual Formation

DANIEL J. BRENDSEL

First Corinthians: Occasional Literature Par Excellence

It is the delight of many first-year seminary students to disabuse their congregations of the assumption that the New Testament letters are timeless
treatises or systematic theologies. On the contrary, these writings are occasional literature. They were written on specific occasions, in and for specific
times, places, and circumstances. When St. James and St. Peter and St. Paul
picked up their pens to write letters, their clear intent was to speak directly
to first-century churches, addressing the contemporary and contextual experiences of those churches.

What we call St. Paul's First Letter to the Corinthians is the poster child
of occasional literature. One would be hard-pressed to find in contemporary
systematic theology textbooks talk of lawsuits among believers or visiting of
prostitutes, much less *direct charges* to readers to stop engaging in such
things! But this is more or less what 1 Corinthians *is*: direct exhortation
concerning specific and time-bound challenges facing a church in Roman
Corinth. Part of the reason for the difference in content between Paul's letter
and contemporary systematic theologies is the differences of intended audience. The latter are typically written for a "general readership." They studi-
ously avoid addressing specific Christians and local congregations, if for no

other reason than that to write for such a localized and historically rooted audience would seem to severely truncate the "shelf-life" of such "resources." Paul in 1 Corinthians clearly has no such concern, boldly and directly speaking his words into the specific disorders manifesting themselves at a particular time and place. What Paul writes is in response to what "Chloe's household have informed me" concerning quarreling and factionalism in the Corinthian church (1 Cor 1:11). He likely takes up topics raised in personal dialogue with Stephanas, Fortunatus, and Achaicus (1 Cor 16:17). Paul addresses several matters concerning which the Corinthian Christians inquired in a letter they wrote to him (1 Cor 7:1). The contents of 1 Corinthians constitute Paul's direct response to a particular set of circumstances in the first-century church at Corinth. This is occasional literature par excellence, certainly a finalist in the (entirely fictitious) contest for "most occasional of the New Testament letters," together with perhaps Paul's Letter to Philemon.

One significant way in which 1 Corinthians differs from Philemon, other than the obvious difference of length, is that the latter is arranged as a single, sustained argument, while the former seems more scattered in its arrangement with no overarching argument. There is in 1 Corinthians 1–4 some sustained focus on wisdom and foolishness, but from 1 Corinthians 5 on, we move rapidly and seemingly randomly through a bevy of topics (see figure 1). There is little difficulty in determining where in 1 Corinthians Paul shifts to new topics, where the minor and major breaks in the letter are. The real difficulty lies in discerning what, if *anything*, provides cohesion and coherence for all of the materials of 1 Corinthians. As Frédéric Godet asked at the end of the nineteenth century, "Will the First Epistle to the Corinthians be a heap or a building?"[1]

NOW ABOUT THE ARRANGEMENT OF WHAT PAUL WROTE

Not surprisingly, some in the history of interpretation have concluded not only that 1 Corinthians is a "heap," but also that this "heap" is something of a garbage collection site for leftover building materials from *different* building projects. That is to say, partition theories concerning 1 Corinthians

---

[1]F. Godet, *Commentary on St. Paul's First Epistle to the Corinthians*, trans. A. Cusin, 2 vols. (Edinburgh: T&T Clark, 1889), 1:27, quoted in Margaret M. Mitchell, *Paul and the Rhetoric of Reconciliation: An Exegetical Investigation of the Language and Composition of 1 Corinthians*, HUT 26 (Tübingen: Mohr [Siebeck], 1991; repr., Louisville, KY: Westminster John Knox, 1993), 184.

Figure 1. The topics addressed in 1 Corinthians

I. Letter Opening: Greeting and Thanksgiving (1 Cor 1:1-9)

II. Letter Body: Ten(ish) Topics (1 Cor 1:10–16:12)

    A. Reports About Wisdom, Rhetoric, and Division at Corinth (1 Cor 1:10–4:21)

       "Some from Chloe's household have informed me that . . ." (1 Cor 1:11)

    B. Reports about Immorality and Lawsuits at Corinth (1 Cor 5:1–6:20)

       "It is actually reported that . . ." (1 Cor 5:1)

       1. An Incestuous Relationship (1 Cor 5:1-13)

       2. Lawsuits with Brothers and Sisters in Christ (1 Cor 6:1-11)

       3. "The Right to Do Anything," Going to Prostitutes (1 Cor 6:12-20)

    C. "Now About" Marriage (1 Cor 7:1-24)

    D. "Now About" Virgins (1 Cor 7:25-40)

    E. "Now About" Food Sacrificed to Idols and Feasts at Idol Temples (1 Cor 8:1–11:1)

    F. On Head Coverings in Corporate Worship (1 Cor 11:2-16)

    G. Reports of Division and Exclusion at the Lord's Supper (1 Cor 11:17-34)

       "I hear that when you come together as a church . . ." (1 Cor 11:18)

    H. "Now About" Spiritual Gifts Used in the Public Assembly (1 Cor 12:1–14:40)

    I. On the Resurrection of Christ and the Body (1 Cor 15:1-58)

       "How can some of you say that there is no resurrection of the dead?" (1 Cor 15:12)

    J. "Now About" the Collection and Future Travel Plans (1 Cor 16:1-12)

III. Letter Closing: Final Exhortations and Greetings (1 Cor 16:13-24)

are not uncommon in the secondary literature.[2] Many others, while persuaded that there is no necessary reason to question the literary integrity of 1 Corinthians, still conceive of 1 Corinthians as more "heap" than "building." As Bruce Winter comments, "There is a tendency in the study of 1 Corinthians to see various sections in the letter as dealing with a discreet issue after which Paul turns to another problem. The issues are judged to be quite independent of each other."[3]

---

[2]For discussion, see Mitchell, *Paul and the Rhetoric of Reconciliation*, 2-5; John Coolidge Hurd Jr., *The Origin of I Corinthians*, 2nd ed. (Macon, GA: Mercer University Press, 1983), 43-47.

[3]Bruce W. Winter, *After Paul Left Corinth: The Influence of Secular Ethics and Social Change* (Grand Rapids: Eerdmans, 2001), 86.

This is not to say that interpreters of 1 Corinthians discern no logic at all
in the structure and arrangement of the letter. At times, for example, coherence in the arrangement of 1 Corinthians has been sought in conformity
with Greco-Roman rhetorical forms.[4] What seems much more common, at
least at the level of popular and ecclesial exposition, is to posit cohesion in
the arrangement of 1 Corinthians in terms of what kinds of reports Paul
responds to from section to section. That is to say, it is often asserted (though
less often *argued*[5]) that Paul responds first to oral reports about Corinthian
disorder received directly from Chloe's people and Stephanas, Fortunatus,
and Achaicus, and second to the Corinthians' written inquiries in the letter
they wrote to him.

Paul's statement in 1 Corinthians 7:1, "Now for the matters you wrote
about . . . ," is seen as the dividing line. Five more times in the rest of the letter,
Paul uses the phrase "now about" (περὶ δὲ at 1 Cor 7:25; 8:1; 12:1; 16:1, 12). Each
time it is typically read as introducing a direct response to a point from the
Corinthian church's letter. It is not hard to find an outline of 1 Corinthians
1–6 that presents those chapters as Paul's "response to oral reports," and
1 Corinthians 7–16 as his "response to the Corinthian letter," something of a
point-by-point reply to their written inquiries.[6] This is to locate the coherence
of the letter's arrangement in the occasion or impetus for the writing, rather
than in the contents of the writing itself. Or to return to the imagery of
Godet's inquiry, if 1 Corinthians is not a "heap" but a "building," then for
many the "building" is less a purposefully planned and well-ordered work of
a master architect, and more a fort built ad hoc with whatever sticks and
stones were at hand. It is my conviction that such a construal of 1 Corinthians
fails to adequately explain the arrangement and structure of the letter, falling
short on at least three counts.

First, it attempts to squeeze out of the phrase περὶ δὲ ("now about") more
than is necessary or justifiable. Clearly, Paul uses this phrase to introduce
his response to a written inquiry about sexual relations at 1 Corinthians 7:1.
But the fact of the matter is that 1 Corinthians 7:1 is the *only* place where Paul,

---

[4]See, particularly, the influential study of Mitchell, *Paul and the Rhetoric of Reconciliation*, 20-64.
[5]Hurd, *Origin of I Corinthians*, 61-94, is one of the few exceptions.
[6]E.g., C. K. Barrett, *The First Epistle to the Corinthians*, HNTC (New York: Harper & Row, 1968),
28-29; Gordon D. Fee, *The First Epistle to the Corinthians*, rev. ed., NICNT (Grand Rapids: Eerdmans, 2014), viii-xi.

in using περὶ δὲ, explicitly says that he is addressing a matter raised by the letter from Corinth. He might be doing so in each of the other uses of περὶ δὲ, but we need not assume it from the outset. In fact, in 1989 Margaret Mitchell put together an impressive survey of the phrase περὶ δὲ in ancient Greek literature and letters. Mitchell concluded,

> The formula περὶ δὲ, as found in a wide variety of ancient Greek texts (with particular emphasis on letters), is simply a topic marker, a shorthand way of introducing the next subject of discussion. Although this formula *can* be used in response to information received by letter, it is surely *not restricted* to this use, even in letters which mention a previous letter. By the formula περὶ δὲ an author introduces a new topic *the only requirement of which is that it is readily known to both author and reader.* In itself the formula περὶ δὲ gives no information about how the author or reader became informed of the topic, nor does it give information about the order of presentation of topics.[7]

I am inclined to agree with Mitchell's analysis. All that the formula περὶ δὲ by itself in 1 Corinthians requires is that the topic to which Paul turns "is readily known to both the Corinthians and Paul *from some element of their shared experience.*"[8] Its presence alone cannot tell us more.

It is worth adding that neither does the absence of περὶ δὲ indicate that Paul must *not* have the Corinthians' letter in view.[9] When Paul clarifies his exhortation "not to associate with immoral people" in 1 Corinthians 5:9-13, or addresses lawsuits among believers in 1 Corinthians 6:1-11, or rebukes the church with reference to the motto "I have the right to do anything" and the visiting of prostitutes in 1 Corinthians 6:12-20, he could very well be responding to issues that the Corinthians touched on in their letter.[10] With respect to that last-mentioned passage, it is reasonable to suppose that Paul

---

[7]Margaret M. Mitchell, "Concerning ΠΕΡΙ ΔΕ in 1 Corinthians," *Novum Testamentum* 31 (1989): 233-34, emphasis original.

[8]Mitchell, "Concerning ΠΕΡΙ ΔΕ," 256, emphasis original. Long before Mitchell's work, Archibald Robertson and Alfred Plummer show proper restraint in their comments concerning περὶ δὲ (see *A Critical and Exegetical Commentary on the First Epistle of St. Paul to the Corinthians*, 2nd ed., ICC [Edinburgh: T&T Clark, 1914], xxiv-xxv). For criticism of Mitchell's basic thesis, see David G. Horrell, *The Social Ethos of the Corinthian Correspondence: Interests and Ideology from 1 Corinthians to 1 Clement* (London: T&T Clark, 1996), 90.

[9]Mitchell, "Concerning ΠΕΡΙ ΔΕ," 256.

[10]See Joseph A. Fitzmyer, *First Corinthians*, AYB 32 (New Haven, CT: Yale University Press, 2008), 263.

knows that "I have the right to do anything" was a motto of the Corinthian Christians because they used it in their letter.[11] The only reason interpreters would not entertain this possibility is that they have already assumed that Paul orders his letter in such a way that direct engagement with and response to the letter from Corinth is reserved for 1 Corinthians 7 and after.

There is a second, more glaring problem with the assumption that 1 Corinthians is arranged neatly to address first oral reports and second written inquiries. Even if Paul does, in fact, use περὶ δὲ to introduce his responses to the Corinthian letter,[12] this does not alter the fact that Paul still clearly responds to what he hears, to oral reportage, in 1 Corinthians 7–16. "I *hear* that when you come together as a church," Paul says in 1 Corinthians 11:18, "there are divisions among you." Paul's rebukes concerning the celebration of the Eucharist in 1 Corinthians 11:17-34 are, at least in part, owing to what he has heard by way of oral report.[13] We might also suggest that 1 Corinthians 15:12, "How can some of you *say* that there is no resurrection of the dead?" implies that Paul has *heard* what some are *saying* by way of spoken communication. But 1 Corinthians 11:18 is sufficient to indicate that the supposed division of the letter into response-to-oral-communication followed by response-to-written-communication does not hold.[14] Whatever accounts for the arrangement of this letter, it cannot be the simple shifting of Paul's attention from one source of news about the state of the church to another.

This brings us to the third and, I believe, the greatest problem with the common take on 1 Corinthians. It strikes me as inherently implausible that Paul's discussion "adopts a merely reactive stance,"[15] more or less following the lead of the reports and letter from Corinth. To say it differently, it is inherently implausible that Paul has no pastoral strategy in the order in which he treats topics in this letter, but is simply reacting in real time to whatever stimuli comes next, whether an oral report or a letter.[16]

---

[11]Cf. Ben Witherington III, *Conflict and Community in Corinth: A Socio-Rhetorical Commentary on 1 and 2 Corinthians* (Grand Rapids: Eerdmans, 1995), 167.

[12]I suspect that he does in most of its occurrences in the letter; I am more circumspect about 1 Cor 16:1, 12.

[13]See also Witherington, *Conflict and Community in Corinth*, 38.

[14]See also Fitzmyer, *First Corinthians*, 51-52, on, e.g., 1 Cor 8:1; 12:1.

[15]A. C. Thiselton, *The First Epistle to the Corinthians*, NIGTC (Grand Rapids: Eerdmans, 2000), 40, in agreement with the point I'm making here.

[16]Martinus C. de Boer, "The Composition of 1 Corinthians," *New Testament Studies* 40 (1994):

There's a mock proverb that says, "Choose your interlocutors with care, for some will try to steal the conversation and change the subject."[17] I propose that Paul is not letting the Corinthians steal the conversation or dictate the subjects, rules, and order of discussion. To do so would be to let a people whose structure of thought and imagination is badly disordered by false, idolatrous wisdom skew the results from the outset. We should not presume that this supremely occasional letter is, for that reason, arbitrary or merely reactive in its arrangement. Rather, Paul is intentionally, strategically, pastorally crafting an overall argument.[18] By the very order of his letter he would seek to order the Corinthian church aright.

SOCIALIZATION AND THE SANCTUARY: CIVIC FORMATION UNTO WISDOM

The crucial question thus arises: How might we articulate the pastoral strategy at work in the ordering of 1 Corinthians? Can we discern any organizational rhyme or reason? In the space remaining, I will offer something of a content and discourse analysis of 1 Corinthians.[19] More precisely, I will seek to articulate, from the perspective of theological subject matter and pastoral responsibility, the strategy of the order in which Paul addresses the disorders at Corinth.

I use the language of *culture* at the broadest level of my proposed outline, though it is admittedly foreign to the text of 1 Corinthians itself. I think it helpfully names some of the key judgments that Paul is making in the letter. Consider it a heuristic device to illuminate what is at stake at Corinth and what Paul is doing for the Corinthians in this letter's arrangement. The language of culture and cultural formation is also useful for underlining the pastoral implications of the order of 1 Corinthians for our own pastoral pursuits in the present.

229-45, accounts for the seeming jerkiness of the contents of 1 Cor in this way—new information arrives from Corinth in various waves, which waves are inscribed in the present form of 1 Cor, as it were, by the shifts in Paul's responses and tones.

[17]Peter J. Leithart, *Against Christianity* (Moscow, ID: Canon, 2003), 53.

[18]In any case, 1 Cor 11:34 clearly indicates that Paul has been selective in writing. We may rightly ask what, if any, principle of selectivity has governed the inclusion (and ordering) of topics.

[19]Mitchell, too, provides a "content analysis" in her study of 1 Cor (*Paul and the Rhetoric of Reconciliation*, 187), while rightly acknowledging that the flow of the contents of the letter (like any complex and profound literary work) is susceptible to several plausible analyses (207).

Figure 2. A conceptual outline of 1 Corinthians

I.   Letter Opening: Greeting to and Thanksgiving for "Saints" by Calling
     (1 Cor 1:1-9)

II. Two Wisdoms, Two Ways/Walks (1 Cor 1:10–4:21)

     A. Corinthian Divisions and Corinthian Rejection of Paul (1 Cor 1:10-17)

     B. The Wisdom of God Versus the Wisdom of the World (1 Cor 1:18–3:4)

     C. The Wise Master Architect and Other True Builders of God's Temple
        (1 Cor 3:5–4:5)

     D. Christlike Servants of Christ: Suffering and *Parousia* (1 Cor 4:6-21)

III. Alignments with Idolatrous Culture (1 Cor 5:1–11:1)

     A. Reports About Immorality and Lawsuits (1 Cor 5:1–6:20)

        1. An Incestuous Relationship (1 Cor 5:1-13)

        2. Lawsuits with Brothers and Sisters in Christ (1 Cor 6:1-11)

        3. Going to Prostitutes: "Flee from Sexual Immorality" (1 Cor 6:12-20)

     B. "Now About" Marriage, Celibacy, and Sexuality (1 Cor 7:1-40)

     C. "Now About" Food Sacrificed to Idols (1 Cor 8:1–11:1)

              a Knowledge, Freedom, and Love: "An Idol Is Nothing at All"
                 (1 Cor 8:1-13)

                   b Paul's Way of Self-Denying Love for the Sake of the Gospel
                      (1 Cor 9:1-27)

              a' Conflicting Communions (or Liturgies): "Flee from Idolatry"
                 (1 Cor 10:1–11:1)

IV. Tackling Cultural Renewal Head-On (1 Cor 11:2–14:40)

     A. On Head Coverings in Corporate Worship (1 Cor 11:2-16)

     B. Reports of Division and Exclusion at the Lord's Supper (1 Cor 11:17-34)

     C. "Now About" Spiritual Gifts (1 Cor 12:1–14:40)

              a Varieties of Gifts but the Same Spirit for the Common Good
                 (1 Cor 12:1-31)

                   b Knowledge, Gifting, and the More Excellent Way of Love
                      (1 Cor 13:1-13)

              a' Prophecy and Practice in Corporate Worship (1 Cor 14:1-40)

V. The Source and Substance of True Culture: The Resurrection of the King
    (1 Cor 15:1–16:12)

     A. On the Resurrection of Christ and the Body (1 Cor 15:1-58)

     B. "Now About" the Collection and Future Travel Plans (1 Cor 16:1-12)

VI. Letter Closing: Final Exhortation to Courage and Final Greetings
    (1 Cor 16:13-24)

Two wisdoms, two "ways" (1 Cor 1:10–4:21). I agree with those interpreters who identify a central problem at the Corinthian church to be idolatrous and disordered "wisdom."[20] This is why Paul spends so much time addressing the "wisdom of the world" versus God's "foolishness" at the outset in 1 Corinthians 1–4.

Commentaries frequently discuss various "isms" and thought structures (e.g., Gnosticism, Stoicism, Hellenistic Judaism, overrealized eschatology) as the key background to the clash of wisdoms that Paul addresses. Some have been debunked or rightly questioned. But whatever the backgrounds of the Corinthian problems, a crucial question remains to be answered: *How* did false wisdom actually infiltrate the church?[21] Many treatments give the impression that such infiltration happened by way of a studious reading of Greco-Roman philosophy, since competing "wisdoms" are typically epitomized by quotation of philosophical texts. But deep engagement with the literary products of what we might call "elite culture" in the first-century Roman world seems unlikely for a community among whom there were "not many . . . wise by human standards; not many were mighty; not many were of noble birth" (1 Cor 1:26).[22] Alternatively, we might think of the Corinthians being formed in various "wisdoms" by way of tutelage at the feet of various orators. But such tutelage would have been important not only for delivery of philosophical content to the mind but also and especially as a "pattern of behavior."[23]

By way of analogy, David Wells points out in *Above All Earthly Pow'rs* that the fall of Enlightenment modernism, and the flourishing relativism and nihilism of Western society, are most likely not the direct products of postmodern textbooks and teachings:

> Intellectuals like Foucault and Derrida are undoubtedly contributors to postmodern thinking, but what is often left unexplained is how we get from

---

[20]See, e.g., Witherington, *Conflict and Community in Corinth*, 337; cf. David R. Hall, *The Unity of the Corinthian Correspondence*, JSNTSup 251 (London: T&T Clark, 2003), 30.

[21]See similarly John M. G. Barclay, "Thessalonica and Corinth: Social Contrasts in Pauline Christianity," *Journal for the Study of the New Testament* 47 (1992): 66-72.

[22]Cf. Bradley J. Bitner, *Paul's Political Strategy in 1 Corinthians 1–4: Constitution and Covenant*, SNTSMS 163 (Cambridge: Cambridge University Press, 2015), 4, 46-47. For a plausible "social profile" of the church at Corinth, see Craig Steven de Vos, *Church and Community Conflicts: The Relationships of the Thessalonian, Corinthian, and Philippian Churches with Their Wider Civic Communities*, SBLDS 168 (Atlanta: Scholars Press, 1999), 197-203.

[23]Witherington, *Conflict and Community in Corinth*, 100.

Foucault to MTV, from Derrida to the centerless young people whose canopy of meaning in life has collapsed, from Fish and Rorty to our movies. Are we really to suppose that this is to be explained by an assiduous reading of these authors? Furthermore, why is the whole far-flung Enlightenment enterprise, which has been deeply entrenched in American society, coming down *now*? Is it credible to think that this massive edifice is being toppled by thinkers whose writing is often elusive, complex, and inaccessible? In an age not given much to reading and thought, this seems unlikely.[24]

For Wells, postmodern sensibilities are planted and watered more by our cultural milieu—our cultural patterns, practices, products, and postures—than by mere information, ideas, and discursive argumentation. Postmodern ideas make more sense, seem more plausible or natural or normal, in certain environments than in others. Ours is one such environment.

Similarly in first-century Corinth, we may rightly assume that the "wisdom" seducing the Corinthian church away from the wisdom of God was instilled in them not only or chiefly through considered study and instruction but also through cultural practice. It was less about didacticism and more about everyday discipleship and practical formation. So a crucial pastoral consideration for Paul (and for us) is how Christians are practically formed in idolatrous wisdom. Paul must attend not only to the Corinthians' thought life but also to their lived life, their enacted way of life and walk. Indeed, Paul rebukes the church in 1 Corinthians 3:3 not for "*thinking* like mere humans" but for "*acting* like mere humans." It is their everyday, culturally conditioned walk that clarifies,[25] crystalizes, and, we can add, *cultivates* their fleshliness, their foolishness, their thrall to the wisdom of the world. If the Corinthians are enamored with "the wisdom of the world," then most likely their infatuation is directly tied to lives practically marked by the way of the world, by worldly, idolatrous culture.

Alignments with idolatrous culture (1 Cor 5:1–11:1). That is precisely what we see in 1 Corinthians 5:1–11:1. The movement from 1 Corinthians 1–4, with its sustained focus on wisdom, to the plethora of "practical" matters in

---

[24]David F. Wells, *Above All Earthly Pow'rs: Christ in a Postmodern World* (Grand Rapids: Eerdmans, 2005), 65, emphasis original.

[25]The καί in the final clause of 1 Cor 3:3 is likely epexegetical (Fee, *The First Epistle to the Corinthians*, 136).

1 Corinthians 5–10 is not arbitrary, or a reflexive reaction to new reports from Corinth. It is Paul cutting off false wisdom at some of its concrete sources. The Corinthian church imbibes, enacts, and reinforces idolatrous wisdom by participating in the social and liturgical ceremonies, customs, and configurations of the idolatrous Corinthian culture. They are "called" to be saints (1 Cor 1:2). They are called to be set apart from the culture around them, called to manifest the striking division between the kingdom of light and the kingdoms of darkness.[26] But far from being peculiar to the broader culture, the Corinthian church looks just like it. They are not divided from "the world" but divided among themselves in self-seeking, like the kingdoms of the world (1 Cor 6:1-11). They mimic worldly sexual ethics (1 Cor 6:12-20), being as ignorant about sexual order as the society around them (1 Cor 7:1-40). In fact, they one-up the pagan culture in immorality (1 Cor 5:1-13), even joining it in its feasts and rituals at the temples of idols (1 Cor 8–10).[27] Is it any wonder that a church so caught up in idolatrous cultural practice is enthralled by the wisdom embodied by such practice?

It is worth pausing to note how hard it would have been for the Corinthians to live any differently. Paul writes to adult converts, and, in fact, to the first converts in Corinthian society—which is to say, he writes to people whose socialization and enculturation, from the cradle on, was pagan and Corinthian. Ben Witherington has rightly highlighted just the kind of challenge this creates for the Corinthians and for Paul writing to them:

> The conversion of an adult to a new religion is a form of *secondary* socialization.
> . . . Usually the values gained in primary socialization, that is, while growing

---

[26]On Paul's concern in 1 Cor for drawing sharp boundaries between church and "world," see, e.g., Edward Adams, *Constructing the World: A Study in Paul's Cosmological Language* (Edinburgh: T&T Clark, 2000), 87-99.

[27]Importantly, 1 Cor 8–10 does not introduce a topic largely disconnected from what precedes. Ciampa and Rosner note that in 1 Cor 6:18, 20, Paul exhorts the Corinthians to "flee from sexual immorality" and "honor God," and in 1 Cor 10:14, 31, Paul exhorts the Corinthians to "flee from idolatry" and "do it all for the glory of God." The slogan "I have the right to do anything" also appears in both sections (see Roy E. Ciampa and Brian S. Rosner, *The First Letter to the Corinthians*, PiNTC [Grand Rapids: Eerdmans, 2010], 23; cf. Stephen C. Barton, "Food Rules, Sex Rules and Idolatry: What's the Connection? An Essay in New Testament Theology," in *Idolatry: False Worship in the Bible, Early Judaism, and Christianity*, ed. S. C. Barton [New York: T&T Clark, 2007], 141-62). The *formal* parallels between the endings of 1 Cor 6 and 10 highlight the *material* parallels in the discussions they conclude. "Flee from immorality" (1 Cor 6:18) and "flee from idolatry" (1 Cor 10:14) are two sides of the same coin: idolatrous commitments and bonds are enacted/reinforced in immoral and disordered cultural pursuits.

up, remain throughout life. A dramatic *volte face* or change in life setting is usually necessary to redirect an adult's life orientation and pattern. Paul's converts remained where they converted, e.g., in Corinth, and Paul encouraged them not to withdraw from the world totally. Deinculturation would have been difficult. Paul's basic strategy in Corinth was to emphasize that eschatological events of the past, present, and future had relativized the present world order and that the schema of this world was passing away (1 Cor. 7:31).[28]

Witherington draws on the influential sociological research of Peter Berger and Thomas Luckmann. As Berger and Luckmann note, one's primary socialization leaves a lasting imprint all through life: "already internalized reality has a tendency to persist."[29] A project in secondary socialization such as Paul's with the Corinthian church begins, as it were, at a major disadvantage. It is necessarily an uphill climb. Witherington rightly emphasizes how hard it would be for the church to turn away from everything they had been socialized and habituated to consider normal. But Witherington does not go far enough in concluding that Paul's "basic strategy" in the face of this challenge is to offer the Corinthians data about history and a new way of thinking about reality. Paul does do that (he is, after all, writing propositions for the Corinthians to consider, know, and respond to); but I think Paul does much more. He has a much more robust pedagogical strategy than the merely propositional.

As Witherington presents the matter, Paul basically adds a few new and true ideas about history and eschatology to the Corinthian mindset.[30] But the Corinthian socialization and enculturation as good, normal pagans was not simply or particularly a matter of a "mindset" that the Corinthians had been taught or had read about and had consciously deliberated over. As Bradley Bitner explains, in direct connection to Paul's strategy in 1 Corinthians, "*patterns of life* propel, delectably if sometimes unsystematically, distinct *patterns of belief* and *patterns of ethical reflection*."[31] The Corinthian

---

[28]Witherington, *Conflict and Community in Corinth*, 8n21, emphasis original.

[29]Peter L. Berger and Thomas Luckmann, *The Social Construction of Reality: A Treatise in the Sociology of Knowledge* (New York: Penguin, 1966), 160; see more generally 149-82.

[30]Witherington is certainly not alone in this. The assumption/insinuation that "right thinking leads to right living" and that Paul would seek to manufacture the "right living" of the Corinthian church simply by giving them the stuff of "right thinking" manifests itself throughout the literature on 1 Cor (and far beyond).

[31]Bitner, *Paul's Political Strategy*, 105, emphasis original. Bitner immediately, and rightly, adds, "The inverse is, of course, true as well."

Christians had pagan sensibilities and pagan outlooks on the world because they had been well-practiced and *long*-practiced in pagan "patterns of life," pagan liturgies and celebrations and rituals and practices. There was no escaping it. Social tics, intellectual tides, cultural habits, artifacts, images, sounds, and smells rendering idolatrous wisdom plausible and shaping idolatrous imaginations would have been ubiquitous in the prevailing society.[32] The Corinthian Christians would have seen and engaged in these things everywhere they turned. They would have been exposed to them from before the time they were crawling. Idolatry was the air they breathed, and pagan sensibilities and ways of living would have been etched into their very bones, as it were, like second nature for them. That kind of deep enculturation and liturgical formation is not best combatted with only a set of new ideas or "truths" to think about. The Corinthians did not *think* themselves into being good, normal pagan people; it stands to reason that neither would countering their socialization and enculturation as pagans be a matter of simply thinking themselves into being some other kind of people.

Tackling cultural renewal head-on: Temple worship (1 Cor 11:2–14:40). With that in mind, we can turn our attention to what comes next in 1 Corinthians 11–14. One unmistakable feature of the topics addressed in these chapters is that they all have to do with the place and practices of the Christian assembly for worship and covenant renewal[33]—head coverings during worship assemblies where public praying and prophesying would take place (1 Cor 11:2-16); the Lord's Supper (1 Cor 11:17-34); the use of "spiritual gifts," especially tongues and prophecy, in liturgical gatherings and enactments (1 Cor 12:1–14:40).[34] Everything in 1 Corinthians 11–14 is related to the public assembly of the church for worship. Why does Paul cluster these similar points together in penultimate position in the body of his letter?

I suggest that if Paul discerns how the Corinthian life was shaped for the worse by idolatrous liturgy and practice, then he also expects the way forward into the life held out for them by God will begin with true liturgy,

---

[32]Consider, e.g., the careful discussion of Mary E. Hoskins Walbank, "Image and Cult: The Coinage of Roman Corinth," in *Corinth in Context: Comparative Studies on Religion and Society*, ed. S. J. Friesen, D. N. Schowalter, and J. C. Walters, NovTSup (Leiden: Brill, 2010), 151-97.

[33]With Jorunn Økland, I believe that emphasizing "the ritual or sanctuary aspect" in these chapters is interpretatively fruitful (see *Women in Their Place: Paul and the Corinthian Discourse of Gender and Sanctuary Space*, JSNTSup 269 [London: T&T Clark, 2004], 31n63).

[34]On the use of such "gifts" in the public assembly, see 1 Cor 12:3, 7; 14:3-5, 16, 19, 23-36, 39-40.

with true worship of the one true God, with rightly ordered practice and ritual.[35] It is not true ideas alone that will most effectively combat one's "primary socialization," but a *new socialization* in a new "place," through a new set of practices and habits, by a new kind of cultural liturgical formation. So Paul gives extended instructions about a rightly ordered culture for the Corinthian church to enact liturgically.[36] As Jorunn Økland has noted, "If Paul really succeeds with his argument in chapter [*sic*] 11–14, the Corinthians will enact ritually the words, acts and bodily gestures he prescribes in these chapters."[37] Reshaped liturgical, ritual enactments are also, in addition to theological knowledge conveyed through writing, part of Paul's pastoral strategy.

Paul's interest in the Corinthian church's corporate worship relates to his larger hope that they be a peculiar people, a people set apart according to their calling (1 Cor 1:2)—that is, that their ways would be distinct from and counter to the prevailing pagan culture. As Nicholas Wolterstorff proposes, what distinguishes Christians most—or at least most palpably and publicly— from the world is not a different set of "beliefs" or "motivations," not a different "interiority." Rather, it is their "*worship*, worship by way of participation in the liturgy of the church."[38] Corporate worship and liturgy is—or should be—the place where Christians are most publicly different from the world, and formed in distinction from the formation of the world that Christians are exposed to constantly in their present sojourn.

This is indicated in a striking way through the distribution of the term κόσμος ("world") in 1 Corinthians. Edward Adams notes that Paul's use of κόσμος in 1 Corinthians is consistently negative, mostly in denotation but sometimes in connotation.[39] In 1 Corinthians, "κόσμος is the 'ordered' and

---

[35]Cf. Barrett, *The First Epistle to the Corinthians*, 21.

[36]On liturgical cultural formation, see James K. A. Smith, *Desiring the Kingdom: Worship, Worldview, and Cultural Formation* (Grand Rapids: Baker, 2009); also Daniel J. Brendsel, "A Tale of Two Calendars: Calendars, Compassion, Liturgical Formation, and the Presence of the Holy Spirit," *Bulletin of Ecclesial Theology* 3 (2016): 15-43.

[37]Økland, *Women in Their Place*, 34-35.

[38]Nicholas Wolterstorff, *Until Justice and Peace Embrace* (Grand Rapids: Eerdmans, 1983), 146-47, emphasis original. More precisely, Wolterstorff proposed that the "rhythmic alternation of work and worship, labor and liturgy is one of the significant distinguishing features of the Christian's way of being in the world" (147).

[39]See Adams, *Constructing the World*, 107-43; the use in 1 Cor 14:10 is neutral, a "simple statement of fact" having "no rhetorical significance in Paul's discussion of glossolalia" (108n2).

'unified' world of opposition to God," and it is a world that is passing away together with its "form."[40] Strikingly, the use of the word is almost entirely front-loaded, appearing only twice in 1 Corinthians 11–16 out of the twenty-one total uses in the letter.[41] In reflection of the expected (and inaugurated) "passing away" of the world, κόσμος fades from view as this letter progresses, and the focus turns to the social location where the inaugurated "new world," the καινὴ κτίσις, is most concretely breaking out—namely, the church assembled in worship, or the sanctuary.[42] Socialization begins in the sanctuary, because the sanctuary (i.e., the church's gathering for worship) is where the new and true society of the new creation is breaking out most publicly.

The church's worship should be the place where the distinctness of Christian culture is most pronounced, and where a counterformation to one's primary socialization begins. But if, in fact, the church's liturgical practice is itself disordered, if it is simply a subcultural reproduction of the majority culture, then what hope is there of being truly transformed and rightly ordered in life? At Corinth, the church's worship simply echoed and reproduced majority pagan culture. At Corinth, there was the same socio-economic division within the church's worship as there was in Corinthian culture at large, with the rich functionally excluding the poor from the Lord's table (1 Cor 11:17-34). There was the same kind of one-upmanship, social ladder-climbing, and competition that marked pagan Corinthian culture (1 Cor 12:1–14:40). There was the same kind of social disorder and unrest, whether in male-female relationships (1 Cor 11:2-16) or in the confusion of uninterpreted tongues (1 Cor 14:1-39), inside the church's worship as outside of it in the worshipful rituals of Corinthian society. Far from combating the deformed primary socialization of the Corinthian Christians, the practices and habits of the Corinthian church's worship further reinforced their primary socialization as pagans. So Paul's extended focus on the rituals and engagements of the sanctuary is his effort to remedy that woeful situation.

---

[40] Adams, *Constructing the World*, 147. On the difficulties of interpreting 1 Cor 7:31, see 132-35.

[41] Adams, *Constructing the World*, 107-8. See 1 Cor 1:20-21, 27-28; 2:12; 3:19, 22; 4:9, 13; 5:10; 6:2; 7:31, 33-34; 8:4; 11:32; 14:10.

[42] Though the term *new creation* is not used in 1 Cor but in 2 Cor 5:17, it adequately expresses the theological significance that Paul in 1 Cor understands the church and its gathering for worship to have.

What is at stake in the Corinthians beginning to enact a truthful and well-ordered worship is the manifestation of new and true culture and human society. This is for the good of the idolatrous society in which they dwell. The best, most needful way to bear witness to the societies of earth is to be an alternative society. Paul's great hope is that the unbeliever might witness the well-ordered worship of the church, the new covenant polis gathered in the presence of its Lord and King, with the result that "they will fall down and worship God, exclaiming, 'God is really among you!'" (1 Cor 14:25).[43] For the life of the world, Paul labors to reorder the worship of the church so that it might be a beginning foretaste of new and true culture.

In 1 Corinthians, Paul is not addressing seriatim the inquiries of the Corinthians, letting them set the tone and determine the shape of the discussion. Instead, Paul strategically develops an argument. Paul moves purposefully from the crucial clash of wisdoms and his dismay at the Corinthian Christians' capitulation to the "wisdom of the world," to how such wisdom is enacted, reinforced, and rendered more plausible by their practices and rituals, which are indistinguishable from the world's, to the place where their difference from the world is (or ought to be) most distinct and discernible—namely, the sanctuary, the assembly for corporate worship. The "culmination of the ages has come" (1 Cor 10:11). And the people of God can begin to live into the form of the end as a testimony to the nations—can begin to experience some of the shape and substance of future resurrection life in the present—in their worship.

The source and substance of true culture: The resurrection of the King (1 Cor 15:1–16:12). Of course, Christ's resurrection is what launched the new age. This helps explain in part why at the end of this letter there appears the only extended Pauline discussion of the resurrection in the New Testament. If the Corinthian church is set apart from the societies of the world as the beginning of new and true society, then their living into that calling is only possible because Christ's resurrection brought the future hope of resurrection into the present as an inaugurated reality. The mysteries experienced

---

[43]On the likelihood, and the spatial-material dynamics, of such an encounter in Corinthian Christian assemblies for worship, see de Vos, *Church and Community Conflicts*, 203-5, 213.

in the sanctuary are possible because of, and indeed they point directly to, the risen Lord Jesus.[44]

Christ Jesus is, as Paul says in 1 Corinthians 15:20, 23, the "firstfruits" of the new age. The future harvest has already begun in the risen Lord's body. Kingdom realities are beginning to break out in the present because the risen Jesus is presently ruling (1 Cor 15:25). By the presence and power of the Spirit—the gift of the risen King, the down payment of the age to come— the Corinthian church can experience the future age and its resurrection life in beginning ways in the present. They can experience, and they can provide in their public and private life, present foretastes of the life of the kingdom. They can offer little previews of life and culture as God intends.

From the general arrangement of this letter and Paul's focalization of the worship of the church in 1 Corinthians 11–14, I think we can say that especially in corporate worship ordered according to God's purposes and intentions, the Spirit of the risen Lord is uniquely present to manifest the reality of resurrection life and culture. But flowing from that gathering, the church sent out on mission is also given opportunities to display kingdom realities in the mundane, everyday responsibilities and engagements of life in the dispersion. Things as apparently mundane as finances and travel plans and ordering of time are of concern in the kingdom (1 Cor 16:1-12) because in raising Christ from the dead, in raising part of the very mundane, dusty material of this world, God has shown that the mundane and material is something he cares deeply about, and is what his kingdom consists of. Since Christ is risen, our mundane labors in the Lord, and the liturgy that they both spring from and lead to, are not in vain (1 Cor 15:58).

Conclusion

In sanctifying the Christians at Corinth and setting them apart as "saints," what God was up to was the building up of his true temple as a beginning

---

[44]The hope of resurrection casts a retrospective shadow on the whole of the letter (cf. Raymond W. Pickett, *The Cross in Corinth: The Social Significance of the Death of Jesus*, JSNTSup 143 [Sheffield, UK: Sheffield Academic Press, 1997], 108). See similarly, with respect to the crucial role of 1 Cor 15 in the letter, Karl Barth, *The Resurrection of the Dead*, trans. H. J. Stenning (London: Hodder & Stoughton, 1933), 13. While differing in specifics from Barth, I am very much in agreement with him when he says, "If we were not accustomed from of yore to regard Christian Corinth in the light of what Paul found to *censure*, instead of, and first of all, in the light of what Paul expressly and positively valued, we should appraise the conditions which the Epistle illuminates quite differently, and also better understand the attitude of Paul" (103, emphasis original).

manifestation of the life of the resurrection age to come. The church as true temple at Corinth was to provide truthful demonstrations and enactments of rightly ordered worship and culture, as a testimony to the kingdom of God in the presence of the idolatrous, disordered culture of Roman Corinth. Such a calling is hard, in large part because taking it up is so palpable, public, and political. Faithful enactment of Christian and ecclesial calling means being a culture, a polis, a kingdom among the cultures of the world. And that inevitably leads to at least some tension and friction, perhaps ostracizing, perhaps even to conflict and battle, with prevailing cultures and kingdoms.

So Paul's concluding exhortation in 1 Corinthians 16:13-14 is quite fitting, though it probably sounds strange to our ears at first. When Paul exhorts the church to "act like men" (au. trans.; more often translated "be courageous"), he uses a word (ἀνδρίζομαι) that in several places in the Greek Old Testament refers not so much to men over against women, but to Israel as the people whom the Lord of hosts is leading to victory,[45] or to armies and soldiers who are called to fight valiantly (and who would have, of course, been male).[46] At the conclusion of his letter, Paul is not really singling out the men of the congregation,[47] but instead calling the church as a whole to act like the kingdom and army of the Lord, which in Christ they are, in the conflict with the kingdoms of the world. That only makes sense, since the content of this letter, if heeded, will likely lead to a good deal of cultural conflict and a clash of *politeias*. Paul offers a concluding battle cry.

But the weapons of this kingdom's warfare are unusual. They are the weapons of worship and liturgy, of holiness and purity, and especially of love (1 Cor 16:14). If the Corinthian Christians join in this holy warfare, then their victory is as sure as the tomb in which Christ was laid is empty.

---

[45]See Deut 31:6-7.

[46]See, referring to Joshua leading Israel in the conquest, Deut 31:23; Josh 1:6-7, 9, 18; and, referring to the armies of Israel or other fighting men, Josh 10:25; 2 Sam 10:12 (with κραταιόω); 13:28; 1 Chron 19:13.

[47]Ciampa and Rosner, *First Letter to the Corinthians*, 855, rightly note that Paul is not singling out men over against women or basing his call to courage on some inherently, exclusively, or paradigmatically *male* quality. They believe that the sense of Paul's exhortation has to do with maturity (i.e., act like "men" as opposed to children); see also Thiselton, *First Epistle to the Corinthians*, 1336. But Paul's immediate juxtaposition of ἀνδρίζομαι with κραταιόω (cf. 2 Sam 10:12), together with the overall argument of the letter, inclines me otherwise.

2

Beyond Imitation

The Image of God as a Vision for Spiritual Formation

MARC CORTEZ

THE *IMAGO DEI* HAS LONG STOOD as a central aspect of how we understand the biblical vision of what it means to be human. It is the first thing the Bible declares about these human creatures (Gen 1:26-27). It also identifies Jesus himself as the true image of God (Col 1:15), the one who is the eternal telos toward which God has called his people (Rom 8:29). Consequently, from the perspective of both creation and redemption, we have good reason to think that the *imago Dei* is central to the biblical vision of humanity.[1] And this matters for spiritual formation because any meaningful attempt to "develop" people spiritually requires some vision of that toward which we want them to develop. Indeed, this holds true for any formational process that involves humans (teaching, parenting, counseling, etc.). If the *imago Dei* is central to our vision of the human person, and if some vision of what it means to be human is necessary for spiritual formation, then we can easily see the essential link between the *imago* and spiritual formation.

---

[1]For a discussion of why we should continue to emphasize the centrality of the *imago Dei* for theological anthropology despite the scarcity of biblical material, see Marc Cortez, *ReSourcing Theological Anthropology* (Grand Rapids: Zondervan, 2017), 102-7.

For many, this link gets teased out through the lens of the *imitatio Christi*.[2] If the *imago Dei* defines what it means to be human, and if Jesus is the true image of God, then the most appropriate way to understand our own humanity is through the imitation of Christ. This becomes the *explicit* link between the *imago* and spiritual formation. Regardless of what we might think about whether the *imitatio* is the best lens through which to understand this link, however, I want us to explore the possibility that the *imago* may have other, subtler implications for spiritual formation, *implicit* links that shape our approach to spiritual formation in unexpected, and often undesired, ways.

Rather than trying to address a broad range of approaches to the *imago Dei*, this essay will focus instead on a single view, offering the following as a case study in how to tease out the links between the *imago Dei* and spiritual formation. To this end, we will spend the majority of our time discussing what might be referred to as a *capacity* view of the *imago Dei*. The purpose of the discussion will not be to persuade anyone for or against this view. Instead, our goal will be to demonstrate a way of thinking through a particular interpretation of the *imago Dei*, drawing out the implications it has for spiritual formation, and then seeing if we can find ways of addressing those worries from within the framework provided by the capacity view itself. That will hopefully provide a model for addressing other views of the image, though that is a task we will not pursue here.

After briefly describing a capacity view of the image, then, I will briefly summarize four key worries that arise with respect to our understanding of spiritual formation, offering some suggestions for how those worries might be addressed.

THE *IMAGO DEI* AND HUMAN CAPACITIES

By far the most prominent approach to the *imago Dei* throughout history has been that which focuses on some capacity or set of capacities in the human person that makes us both *like* God and *unlike* the rest of creation.[3]

---

[2]See, for example, Jeremy Moiser, "Dogmatic Thoughts on Imitation of Christ," *Scottish Journal of Theology* (1977): 201-13; William L. Power, "*Imago Dei—Imitatio Dei*," *International Journal for Philosophy of Religion* (1997): 131-41.

[3]For a brief survey of the major views, see Marc Cortez, *Theological Anthropology: A Guide for the Perplexed* (Edinburgh: T&T Clark, 2010).

For the purposes of our discussion, we will focus primarily on humanity's capacity for *rationality*, which has been the most influential version of this view of the *imago Dei*.[4]

Although the *imago Dei* texts themselves do not highlight such capacities, the intuition behind the argument runs something like this. First, the very idea of being an "image" or "likeness" of God suggests that there is something about the human person that "reflects" or "mirrors" one or more of God's own attributes in creation. Second, since only human persons are said to be made in the image of God, and since we typically differentiate humans from nonhuman creatures by virtue of the distinct capacities that make us uniquely human, it stands to reason that the *imago Dei* would involve just such capacities. As it relates to the specifics of our discussion, then, if we define the *imago Dei* according to some capacity or set of capacities, we will orient our understanding of spiritual formation around the development of that capacity.

Worry #1: The spiritual formation of a brain in a vat. One of the primary worries about this view arises from something akin to those famous philosophical thought experiments that involve some form of the "brain in a vat" argument. Such arguments ask whether *I* would continue to be *me* if my brain were removed from my body and hooked up to some kind of complex technology that could sustain all of my brain's processes. Whatever we might think about the validity, or even usefulness, of such thought experiments, the analogy still expresses one of the primary worries about such a capacity view of the *imago Dei*, which is that such a view results in an unavoidably reductive view of the human person with negative implications (at least) for our understanding of spiritual formation.[5] Indeed, much of the contemporary literature on spiritual formation focuses precisely on a rejection of such an apparently "cognitive" understanding of the human person and human flourishing, pushing toward more "holistic" approaches to spiritual formation. And although the corresponding worries will shift if we identify the image with some other capacity, the fundamental problem remains. Whether it's a will in a vat, affections in a vat, creativity in a vat, or whatever,

---

[4]See esp. Thomas Aquinas, *Summa Theologica*, Ia, Q.93, A.1-9.
[5]See, for example, Rosemary Radford Ruether, *Sexism and God-Talk: Toward a Feminist Theology* (Boston: Beacon, 1983).

we still seem to end up with a fairly reductive understanding of a human person and a correspondingly reductive view of spiritual formation.

I will admit here that I have a rather sizeable soft spot for a view that focuses on rationality as central to humanity and human flourishing. While I appreciate worries about an overly cognitive approach, I wonder at times if we have swung the pendulum too far in the other direction. In our zeal to emphasize the importance of the affections, personal experiences, and embodied practices in our understanding of spiritual formation, I think we run the risk of downplaying the clear biblical emphasis on the knowledge of God in his self-revelation.[6]

Nonetheless, I am also sympathetic to the worry that we often tend to think of this knowledge in overly rational/cognitive terms, missing the Bible's emphasis on a holistic form of knowledge that involves the entire person. One frequently encounters what could be interpreted as notable examples of this worry in songs that are routinely sung in many children's ministries. According to those songs, you will grow as a Christian if you read your Bible and pray every day. Fail to do those things, and you will certainly shrivel spiritually. Now, to be fair, such songs are of course offering intentionally simplified versions of things to make it easier for children to remember. And they do frequently emphasize both prayer and Scripture reading, suggesting that they are at least trying to offer more holistic visions of spiritual formation. Nonetheless, when I ask my middle school students what they think such songs are trying to say, they generally offer a straightforwardly cognitive understanding of spiritual formation. Growing spiritually is about knowing the stuff in the Bible; praying (in this context) is important because it somehow helps you know the stuff better.

We could try to address this first worry by arguing that the mistake lies in assuming that the image of God should drive our spiritual formation practices in such a straightforward way. Instead, we could maintain that although the *imago Dei* stands at the center of our vision of humanity, we must still recognize other aspects of humanity as having tremendous significance. Thus, even if I defend a rationality view of the *imago Dei*, I might contend that we cannot understand human rationality adequately apart

---

[6]E.g., Prov 1:7; Is 11:2; Phil 1:9.

from knowing how it is in turn shaped by things like affections, personal relations, and so forth. As important as such a counterargument might be, though, I suspect that those concerned about overly rationalized definitions of the human person will continue to worry that this approach continues to privilege rationality in ways that will inevitably skew our approach to spiritual formation. In contrast to such a view, the biblical authors shift smoothly from emphasizing knowledge, to love, to obedience, to action, and back to any of the above, avoiding any suggestion that we should view rationality as somehow more fundamental to biblical anthropology and spiritual formation than the others.

Such a problem is likely to plague any attempt to identify a single capacity that can serve as the definition of the *imago Dei* and thus as the central feature of a biblical anthropology. A likelier approach, then, would be to drop the emphasis on a particular capacity as constituting the meaning of the *imago Dei*, focusing instead on a broader *set* of capacities that are somehow jointly necessary or sufficient for making us *imago Dei* creatures. Although we will see in some of the following worries that such a strategy runs into problems elsewhere, it would at least allow us to retain the intuition that we image God by virtue of our capacities without lapsing into the kind of reductionism that we have encountered here.

Worry #2: The spiritual formation of "normal" people in a vat. Sticking with the vat metaphor, the analogy once again conveys the idea that our view of the *imago Dei* leads us into a kind of reduction. But here the worry has more to do with the idea that by focusing on one capacity—or, as we will see in a moment, even a set of capacities—we inevitably end up focusing on one way of being human (i.e., the "normal" way of being human) to the neglect of those at the margins. The most common form of this criticism focuses on the idea that any capacity view of the *imago Dei* necessarily denigrates the full humanity of those human persons in whom the relevant capacity seems significantly diminished or even nonexistent.[7] Thus, for example, many worry that the rationality view of the image implicitly, or even explicitly, denigrates those with severe intellectual disabilities.

---

[7]See esp. John Kilner, *Dignity and Destiny: Humanity in the Image of God* (Grand Rapids: Eerdmans, 2015).

Now, to be fair to the capacity view under consideration, we need to recognize that the criticism needs to be modified somewhat. According the capacity view, it is the *capacity* that constitutes the image of God, not any particular *exercise* of that capacity. Just as I remain rational—in the sense of retaining the capacity for rationality—when I am asleep and not exercising that capacity, so I would remain a rational creature even if some accident or disease rendered me unable to manifest my capacity for rationality. Similarly, we might say that a person with a severe intellectual disability still has the capacity for rationality (insofar as he or she is human), even if something has happened to render that person unable to exercise that capacity.

Consequently, we cannot argue that a capacity view of the image necessarily denigrates the full humanity of those with significant disabilities. Nonetheless, I think there is a real worry here that we need to address with regard to spiritual formation. On this account, it would seem that whatever capacity we identify as being the core of the *imago Dei* raises questions about whether those who experience a significant disability with respect to the relevant capacity can participate in any meaningful kind of spiritual formation.

As a practical example of this worry, I recently received the following in an email from a student in one of my theological anthropology classes:

> I'm . . . thinking of a young girl I know who is profoundly developmentally disabled. She is a teenager but has the IQ of an infant. Yet, at her baptism, at the name of Jesus she smiled and wiggled with joy. (There was not a dry eye in the house.) Though this does not give "proof" of anything, I wonder if there is a means of recognition and consciousness beyond the brain. Just wondering.[8]

Although this student was "just wondering," the question finds support from a broad range of those working alongside persons with disabilities.[9] According to them, capacity views like this are precisely why we tend to marginalize those with intellectual disabilities in our churches. Since we envision spiritual formation largely in terms of intentionally actualized capacities, typically those associated with cognition, we have no room in our theological imaginations

---

[8]Used with permission.
[9]The literature on disability and spiritual formation has grown considerably in recent years. For one good example, see John Swinton, *Becoming Friends of Time: Disability, Timefullness, and Gentle Discipleship* (Waco, TX: Baylor University Press, 2016).

for a kind of spiritual formation that might be able to include those who cannot exercise the relevant capacities in the expected ways.

We should also note here that it's not entirely clear how the earlier strategy of appealing to a set of capacities will suffice to address this particular concern. Indeed, if we emphasize the entire set in such a way that all of those capacities are necessary to the image of God, we make the problems encountered here even worse since we would be requiring people to manifest an even broader array of capacities. If we maintain instead that only some portion of the set is required—presumably also maintaining that we cannot stipulate any necessary subset, which would just result in a smaller version of the same set problem—then we seem to end up with a rather vague and unhelpful concept of the image. On this account, the image involves some set of capacities, but we can't tell you what.

I could be wrong, but it seems to me that the likeliest way to address this worry would be to make some kind of appeal to mystery, in that a person may be able to exercise the relevant capacity or capacities in ways that transcend our current ability to understand. So maybe it's the case that a person with severe intellectual disabilities is in fact able to exercise their rational capacity (or some broader set of capacities) in a way that is sufficient to ground their full participation in the *imago Dei* and at least some involvement in the spiritual formation practices of the church, even if we are not able to identify precisely how they are able to do so. While I will admit that I do not find this strategy entirely satisfying, in that it seems to retain the appeal to a capacity even while depriving that capacity of any meaningful, or at least identifiable, content, it does at least provide a way of addressing this particular concern.

Worry #3: The spiritual formation of a soul in a vat. A third worry arises for certain forms of the capacity view. Here the concern is neither with the reduction of the human person to a particular capacity or set of capacities, nor with the reduction of the human person only to certain "normative" expressions of humanity. Instead, the worry here is that a capacity view may involve an inappropriate reduction of the human person to the spiritual dimension alone, resulting in a denigration of the body as having merely instrumental value in spiritual formation.[10]

---

[10]Feminist theologians in particular have criticized this tendency to downplay the centrality of the body for theological anthropology (e.g., Ruether, *Sexism and God-Talk*).

To understand this concern, we need to recognize that according to many traditional ontologies of the human person, the relevant capacities should be understood as capacities of the soul that are only expressed through the body.[11] Although such views often involve complex philosophical claims about a fundamental difference between mental/spiritual realities and biological/physical processes, the easiest way to appreciate the distinction between the soul and the body as it relates to these capacities is to recognize that the relevant capacities are the kinds of things that Christians have long thought that immaterial beings were capable of actualizing (i.e., angels, God, and humans in the intermediate state are all capable of being rational, exercising free will, etc.). If this is the case, and if human persons remain human in the intermediate state, then it seems to follow that the capacities relevant for understanding the *imago Dei* are capacities of the soul and not capacities of the body. Even if we subsequently affirm that the body has value as the necessary means by which an immaterial entity (i.e., the soul) actualizes its capacities in a material world, such a view seems inevitably committed to the idea that the soul has greater significance for humanity and human flourishing than the body. With regard to spiritual formation, the body seems to have been reduced to having merely instrumental value. It is the means by which the immaterial soul accomplishes its own spiritual formation.

This is precisely what I hear from many of my students when I ask about their own spiritual life. I often ask them to brainstorm with me the kinds of things that are relevant to spiritual growth, listing them on the whiteboard as we go. When we're done, almost without exception they will have failed to mention things like sleep, nutrition, exercise, and so forth. When I point this out, many students will respond with some version of the argument that such things are only instrumentally related to spiritual formation. In other words, if I don't get enough sleep or eat properly, I won't be able to pray or read my Bible effectively. Such an instrumentalized view of the body not only runs contrary to the emphasis of the Bible on the whole person as made in the image of God, but it also fails to do justice to the clearly embodied approach to spiritual formation exemplified in the Bible.

---

[11]For a classic formulation of this, see Gregory of Nyssa, *On the Making of Man,* in *A Select Library of the Nicene and Post-Nicene Fathers,* ed. Philip Schaff, vol. 5, series 2 (Grand Rapids: Eerdmans, 1978).

We already identified in the prior worry a reason that the "set of capacities" response might prove inadequate to handle some concerns. Here the issue becomes even more clear. No matter how many capacities you use to define the *imago Dei*, if they are fundamentally capacities of the soul that are only instrumentally realized through the body, this worry will remain. Consequently, we cannot address these worries merely by supplementing a capacity view with additional capacities.

The most obvious way of addressing this concern would be to drop the commitment to the idea that the body is only instrumentally related to the relative capacities of the human person. Instead, we could reject the substance dualism at work here and affirm a kind of Christian physicalism in which the human person just *is* their body.[12] This would require us to affirm as well that any of the capacities relevant to the *imago Dei* are fully embodied capacities, making the body intrinsic to the meaning of the image and not merely instrumental.

However, for many such a solution would require a rather radical revisioning of the human person. A likelier option would be to reject the argument that the instrumentalization of the body is a problem. Instead, we could point out that instrumentalization only undermines the value of the instrument if it's not a *necessary* instrument. For example, suppose that I'm building a set of bookcases for my daughter's bedroom and I need to hammer a series of small nails into the back of the bookcase to attach it to the frame. For such a purpose, it seems reasonable to think that I would grab a hammer from my toolbox. After all, a hammer is precisely the tool that has been designed for this purpose, making it the most efficient instrument to use in completing my daughter's bookcase. But suppose that my wife has used my hammer for some other project around the house, so when I go to grab my trusty hammer, it isn't there. Do I have to give up on the project completely? Of course not. There are all manner of objects laying around the house that I might use instead of a hammer for the purpose of driving those nails (a book, a rock, my wife's cat, etc.). These objects might not be as efficient, of course, but they'll get the job done. Consequently, while the hammer is *important* in the sense of efficiency, it is not *necessary* in any strong sense of the word.

---

[12]For some critical responses to Christian physicalism, see R. Keith Loftin and Joshua R. Farris, *Christian Physicalism? Philosophical Theological Criticisms* (Minneapolis: Lexington, 2017).

Suppose instead, though, that I was a mad scientist creating an artificial intelligence machine capable of taking over the internet and controlling online technology throughout the world. And suppose that to bring my evil plan to fruition, I needed a particular device, the only tool capable of making the final connection that would bring the device online. Technically that tool is only an instrument, but it's a rather vital one. Without that instrument, the plan won't work.

We could go a long way toward addressing this particular weakness of the capacity view if we were to emphasize that even if the body plays only an instrumental role with respect to the image, it's a necessary instrument. God created us with bodies, incarnated himself in a body, and will resurrect us to future lives in bodies, suggesting that our bodies play a rather significant role in the story of humanity. If we cast a similar vision for the *imago Dei*, it would help people understand the significance of their bodies in their own spiritual formation. To do this, though, we not only need to modify how we speak of the *imago Dei*, making it more clear that our bodies are central (even if instrumental) to the definition of what it means to be human, but we also need to be more careful how we speak about the "afterlife," particularly the intermediate state. To the extent that we cast a vision of the full flourishing of human persons when they are separated from their bodies, we send the clear message that the body is *merely* instrumental rather than *necessarily* instrumental. Such a message can only continue to have deleterious effects on how people view the body in their own spiritual formation.

Worry #4: The spiritual formation of an individual in a vat. Finally, even if we develop a robust concept of the relevant capacities that allows for a more holistic vision of the human person as an *imago Dei* creature, allow for a more chastened sense of the extent to which we can be confident about whether a person is actually utilizing those capacities, thus creating more room in our understanding of spiritual formation for a broader range of human experience, and emphasize the irreplaceable significance of the body as a necessary instrument in our spiritual growth, we are still left with the fact that such a vision is inherently individualistic. After all, if the image involves some capacity or set of capacities that renders a human person essentially human, then presumably Adam was in the image of God even before Eve was created (i.e., he had the relevant capacities). Even after Eve was created, they were both fully in the image as their own individual persons with their own individual capacities. And even if we then go on to affirm the obvious point that God wanted these individuals to be involved in relationship with each other, it still seems to be the case that the individual has both logical and temporal priority over the community in such an anthropology.[13]

It should not take much effort to see the consequences such a view might have for spiritual formation in the church today. An obvious example would be the increasing number of "solo Christians" who pursue some form of spiritual growth at home on their own. But I think we see a similar dynamic at work in how many Christians in our own churches view the relationship between the church and their spiritual formation, one that mimics what we said in the prior worry about the instrumentalization of the body. When I ask my students why they should go to church, they quickly focus on the church's role in helping them grow spiritually. In other words, their focus isn't on the church as something that has intrinsic value of its own. Instead, they emphasize the church's instrumental value for producing what they think is primarily important: their own spiritual formation as individual believers before God.

We could try to address this difficulty using the same resources developed when discussing the body, contending that the church is necessarily rather than merely instrumental to the formation of the individual. But that seems rather problematic since it retains the notion that the church is an instrument for the production of the higher end of individual spiritual formation, which is the precise opposite of what we find in the New Testament, where individual formation is always there to serve the greater reality of the church. In other words, if we were going to instrumentalize anything in this account, it would be the formation of the individual, not the church. And since it's unlikely that the New Testament wants us to think of the formation of individuals as having only instrumental value either, we should probably just avoid this option altogether.

A better approach would be to think of the capacities of the human person as the kinds of things that cannot be fully and adequately actualized

---

[13]E.g., F. LeRon Shults, *Reforming Theological Anthropology after the Philosophical Turn to Relationality* (Grand Rapids: Eerdmans, 2003).

in isolation from other human persons. In other words, whatever it means for an individual to have a capacity for rationality, we can and should emphasize that the individual can only actualize that capacity such that they come to know things rightly in the context of human community. If we imagine a human person growing up in isolation somewhere, although they would still be able to exercise their rational capacity to some degree, it does not seem a stretch to suggest that they would hardly be flourishing with respect to their cognitive abilities! Rather than being merely instrumental to the utilization of individual capacities, we might think of the community as playing an intrinsic role with respect to those very capacities. I can't be the fully rational (volitional, affective, creative, etc.) creature that I am supposed to be apart from the community that constitutes me as a rational creature. In an important sense, then, Adam and Eve are not fully human apart from one another. Though there is a sense in which they have all of the requisite capacities as isolated individuals, those capacities are fitted *for* community in such a way that we might also think of them as capacities of the community.

If this is our vision of the human person, we can now return to my middle school students and encourage them to reconsider how they understand the relationship between the church and their own spiritual formation. It remains the case that they need the church to flourish as human individuals, not because the church plays a merely or even a necessarily instrumental role with respect to the individual who has some kind of logical or ontological primacy, but because this understanding of the human person as an *imago Dei* creature requires us to emphasize the inseparable relationship between the individual and the community in God's purposes for humanity.

CONCLUSION

As I mentioned at the beginning of this essay, we have focused our attention on a capacity view of the *imago Dei*, not because it is the only option or even the best option, but merely because its historic and contemporary significance makes it an excellent case study for thinking through (1) how our definition of the *imago Dei* relates to our understanding of spiritual formation, (2) how to identify the difficulties that might arise from that relationship, and (3) how we might address those difficulties. Hopefully, that will give us resources for thinking about how to take a similar approach with regard to other views of the image, a task we cannot pursue here.

Nonetheless, I think we have already seen from this brief case study that the *imago Dei* is a concept that has the potential to shape our understanding of spiritual formation and human flourishing in powerful and often unexpected ways. We would be well served to reflect and teach more intentionally about the relationship between *what* we think humans are and *how* we think humans are best formed spiritually.

3

The Holy Spirit and Positive Psychology in Spiritual Formation

SIANG-YANG TAN

CHRISTIAN SPIRITUAL FORMATION, referring to the process of sanctification into deeper Christlikeness for every Christian, has received widespread attention and great interest in the last few decades, especially in the area of traditional spiritual disciplines. Richard Foster's classic book *Celebration of Discipline* is now available in a special fortieth anniversary edition, and several other notable books have been recently published.[1]

There has been much emphasis in Christian spiritual formation on the crucial role of the traditional spiritual disciplines as means of grace to help Christians grow to become more like Jesus (Rom 8:29; Gal 4:19), especially since Foster's *Celebration Of Discipline* was first published in 1978. The late

---

[1]R. J. Foster, *Celebration of Discipline: The Path to Spiritual Growth*, special anniversary edition (New York: HarperOne, 2018); K. D. Bennett, *Practices of Love: Spiritual Disciplines for the Life of the World* (Grand Rapids: Brazos Press, 2017); A. A. Calhoun, *Spiritual Disciplines Handbook: Practices That Transform Us*, rev. and expanded ed. (Downers Grove, IL: InterVarsity Press, 2015); D. J. Chandler, *Christian Spiritual Formation: An Integrated Approach for Personal and Relational Wholeness* (Downers Grove, IL: IVP Academic, 2014); E. B. Howard, *A Guide to Christian Spiritual Formation: How Scripture, Spirit, Community and Mission Shape Our Souls* (Grand Rapids: Baker Academic, 2018); J. Ortberg, *Soul-Keeping: Caring for the Most Important Part of You* (Grand Rapids: Zondervan, 2014); S. S. Phillips, *The Cultivated Life: From Ceaseless Striving to Receiving Joy* (Downers Grove, IL: InterVarsity Press, 2015); A. J. Swoboda, *Subversive Sabbath: The Surprising Power of Rest in a Nonstop World* (Grand Rapids: Brazos Press, 2018); G. T. Smith, *Called to Be Saints: An Invitation to Christian Maturity* (Downers Grove, IL: IVP Academic, 2014); T. H. Warren, *Liturgy of the Ordinary: Sacred Practices in Everyday Life* (Downers Grove, IL: InterVarsity Press, 2016).

Dallas Willard was also well-known for this emphasis.[2] In his V-I-M model, he asserted that the renovation of the heart into deeper Christlikeness should be the exclusive or primary goal of the local church: "*Vision* of life in the kingdom of God (referring to the range of God's effective will, where what God wants done is done) now and forever, *Intention* to be a kingdom person (we can and need to *decide* to live life in the kingdom, fully relying on Jesus and *intending* to obey him), and *Means* of spiritual transformation into Christlikeness and maturity in Christ which include the practice of spiritual disciplines."[3] Willard described two major categories of spiritual disciplines: *disciplines of abstinence* (solitude, silence, fasting, frugality, chastity, secrecy, and sacrifice), and *disciplines of engagement* (study, worship, celebration, service, prayer, fellowship, confession, and submission).[4] Foster's list includes the following twelve spiritual disciplines applicable for both individuals as well as groups: the *inward disciplines* of meditation, prayer, fasting and study; the *outward disciplines* of simplicity, solitude, submission, and service; and the *corporate disciplines* of confession, worship, guidance, and celebration.[5]

Adele Calhoun has recently revised and expanded her *Spiritual Disciplines Handbook* with descriptions of at least seventy-five spiritual disciplines that can help us to grow in deeper Christlikeness. Several recent books on spiritual disciplines have emphasized them as practices of love for the sake of others or for the life of the world, or as sacred practices in everyday life, serving as liturgy of the ordinary.[6]

While the traditional spiritual disciplines are well known as means of grace in Christian spiritual formation, it is also important to emphasize what Gary Thomas has called the "authentic disciplines," or circumstantial spiritual disciplines in our lives over which we have little or no control or choice, in helping us to become more like Jesus. The following are authentic disciplines as listed and described by Thomas: selflessness, waiting, suffering,

---

[2]D. Willard, *Renovation of the Heart: Putting on the Character of Christ* (Colorado Springs, CO: NavPress, 2002); see also Willard, *The Spirit of the Disciplines* (San Francisco: HarperSanFrancisco, 1988).

[3]S. Y. Tan, *Full Service: Moving from Self-Serve Christianity to Total Servanthood* (Grand Rapids: Baker Books, 2006), 140; see Willard, *Renovation of the Heart*, 77-92.

[4]Willard, *Spirit of the Disciplines*.

[5]Foster, *Celebration of Discipline*.

[6]Bennet, *Practices of Love*; Warren, *Liturgy of the Ordinary*.

persecution, social mercy, forgiveness, mourning, contentment, sacrifice, hope, and fear. The traditional spiritual disciplines can be potentially harmful or dangerous if they are practiced by self-effort in the flesh or sinful nature legalistically because they can lead to self-righteousness, spiritual pride, and self-sufficiency. The authentic disciplines, however, are usually not initiated or chosen by us and they are therefore a vital addition to the traditional spiritual disciplines. Thomas has emphasized that

> they turn us away from human effort—from men and women seeking the face of God—and turn us back toward God seeking the face of men and women. . . . God brings them into our life when he wills and as he wills. . . . This is a God-ordained spirituality, dependent on his sovereignty. . . . There's no pride left when God takes me through a time of suffering. There is no self-righteousness when I am called to wait. There is no religiosity when I am truly mourning. This is a spirituality I can't control, I can't initiate, I can't bring about. It is a radical dependence on God's husbandry. All I can do is try to appreciate it and learn from it.[7]

The ultimate result is "learning to love with God's love and learning to serve with God's power."[8] I have similarly written elsewhere on a biblical perspective on the crucial role of suffering in Christian spiritual formation that goes beyond resilience, posttraumatic growth, and self-care.[9]

THE HOLY SPIRIT AND CHRISTIAN SPIRITUAL FORMATION

While both the traditional spiritual disciplines and the authentic or circumstantial disciplines are crucial means of grace in Christian spiritual formation into deeper Christlikeness, it is also essential to point out that such spiritual disciplines, in and of themselves, are nothing and can do or accomplish nothing. Ultimately, it is by God's grace alone and the work and ministry of the Holy Spirit that we are transformed and conformed

---

[7]G. Thomas, *Authentic Faith: The Power of a Fire-Test Faith* (Grand Rapids: Zondervan, 2002), 18-19.
[8]Thomas, *Authentic Faith*, 16.
[9]S. Y. Tan, "Beyond Resilience, Posttraumatic Growth, and Self-Care: A Biblical Perspective on Suffering and Christian Spiritual Formation," in *Psychology and Spiritual Formation in Dialogue: Moral and Spiritual Change in Christian Perspective*, ed. T. M. Crisp, S. L. Porter, and G. A. Ten Elshof (Downers Grove, IL: IVP Academic, 2019), 104-22; see also J. Goggin and K. Strobel, *The Way of the Dragon or the Way of the Lamb: Searching for Jesus' Path of Power in a Church That Has Abandoned It* (Nashville: Nelson Books, 2017).

into the image of Christ (Rom 8:29) in union with Christ (Jn 15:5).[10] Zechariah 4:6 asserts that it is not by might or by power but by the Holy Spirit, and Ephesians 5:18b emphasizes our need to be continuously filled with the Holy Spirit. We read in 2 Corinthians 3:18, "And we all, who with unveiled faces contemplate the Lord's glory, are being transformed into his image with ever-increasing glory, which comes from the Lord, who is the Spirit."

It is therefore the Holy Spirit who transforms us into deeper Christ-likeness, or the image of Christ. It is not the spiritual disciplines per se. Surrender to the Spirit and being filled with the Spirit (Eph 5:18), daily walking in or by the Spirit and thereby not gratifying the desires of the flesh or sinful nature (Gal 5:16), and keeping in step with the Spirit (Gal 5:25), are the keys to the Spirit's deep work of transformation within us, for God's glory and our ultimate fulfillment in Christ. It is not by self-effort or effort in the flesh or sinful nature that we become more like Jesus. Christlike character is manifested as the one, holistic fruit of the Holy Spirit: love, joy, peace, forbearance, kindness, goodness, faithfulness, gentleness, and self-control (Gal 5:22-23). Christian spiritual formation is the work of the Holy Spirit, who produces such fruit, not ourselves. The role of the Holy Spirit is crucial, central, and comprehensive in Christian spiritual formation.[11] We need to surrender to the Spirit's control and ask by faith to be filled with the Spirit, day by day, and moment by moment.

Gordon Fee has underscored the need to get the Holy Spirit back into spirituality from a biblical perspective:

> The biblical texts . . . are quite clear that [Jesus'] miracles and insights into people's lives were the direct result of his living by the Spirit; or to put it in Lukan terms, "who went around doing good . . . because God was *with* him." Looking just at Luke, we see that Jesus is the Spirit person par excellence. Jesus is prophesied to be filled with the Spirit from birth (Lk 1:15). At his baptism, the Holy Spirit descends on him to empower his future ministry (Lk 3:22). Full of the Holy Spirit, he is led into the wilderness to be tempted (Lk 4:1),

---

[10]See R. Wilbourne, *Union with Christ: The Way to Know and Enjoy God* (Colorado Springs, CO: David C. Cook, 2016).

[11]E.g., see D. J. Chandler, ed., *The Holy Spirit and Christian Formation: Multidisciplinary Perspectives* (Cham, Switzerland: Palgrave MacMillan, 2016); J. P. Greenman and G. Kalantzis, eds., *Life in the Spirit: Spiritual Formation in Theological Perspective* (Downers Grove, IL: IVP Academic, 2010).

returns to Galilee in the power of the Spirit (Lk 4:14) and announces his "manifesto" with the recognition that the Spirit is on him (Lk 4:18). He is filled with joy through the Holy Spirit (Lk 10:21).[12]

He concludes with a plea that

> we more consciously allow the Spirit to have a much more major and fo- cused role in our thinking about "spirituality." As long as we continue to use this word in the way it has evolved, and thus totally separated from its singular origins in the person and work of the Holy Spirit, we will keep on talking about "spiritual exercises" rather than about genuine *Spirituality* related to what Paul calls "living in and by the Spirit." Paul means by this that the Spirit is both the "locus" and the "enabler" of our lives as believers. In an explicitly Christian context, where *Spirituality* has often deteriorated into a series of scripted or traditional routines undertaken by sheer human willpower, I would press for a meaning that is more closely related to our becoming more aware of the person and role of the Spirit in every aspect of Christian life.[13]

Fee has elsewhere described the Holy Spirit as "God's empowering presence."[14] In Acts 10:38, we read "how God anointed Jesus of Nazareth with the Holy Spirit and power, and how he went around doing good and healing all who were under the power of the devil, because God was with him."

I have therefore coauthored a book, *Disciplines of the Holy Spirit*, which emphasizes the central and crucial role and work of the Spirit in the practice of traditional spiritual disciplines in the process of Christian spiritual for- mation into deeper Christlikeness.[15] However, the Holy Spirit can work in many other ways besides the traditional spiritual disciplines or the authentic disciplines. The Holy Spirit, as God, is sovereign and is everywhere working in all kinds of situations, circumstances, and people throughout history in the whole realm of creation. He can work in his own sovereign, mysterious, and spontaneous ways to fall afresh on us or to anoint us with his power (even though he is already in us as Christians) at any time and in any place

---

[12]G. D. Fee, "On Getting the Spirit Back into Spirituality," in Greenman and Kalantzis, *Life in the Spirit*, 43-44. Emphasis original.

[13]Fee, "On Getting the Spirit Back," 44. See also Chandler, *Holy Spirit and Christian Formation*.

[14]Fee, *God's Empowering Presence: The Holy Spirit in the Letter of Paul* (Grand Rapids: Eerdmans, 1994).

[15]S. Y. Tan and D. H. Gregg, *Disciplines of the Holy Spirit* (Grand Rapids: Zondervan, 1997).

with anyone, apart from our doing anything or following any steps or practicing any spiritual disciplines.[16]

Spiritual formation from a Christian perspective therefore needs more precise definition, with the emphasis on the central and essential role and work of the Holy Spirit. Jeffrey Greenman has offered the following theologically oriented, succinct, and comprehensive definition: "Spiritual formation is our continuing response to the reality of God's grace shaping us into the likeness of Jesus Christ, through the work of the Holy Spirit, in the community of faith, for the sake of the world."[17]

POSITIVE PSYCHOLOGY OR THE SCIENCE OF VIRTUE AND CHRISTIAN SPIRITUAL FORMATION

I now turn my attention to the field of positive psychology, focusing especially on the science of virtue as Mark McMinn has described it, which includes positive psychology's theoretical and empirical work on virtues such as wisdom, forgiveness, gratitude, humility, hope, and grace, and how it may or may not be helpful or applicable to Christian spiritual formation.[18]

Positive psychology has been around as a relatively new field in psychology for about two decades. It refers to the scientific study of positive emotion, positive character, and positive institutions, and has been a widely welcome change from a traditional focus on psychopathology that has dominated clinical psychology for many decades. Seligman and Csikszentmihalyi first provided the following definition of positive psychology almost twenty years ago:

> The field of positive psychology at the subjective level is about valued subjective experiences: well-being, contentment, and satisfaction (in the past); hope and optimism (for the future); and flow and happiness (in the present).

---

[16]See S. Y. Tan, *Shepherding God's People: A Guide to Faithful and Fruitful Pastoral Ministry* (Grand Rapids: Baker Academic, 2019); see also J. R. Levison, *Filled with the Spirit* (Grand Rapids: Eerdmans, 2009); Levison, *Fresh Air: The Holy Spirit for an Inspired Life* (Brewster, MA: Paraclete Press, 2012); Levison, *Inspired: The Holy Spirit and the Mind of Faith* (Grand Rapids: Eerdmans, 2013); and A. Thiselton, *The Holy Spirit—In Biblical Teaching, Through the Centuries, and Today* (Grand Rapids: Eerdmans, 2013).

[17]J. P. Greenman, "Spiritual Formation in Theological Perspective: Classic Issues, Contemporary Challenges," in Greenman and Kalantzis, *Life in the Spirit*, 24.

[18]M. McMinn, *The Science of Virtue: Why Positive Psychology Matters to the Church* (Grand Rapids: Brazos Press, 2017).

At the individual level, it is about positive individual traits: the capacity for love and vocation, courage, interpersonal skill, aesthetic sensibility, perseverance, forgiveness, originality, future-mindedness, spirituality, high talent, and wisdom. At the group level, it is about the civic virtues and the institutions that move individuals toward better citizenship: responsibility, nurturance, altruism, civility, moderation, tolerance, and work ethic.[19]

Much progress has been made in positive psychology.[20] The earlier emphasis on happiness[21] has been expanded to a more comprehensive and visionary understanding of happiness and well-being that Martin Seligman has described as flourishing with five major pillars or dimensions, summarized as PERMA: *Positive Emotion, Engagement, Relationships, Meaning,* and *Accomplishment.*[22] Such an approach to positive psychology can be somewhat integrated with biblical teaching on the abundant life in Christ (Jn 10:10) and what Ellen Charry has described as "positive theology"; it emphasizes creation and the *imago Dei* and baptismal identity, and God and the art of happiness here and now, and not only in heaven to come.[23] However, as I have pointed out elsewhere, positive psychology does not sufficiently deal with sin, the fallenness of human beings, and evil with

---

[19]M. E. P. Seligman and M. Csikszentmihalyi, "Positive Psychology: An Introduction," *American Psychologist* 55 (2000): 5.

[20]For an early report, see M. E. P. Seligman, T. A. Steen, N. Park, and C. Peterson, "Positive Psychology Progress: Empirical Validation of Interventions," *American Psychologist* 60 (2005): 410-21; for more recent updates, see also S. Joseph, ed., *Positive Psychology Practice: Promoting Human Flourishing in Work, Health Education, and Everyday Life,* 2nd ed. (Hoboken, NJ: Wiley, 2015); S. J. Lopez and C. R. Snyder, eds., *The Oxford Handbook of Positive Psychology,* 2nd ed. (New York: Oxford University Press, 2011); C. Proctor, ed., *Positive Psychology Interventions in Practice* (New York: Springer, 2017); and A. M. Wood and J. Johnson, eds., *The Wiley Handbook of Positive Clinical Psychology* (Malden, MA: Wiley-Blackwell, 2016).

[21]E.g., see E. Diener and R. Biswas-Diener, *Happiness: Unlocking the Mysteries of Psychological Wealth* (Malden, MA: Blackwell, 2008); S. Lyubomirsky, *The How of Happiness: A Scientific Approach to Getting the Life You Want* (New York: The Penguin Press, 2007); Lyubomirsky, *The Myths of Happiness: What Should Make You Happy, but Doesn't; What Shouldn't Make You Happy, but Does* (New York: The Penguin Press, 2013); M. E. P. Seligman, *Authentic Happiness: Using the New Positive Psychology to Realize Your Potential for Lasting Fulfillment* (New York: Free Press, 2002).

[22]M. E. P. Seligman, *Flourish: A Visionary New Understanding of Happiness and Well-Being* (New York: Free Press, 2011).

[23]E. T. Charry, *God and the Art of Happiness* (Grand Rapids: Eerdmans, 2010); Charry, "Positive Theology: An Exploration in Theological Psychology and Positive Psychology," *Journal of Psychology and Christianity* 30 (2011): 284-93; see also R. Alcorn, *Happiness* (Carol Stream, IL: Tyndale House, 2015); C. H. Hackney, "Possibilities for a Christian Positive Psychology," *Journal of Psychology and Theology* 35 (2007): 211-21.

its tendency to overemphasize happiness, virtues, and strengths.[24] There is a need, from a biblical perspective, to focus more on godly sorrow and repentance (2 Cor 7:9, 10), or "positive sadness," including suffering and pain,[25] and not only on positive emotion or happiness, and therefore to note the dark side of happiness.[26] Crabb has therefore described a different kind of happiness, from a biblical perspective, that emphasizes joy that comes from sacrificial love.[27]

Despite the tendency of positive psychology to focus more on positive emotion, and especially happiness, there has also been an emphasis on virtue development and character strengths, as Schnitker, Houltberg, Dyrness, and Redmond recently pointed out.[28] Peterson and Seligman some years ago published a handbook of classification of character strengths and virtues, with six virtues and twenty-four character strengths:[29] (1) *wisdom and knowledge* (creativity, curiosity, open-mindedness, love of learning, perspective); (2) *courage* (authenticity, bravery, persistence, and zest); (3) *humanity* (kindness, love, social intelligence); (4*) justice* (fairness, leadership, teamwork); (5) *temperance* (forgiveness, modesty, prudence, self-regulation); (6) *transcendence* (appreciation of beauty and excellence. gratitude, hope, humor, religiousness).[30] This focus on virtues and character

---

[24]S. Y. Tan, "Applied Positive Psychology: Putting Positive Psychology into Practice," *Journal of Psychology and Christianity* 25 (2006): 68-73; Tan, *Counseling and Psychotherapy: A Christian Perspective* (Grand Rapids: Baker Academic, 2011); Tan, "Principled, Professional, and Personal Integration and Beyond: Further Reflections on the Past And Future," *Journal of Psychology and Theology* 40 (2012): 146-49; see also D. N. Entwistle and S. K. Moroney, "Integrative Perspectives on Human Flourishing: The *Imago Dei* and Positive Psychology," *Journal of Psychology and Theology* 39 (2011): 295-303.

[25]Tan, "Applied Positive Psychology," 73; see also L. Crabb, "Positive Psychology: More Narcissism? Or a Welcome Corrective?," *Christian Counseling Today* 12 (2004): 64.

[26]J. Gruber, I. B. Mauss, and M. Tamir, A Dark Side of Happiness: How, When, and Why Happiness Is Not Always Good," *Perspectives on Psychological Science* 6 (2011): 222-33; see also B. S. Held, "The Negative Side of Positive Psychology," *Journal of Humanistic Psychology* 44 (2004): 9-46; D. Horowitz, *Happier? The History of a Cultural Movement That Aspired to Transform America* (New York: Oxford University Press (2018).

[27]L. Crabb, *A Different Kind of Happiness: Discovering the Joy That Comes from Sacrificial Love* (Grand Rapids: Baker Books, 2016); see also Alcorn, *Happiness.*

[28]S. A. Schnitker, B. Houltberg, W. Dyrness, and N. Redmond, "The Virtue of Patience, Spirituality and Suffering: Integrating Lessons from Positive Psychology, Psychology of Religion and Christian Theology," *Psychology of Religion and Spirituality* 9 (2017): 264-75.

[29]C. Peterson and M. E. P. Seligman, *Character Strengths and Virtues: A Handbook and Classification* (Washington, DC: American Psychological Association, 2004).

[30]As summarized by Seligman et al., "Positive Psychology Progress"; see also Tan, "Applied Positive Psychology," 68-69.

strengths in positive psychology overlaps much with the field of the psychology of religion, which focuses on the psychological processes related to spirituality, religious behavior, and religious experience, and especially on meaning in life and stress-related growth.[31] Park years ago emphasized the need for positive psychology to draw more from the psychology of religion, with its many years of previous research and theoretical work on related topics that positive psychology has only more recently investigated.[32] A recent special issue of *Psychology of Religion and Spirituality*, the official journal of the Society for the Psychology of Religion and Spirituality (Division 36 of the American Psychological Association), therefore focused on the psychology of virtue.[33]

Kaczor has thoughtfully critiqued some definitions of key virtues in positive psychology that may need more sharpening from a Christian biblical perspective.[34] For example, humility has been defined by Davis and others thus: "We argue that humility involves being other-oriented rather than self-focused, marked by behaviors that indicate a lack of superiority within a relational and cultural context."[35] Kaczor critiques this definition of humility by pointing out the need to include an awareness of one's limitations, as in intellectual humility. He writes, "Humility in a more generic sense consists in a proper attentiveness to, and owning of, one's limitations of whatever nature (moral, intellectual, spiritual, psychological, physical). Humble

---

[31]R. W. Hood Jr., P. C. Hill, and B. Spilka, *The Psychology of Religion: An Empirical Approach* (New York: Guilford Press, 2018); R. F. Paloutzian and C. L. Park, eds., *Handbook of the Psychology of Religion and Spirituality*, 2nd ed. (New York: Guilford Press, 2013); C. L. Park, "The Psychology of Religion and Positive Psychology," *Psychology of Religion Newsletter* 28 (2003): 1-8.

[32]Park, "Psychology of Religion."

[33]"The Psychology of Virtue: Integrating Positive Psychology and the Psychology of Religion," ed. Sarah Schnitker and Robert Emmons, special issue, *Psychology of Religion and Spirituality* 9, no. 3 (August, 2017). The following were the major articles published in this special issue: D. E. Davis, J. N. Hook, R. McAnnally-Linz, E. Choe, and V. Placeres, "Humility, Religion, and Spirituality: A Review of the Literature," 242-53; P. Van Cappelen, "Rethinking Self-Transcendent Positive Emotions (e.g., Awe, Gratitude, Elevation and Admiration, Love and Compassion, Peacefulness, and Joy) and Religion: Insights from Psychological and Biblical Research," 254-63; Schnitker et al., "Virtue of Patience," 264-75; R. A. Emmons, P. C. Hill, J. L. Barrett, and K. M. Kapic, "Psychological and Theological Reflections on Grace and Its Relevance for Science and Practice," 276-84; and S. A. Hardy and B. J. Willoughby, "Religiosity and Chastity Among Single Young Adults and Married Adults," 285-95.

[34]C. Kaczor, "Commentary: On Definition and Traditions," *Psychology of Religion and Spirituality* 9 (2017): 296-98.

[35]Davis et al., "Humility, Religion, and Spirituality," 243.

people recognize their own imperfections, faults, failings, and weaknesses. The one who is humble 'owns' these limitations."[36] Another example is the definition of *patience* provided by Schnitker and others as "a willingness to suffer—to bear under or tolerate—what are perceived as negative circumstances."[37] Kaczor suggests considering other alternative understandings of the term *patience* for research purposes in the future, and more specifically following Thomas Aquinas and Augustine: "Thomas Aquinas understood patience following Augustine, as bearing evils with equanimity so as not to be disturbed by sorrow from pursuing the good. . . . Obviously, these definitions do not differ radically from one another, but they are not also identical. Aquinas added the point that the patient person maintains a tranquility of mind against sorrow that enables the person to advance toward a better life."[38]

Mark McMinn has recently written a very helpful book on the science of virtue, focusing on why positive psychology matters to the church.[39] He reviews a large body of literature and empirical work in positive psychology, specifically on the science of virtue, covering six major virtues: wisdom, forgiveness, gratitude, humility, hope, and grace. He also provides biblical perspectives on these virtues, and shares from his own life and experiences in a gracious, humble, and vulnerable way. He noted that some of the leading figures in positive psychology and especially in the scientific study of virtues include outstanding Christian psychologists and researchers, such as Everett Worthington on forgiveness and humility, and Robert Emmons on gratitude and grace. Worthington, Griffin, and Lavelock have also written a recent chapter emphasizing how the science of positive psychology and its focus on eudaimonic virtue and the theory of virtue can help in spiritual formation.[40]

McMinn writes,

> The church can help the science of positive psychology. In many ways it already has helped by providing many of the leading positive psychology

---

[36]Kaczor, "Commentary," 296.
[37]Schnitker et al., "Virtue of Patience," 265.
[38]Kaczor, "Commentary," 298.
[39]McMinn, *Science of Virtue.*
[40]E. L. Worthington Jr., B. J. Griffin, and C. R. Lavelock, "Cultivating the Fruit of the Spirit: Contributions of Positive Psychology to Spiritual Formation," in Crisp et al., *Psychology and Spiritual Formation*, 206-34.

scholars. . . . The church can also contribute by providing a metaphysic for positive psychology. Why is gratitude worthwhile? What about forgiveness makes it good? In what ways might humility promote a better way of living than self-interest does? . . . Left on its own, positive psychology tends to settle back to a place of self-interest. I forgive because it's good for me. I practice gratitude because it lowers my blood pressure. I pursue hope because it adds to my quality of life. Me, me, me. Many scientists fail to see the paradox of how a science of virtue can be twisted to be so very self-centered. And to this, the church offers a nudge toward the love of God and neighbor.[41]

McMinn concludes with four recommendations for redeeming virtue:

First, positive psychology helps us to reclaim the language of virtue—a language that has been mostly lost in contemporary times. . . . Second, if we in the church engage the science of virtue, and those of us in science engage the church, we can help make the science better. When scientists lean toward the personal health effects of virtues, those in the church can nod and remind them of the larger context of virtues as well. Yes, we may live longer if we forgive our foes, but we will also forge stronger communities and encourage others who observe our forgiveness to forgive their foes as well. . . . Third, the church can be stronger by engaging science in conversation. Even if we in the church know that forgiveness is about more than personal health, we may not know how to go about forgiving very well. But the science can help us. Worthington has offered compelling evidence for his REACH method of forgiveness. . . . Finally, the science of virtue can help transform the way we understand Christian counseling. So much of contemporary counseling is focused on alleviating suffering, and this is a high calling. . . . Once the weeping together is done, and the comfort is offered, and trust is established, counselors and clients can together envision a telos. What might it be like to move forward in life toward full functioning and wholeness? Here's an adventure worth considering: maybe Christian counselors, working in the guiding light of God's spirit, can lead the way in bringing virtue back into the counseling office.[42]

Stanton Jones has also provided a brief Christian critique of positive psychology (PP).[43] He points out that it is problematic that there seems to be

---

[41]McMinn, *Science of Virtue*, 163.
[42]McMinn, *Science of Virtue*, 168-70.
[43]S. L. Jones, *Psychology: A Student's Guide* (Wheaton, IL: Crossway, 2014), 100-105.

nothing transcendent or that is beyond self-interest in PP. He writes, "It comes as no surprise, then, that the virtues as articulated by secular PP and the virtues as understood within Christian faith do not quite line up."[44] Following Watts and others,[45] Jones critiques the following specific virtues emphasized in PP: (1) *Forgiveness*—PP often presents forgiveness as a practice that makes one happy and benefits oneself, and is therefore mainly about feeling better, whereas forgiveness can be profoundly sacrificial from a Christian perspective. PP also focuses almost exclusively on giving forgiveness, whereas a religious perspective emphasizes both receiving and giving forgiveness. (2) *Gratitude*—Gratitude for a gift or kindness from someone else is understandable, but it may be more difficult to comprehend being grateful to a meaningless universe for benefits that may be experienced by an unbeliever. Also, a Christian perspective on thankfulness emphasizes giving thanks at all times for whatever comes from God, and not being grateful for only whatever makes us happy. (3) *Hope*—PP often uses the term *hope* or *hopefulness* to refer more to optimism and a person expecting good outcomes for himself or herself. Religious hope however has to do more with hoping in God, and not in certain good outcomes per se, and is therefore more concerned with the will or desires of God than with positive outcomes for oneself.[46]

Jones therefore concludes, "Positive psychology seems to be confidently, if naively, seeking to do the kind of character formation in fostering virtue that can be ultimately grounded rightly only in Christian faith. There are positive lessons to learn, nonetheless, from the endeavors of PP and how we understand human virtue and develop well-being."[47]

Conclusions

The crucial and essential role of the Holy Spirit in Christian spiritual formation into deeper Christlikeness has been emphasized from a biblical perspective.[48] While traditional spiritual disciplines (e.g., solitude and silence,

---

[44]Jones, *Psychology*, 103.

[45]F. Watts et al., "Human Spiritual Qualities: Integrating Psychology and Religion," *Mental Health, Religion and Culture* 9 (2006): 277-89.

[46]Jones, *Psychology*, 103-4.

[47]Jones, *Psychology*, 105.

[48]See Fee, "On Getting the Spirit Back."

prayer, Scripture meditation and study, confession, submission, fasting, worship, fellowship, simplicity, service, and witness) and authentic or circumstantial disciplines (e.g., waiting, suffering, persecution, forgiveness, mourning, contentment, and sacrifice) are means of grace that the Holy Spirit can use in Christian spiritual formation, it is ultimately the Holy Spirit who transforms us to become more like Jesus (2 Cor 3:18; see also Zech 4:6; Eph 5:18). Surrender, and not self-effort in the flesh or sinful nature, is the key to the Spirit's deep work within us, and among us, for God's glory and our ultimate fulfillment in Christ. The Holy Spirit can work anywhere, anytime, with anyone in whatever way he sovereignly and sometimes mysteriously and paradoxically wants to, to empower and transform us to become more like Jesus and to do the works of Jesus.

The recent work in positive psychology and especially in the science of virtue can be of some benefit to Christian spiritual formation, for example, in helping to delineate helpful steps to forgiving others, as in Everett Worthington's REACH (Recall the Hurt, Empathize, Altruistic Gift, Commit, Hold On) model of forgiveness.[49] However, there are some problematic aspects of positive psychology and the science of virtue that have been pointed out. Positive psychology can be too positive, with an ever-present danger of emphasizing self-effort and self-improvement with a focus on benefits to the self in the development of virtues and character strengths. A biblical perspective on virtues and spiritual formation will emphasize more the work of the Holy Spirit, producing the fruit of the Spirit that is ultimately Christlike character: love, joy, peace, forbearance, kindness, goodness, faithfulness, gentleness, and self-control (Gal 5:22-23). Christian spiritual formation or virtue and character development focuses on loving God and loving others (Mk 12:30, 31). It is centered in God and his glory and the blessing of others, including ourselves, but without a need to be self-obsessed. The virtues and character strengths in positive psychology also need further refinement and even correction, using more biblical definitions and perspectives on virtues and Christian spiritual formation or Christlike character development.

---

[49]See McMinn, *Science of Virtue*, 60; E. L. Worthington Jr., *Forgiving and Reconciling: Bridges to Wholeness and Hope* (Downers Grove, IL: InterVarsity Press, 2003).

4

"That's the Spirit!" Or, What Exactly Does Spiritual Formation Form?

Toward a Theological Formulation of a Biblical Answer

KEVIN J. VANHOOZER

Introduction: A Working Hypothesis

"That's the spirit!" is a common rather than a Christian idiom, something you might say in order to encourage someone to persevere in some endeavor. Generally speaking, people are much more comfortable using such expressions than explaining what *spirit* actually means, or in specifying that to which it actually refers. Pastors do not have this luxury. They need to have some idea of what the spirit *is* in order to engage in spiritual formation: *spiritual formation without ontological presuppositions is impossible.* Hence my central question: What exactly does spiritual formation form?

What we think spirit *is* will invariably orient what we *do* in our spiritual formation. This essay, on the nature of the human spirit, ought to be of interest to pastors and theologians alike, inasmuch as it attempts to spell out the theological assumptions, often unstated, that fund our pastoral practices.

My working hypothesis is that we will get nearer to the ontological core of the human spirit if we follow the way the (biblical) words go in speaking about it. J. L. Austin, the ordinary language philosopher, viewed words as highly sensitive instruments for describing reality and discerning differences between things—able to "penetrate . . . even to dividing soul and spirit" (Heb 4:12): "The fact is . . . that our ordinary words are much subtler in their uses, and mark many more distinctions, than philosophers have realized."[1] Ordinary language is not a blunt conceptual instrument, but rather, for those who have the ears to hear it, a finely tuned precision tool.[2] In following the way the biblical words go, my hope is that we can turn the water of ordinary discourse about the spirit into the wine of theological concept, and thereby attain faith's search for understanding.[3]

We begin, then, with a sampling of how *spirit* shows up in ordinary discourse, both contemporary and biblical. I then examine "general" human pneumatology, that is, attempts to explain or express the human spirit from the humanities and the human sciences. I turn next to "special" human pneumatology, namely, a survey of how Christian psychologists and others involved in spiritual formation define or identify the human spirit. In what follows I stake some constructive theological claims that synthesize and focus the discussion by providing four "theses on the human spirit." I conclude with some suggestions for how to apply my proposed theological understanding of spirit to the pastoral practice of spiritual formation.

THE WAY THE WORDS GO: "SPIRIT" IN
ORDINARY AND BIBLICAL DISCOURSE

Ordinary discourse. Consider the expression, "a spirited horse." This is an anthropomorphism that refers to a horse's energy and determination. The adjectival form often describes a prevailing or typical quality of human persons too (e.g., "Ebenezer Scrooge was mean-spirited"). As to the nominative form, the first entry in the *Oxford English Dictionary* under "spirit" is "the non-physical part of a person which is the seat of emotions and character." Together, these two uses illustrate the baseline meaning: spirit is the typical or prevailing disposition displayed by a person's bearing and behavior.

---

[1] J. L. Austin, *Sense and Sensibilia* (Oxford: Oxford University Press, 1962), 3.
[2] J. L. Austin describes this approach as a "linguistic phenomenology" (*Philosophical Papers*, 3rd ed. [Oxford: Oxford University Press, 1976], 182).
[3] Cf. John Cooper's similar commitment to "ordinary-language realism" ("Scripture and Philosophy on the Unity of Body and Soul," in *The Ashgate Research Companion to Theological Anthropology*, ed. Joshua R. Farris and Charles Taliaferro [New York: Routledge, 2017], 28).

Not only persons but seasons too have certain qualities. Toward the end of his story, Scrooge displays the true "spirit of Christmas," which for Dickens meant displaying generosity and good cheer. There's also "spirit week," a time for young people to show enthusiastic support for their schools' activities. This use touches on one of Anthony Thiselton's pet peeves. He objects to the way "spirituality" has migrated from its original reference to the work of the third person of the Trinity to a way of talking about "excited" human experience. If only speakers respected this distinction, he laments, we might not make the mistake of thinking that people are divinely gifted for church ministry simply because they are full of enthusiasm.[4] As Fred Sanders puts it, "Not every tingle you feel is the Holy Ghost! Sometimes it's just the good old animal spirits getting riled up."[5]

Biblical discourse. According to Nancey Murphy, a nonreductive physicalist, "there is no such thing as *the* biblical view of human nature *insofar as we are interested in a partitive account*."[6] By "partitive" account, she means one that views human beings as made up of different parts, like body and soul. The question, then, is how to interpret the Bible's references to human spirit. To recall our primary question: What exactly does spiritual formation form? To take but one scenario: if humans are essentially individual souls who just happen to have bodies, we might conclude that the body is of no concern to spiritual formation.

Old Testament. J. A. T. Robinson dents our high hopes of letting ordinary biblical language be our guide: "From the standpoint of analytic psychology and physiology the usage of the Old Testament is chaotic: it is the nightmare of the anatomist when any part can stand at any moment for the whole."[7] Herman Bavinck is more realistic, and in keeping with ordinary language analysis, in admitting that the Bible no more gives us a scientific psychology than it does a scientific account of astronomy: "Holy Scripture never makes

---

[4]Anthony C. Thiselton, *A Shorter Guide to the Holy Spirit: Bible, Doctrine, Experience* (Grand Rapids: Eerdmans, 2016).

[5]Fred Sanders, "Thiselton, Briefly, on the Holy Spirit," *The Scriptorium Daily*, Nov. 1, 2017, http://scriptoriumdaily.com/thiselton-briefly-on-the-holy-spirit/.

[6]Nancey Murphy, *Bodies and Souls, or Spirited Bodies?* (Cambridge: Cambridge University Press, 2006), 22 (emphasis original).

[7]J. A. T. Robinson, *The Body* (London: SCM Press, 1952), 16.

use of abstract, philosophical concepts, but always speaks the rich language of everyday life."[8]

Genesis 2:7 depicts human beings as dust from the ground into which God breathes life so that Adam becomes "a living being" or "soul" (*nephesh*). Animals have *nephesh* too, for they also are living beings that breathe. The LXX translates 600 of the 755 occurrences of *nephesh* in the OT by *psyche*, from which we get our term *psychology*. *Nephesh* appears frequently as the seat of emotions: it is troubled (Ps 6:3), depressed (Ps 42:11 NET), angry (Judg 18:25), weeps (Jer 13:17), and rejoices (Ps 35:9). According to Hans Walter Wolff, *nephesh* "is never given the meaning of an indestructible core of being, in contradistinction to the physical life."[9] It is not that humans *have nephesh*, as much as they *are nephesh*.[10] The idea of an immortal bodiless soul only turns up in later Jewish authors such as Philo: "It is indebted to Plato rather than to the Bible."[11]

The Old Testament Hebrew term for "spirit" is *ruach*. *Ruach* means wind power, both when it refers to God's Spirit moving over the face of the waters (Gen 1:2) or when it refers to the lesser human spirit/wind—our breath. God gives his own Spirit to certain individuals to perform certain tasks (Judg 3:10). Ezekiel 37:1-10 describes how God breathes into a valley of dry bones to bring them to life. Yet it is also possible to speak of the human spirit, which appears to be the seat of emotion, will, and intellect (Prov 18:14 "The human spirit can endure in sickness, but a crushed spirit who can bear?"; Num 14:24 "Because my servant Caleb has a different spirit and follows me wholeheartedly, I will bring him into the land"; Prov 17:27 "Whoever restrains his words has knowledge, and he who has a cool spirit [*ruach*] is a man of understanding" ESV). According to the psalmist, when our breath departs, so do we (Ps 146:4). In sum, *ruach* "empowers humans to do whatever they were created to do."[12]

---

[8]Translation by Anthony A. Hoekema of Bavinck's *Biblical and Religious Psychology*, cited in Hoekema, *Created in God's Image* (Grand Rapids: Eerdmans, 1986), 204.

[9]Hans Walter Wolff, *Anthropology of the Old Testament* (London: SCM, 1974), 20.

[10]Cf. Kenneth A. Mathews on Gen 2:7: "In our passage man does not possess a *nephesh* but rather is a *nephesh* (individual person)" (*Genesis 1–11:26* ACC 1A [Nashville: Broadman & Holman, 1996], 196).

[11]Brian Rosner, *Known by God: A Biblical Theology of Personal Identity* (Grand Rapids: Zondervan, 2017), 67.

[12]John W. Cooper, *Body, Soul & Life Everlasting: Biblical Anthropology and the Monism-Dualism Debate*, 2nd ed. (Grand Rapids: Eerdmans, 1989), 40.

The Old Testament employs many more terms to speak of human beings, including *basar* ("flesh") and *lev* ("heart"), but most scholars agree with H. Wheeler Robinson's judgment that "the final emphasis must fall on the fact that the four terms [*nephesh, ruach, lev,* and *basar*] . . . simply present different aspects of the unity of personality."[13] According to Richard Averbeck, "*ruach* can refer either to an immaterial element of the human person . . . or to the whole of the immaterial person."[14] Interestingly, Scripture describes God as *spirit*, but never as *soul*.

New Testament. There are some forty New Testament instances of *pneuma* denoting the human spirit.[15] It is the presence of *pneuma* that enlivens a body: "As the body without the spirit is dead, so faith without deeds is dead" (Jas 2:26).[16] While all human persons have *pneuma*, Paul sees it as taking on "a new character and a new dignity" in the regenerate thanks to their fellowship with the Spirit of God (Rom 8:10).[17] Paul does not view human beings as essentially spiritual or immaterial, for he exhorts Christians in Rome to "offer your bodies as a living sacrifice" (Rom 12:1).

The situation is different with flesh (*sarx*). Whereas Paul cannot imagine human existence without a body, he contrasts living "according to the flesh" with living "by the [Holy] Spirit" (Rom 8:12-13). Flesh here is not a physical but an eschatological notion, a way of referring to human existence in the present evil age.[18] The Christian hope for the last day is for a "spiritual body," that is, "a physical body wholly belonging to the new age, wholly like Christ, wholly under the Spirit's direction (Rom 8:11, 23; 1 Cor 15:44-49)."[19]

---

[13]H. Wheeler Robinson, *The Christian Doctrine of Man* (Edinburgh: T&T Clark, 1911), 27.

[14]Richard E. Averbeck, "Breath, Wind, Spirit and the Holy Spirit in the Old Testament," in *Presence, Power, and Promise: The Role of the Spirit of God in the Old Testament*, ed. David G. Firth and Paul D. Wegner (Downers Grove, IL: IVP Academic, 2011), 11.

[15]It is occasionally hard to tell whether the reference is to the human spirit or the Holy Spirit. See, for example, Matthew 26:41—"The spirit is willing, but the flesh is weak"—which might be a contrast between physical and nonphysical aspects of our humanity or between unaided human effort and enablement by the Holy Spirit.

[16]See further Marjorie O'Rourke Boyle, *The Human Spirit: Beginnings from Genesis to Science* (University Park, PA: Penn State University Press, 2018).

[17]W. D. Stacey, *The Pauline View of Man* (London: Macmillan, 1956), 135.

[18]See Susan Grove Eastman: "*Sarx* participates exclusively in what Paul calls 'the present evil age' (Gal 1:4)," *Paul and the Person: Reframing Paul's Anthropology* (Grand Rapids: Eerdmans, 2017), 89.

[19]Moises Silva, "*Pneuma*," in *New International Dictionary of New Testament Theology and Exegesis*, 2nd ed., vol. 3 (Grand Rapids: Zondervan), 816.

As to the difference of spirit and soul (*psyche*), New Testament scholars detect a subtle yet significant distinction. George Ladd comments, "Spirit is often used of God; soul is never so used. This suggests that *pneuma* represents man in his Godward side, while *psyche* represents man in his human side."[20] Moises Silva concludes his analysis of *pneuma* with these words: "Thus the spirit is that aspect of our human nature through which God most immediately encounters us . . . that dimension whereby we are most directly open and responsive to God."[21]

Susan Eastman's *Paul and the Person: Reframing Paul's Anthropology* deserves special mention in connection with this last point, particularly as it relates to Paul's claim that "the Spirit himself testifies with our spirit that we are God's children" (Rom 8:16). To this point, the concept of person has been conspicuous by its absence. Eastman argues that Paul did indeed think about persons, not as individualized thinking subjects, but "as relationally constituted agents who are both embodied and embedded in their world."[22] She is particularly struck by expressions that take the form "I no longer [verb] but [subject plus verb] in me," as in "I no longer live, but Christ lives in me" (Gal 2:20).[23] Such expressions suggest that a person is never on his or her own "but always socially and cosmically constructed in relation to external realities that operate internally as well."[24] Eastman self-consciously adopts a "second-person hermeneutics," that is, an approach based on second-person encounters rather than first-person (i.e., self-referential) or third-person (i.e., objectifying) accounts. Her key insight: if we want to understand persons, we must begin with the self in relationship to another. This will prove to be a key point when below I present spiritual formation as a dialogical relationship that gives pride of place to the Holy Spirit's witness to our spirit.[25]

---

[20]George Ladd, *A Theology of the New Testament* (Grand Rapids: Eerdmans, 1974), 459.
[21]Silva, "*Pneuma*," 807.
[22]Eastman, *Paul and the Person*, 2.
[23]Eastman, *Paul and the Person*, 6.
[24]Eastman, *Paul and the Person*, 8.
[25]For more on second-person perspectives, see the sources referred to in Eastman, *Paul and the Person*, 15-16.

IS SPIRIT A PART OR ASPECT OF A PERSON?
MONISM, DUALISM, AND TRICHOTOMY

Thinking of the human spirit in terms of an immaterial substance raises the pastoral concern of dualism, which distinguishes the spiritual from the secular and relegates the body to the latter, making one's interior life the exclusive focus of spiritual formation. Nancey Murphy, a critic of such dualism, wonders whether church history would have gone differently if a physicalist anthropology had prevailed instead. At the very least, spiritual formation would not have been reduced to soul care.[26] What conclusions, then, should we draw from the biblical discourse about the human constitution? What exactly does spiritual formation form?

Spirit as part of human being. Monists like Nancey Murphy reject the picture of immortal souls temporarily housed in physical bodies, insisting instead that we *are* our bodies: complex physical organisms in relationship to other humans and to God. She claims that Scripture teaches a holistic view and that dualism came later, with Plato, and cites James Dunn in support: "while Greek thought tended to regard the human being as made up of distinct parts, Hebraic thought saw the human being more as a whole person existing on different dimensions."[27]

Dualists view soul and spirit as roughly synonymous, insisting they denote an immaterial part of human being that lives on after the death of the body. It is noteworthy for present purposes that dualists tend to speak of the two parts as body and soul (rarely *spirit*). Dualists are on strongest biblical ground with regard to postmortem, preresurrection existence, arguing that the soul exists in an intermediate state after death until it is reunited with a resurrection body. A key text here is 2 Corinthians 5:8: "We . . . would prefer to be away from the body and at home with the Lord."

Trichotomists maintain that spirit, soul, and body, mentioned together in 1 Thessalonians 5:23, refer to three separate human elements. Franz Delitzsch quotes Luther: "Scripture divides man into three parts. . . . The spirit is the highest, noblest part of man, wherewith he is fitted to apprehend intangible, invisible, eternal things; and it is briefly the house within which the faith and

---

[26]Murphy, *Bodies and Souls,* 27.
[27]Dunn, *Theology of the Apostle Paul,* 54.

word of God dwells."[28] Witness Lee similarly distinguishes soul/mind from
spirit: "When you go to school to study, you have to use your mind. But when
you come to the church to contact God, you have to use your human spirit."[29]
Such sharp distinctions provoke concerns about dualism in the Christian life,
where only certain experiences or activities are deemed spiritual—apparently
to the detriment of thinking, which is not one of them.

There is conclusive biblical evidence against trichotomy. Scripture often
uses "soul" and "spirit" interchangeably.[30] Sometimes body is linked to soul
(Mt 10:28), at other times to spirit (1 Cor 7:34). Human emotions like grief can
be ascribed either to *soul* or *spirit* (e.g., Jn 12:27; 13:21). Finally, Scripture describes dying as the departure either of the soul or spirit (Gen 35:18; Eccles 12:7).

Spirit as aspect of human being. I am less interested in taking side in
these debates than in articulating some common concerns and finding
common ground.[31] First, almost everyone affirms the unity of human being:
"Monists and dualists agree that body, soul, spirit, heart, mind, and will—
whatever their metaphysical nature and relation—are diverse but interde-
pendent, interactive, and integrated aspects or parts of living, active
humans."[32] Biblical scholars agree that "such terms as body, soul, and spirit
are not different, separable faculties of man but different ways of viewing the
whole man."[33] John Cooper draws an important practical implication: "all
of life images God, is a gift from him, and should be lived for God. . . . All
of life is religious or spiritual."[34]

Second, everyone affirms the diversity of human being, as Cooper notes:
"Dualists hold that God has integrated metaphysically distinct ingredients.
. . . Monists counter that God has elicited the interconnected diversity from

---

[28]Luther, *Exposition of the Magnificat of the Year* 1521, cited in Franz Delitzsch, *A System of Biblical Psychology* (Edinburgh: T&T Clark, 1867), 460. Some trichotomists say that only humans have spirits, others say that only believers are given spirits, the key point being that spirit is that part of human being that enters into contact with God.

[29]Witness Lee, *Our Human Spirit* (Anaheim, CA: Living Stream Ministry, 1984), 8.

[30]Cf. J. Gresham Machen: "The Bible does not distinguish the human spirit from the human soul. No doubt these two words designate the same thing in two different ways" (*The Christian View of Man* [Grand Rapids: Eerdmans, 1947], 167-68).

[31]Having said that, my own position is akin to the "moderate dualism" defended by Cooper and described by Cornelis van der Kooi and Gijsbert van den Brink, *Christian Dogmatics: An Intro-duction* (Grand Rapids: Eerdmans, 2017), 270-71.

[32]John Cooper, "Scripture and Philosophy," 30.

[33]Ladd, *Theology of the New Testament*, 457.

[34]Cooper, "Scripture and Philosophy," 30-31.

a single primordial ingredient. But neither group can declare victory or disqualify the other on the basis of the biblical data."[35] Cooper grants this as a convinced "holistic dualist" who has written a book defending his position.

In sum: we can affirm the unity of human being without falling into monism, and the diversity of our constitution without succumbing to dualism: "Man is *one* person who can . . . be looked at from *two* sides," as a "psychosomatic duality." Some prefer to speak of "psychosomatic holism" out of a concern that duality "implies that the distinction between soul and body is more basic than its unity. The important point is . . . the 'real self' is the whole self—body and soul."[36]

What is noteworthy is how these developments enable monists and dualists to become positively chummy. They still disagree over the basic constitution of human nature—one lump or two?—yet both affirm holism. Nancey Murphy, a leading nonreductive physicalist, speaks of humans as psycho-physical unities, and John Cooper, a dualist, now concedes that "dualistic holism" is an equally acceptable expression of the biblical picture of the human constitution as "holistic dualism."[37] Even the Eastern Orthodox want to get in on the diplomatic action. Kallistos Ware notes that the Greek fathers use "heart" to designate "the human being as a psycho-somatic whole."[38] Such holism also coheres with the consensus outside biblical studies: "Developments in biology, psychology, and the neurosciences all tend toward the conclusion that humans are much more of an organic unit of soul/spirit and body than has been traditionally thought."[39]

I usually find myself on the side of the peacemakers, happy to help theologians resolve longstanding disputes. Yet, in this case, where the lion of monism can lie down with the dualist lamb, I'm not so sure. The good we have gained is our embodied souls, yet we appear to have forfeited our spirits. Whichever way one cuts holism, the privileged terms are "soul" and "body," leaving no place for *pneuma* in the psychosomatic inn.

---

[35]Cooper, "Scripture and Philosophy," 31.

[36]Michael Horton, *The Christian Faith* (Grand Rapids: Zondervan, 2011), 377.

[37]Cooper, *Body, Soul & Life Everlasting*, xxvii. Robert Gundry opts for "psychosomatic unity" with "ontological duality" as the best description of the apostle Paul's position (*Soma in Biblical Theology with Emphasis on Pauline Anthropology* [Cambridge: Cambridge University Press, 1976], 83-84).

[38]Kallistos Ware, "The Soul in Greek Christianity," in *From Soul to Self*, ed. James C. Crabbe (London: Routledge, 1999), 59.

[39]Van der Kooi and van den Brink, *Christian Dogmatics*, 267.

"GENERAL" VERSUS "SPECIAL" HUMAN PNEUMATOLOGY

I am not yet ready to give up the ghost (i.e., the human spirit). I here examine what for lack of a better term we could call "general" human pneumatology—what people in the humanities and human sciences are saying about the human spirit on grounds other than explicit Christian faith. This detour into the humanities unexpectedly yields a precious insight into what spiritual formation forms.

"General" human pneumatology: What culture cultivates. "Generic" as opposed to Christian spirituality pertains to how human thinking and behavior are partially formed through a person's social relationships. If proverbial wisdom is correct—that we can know a person by the company she keeps—then it is equally true that we can know a person by the culture she inhabits. Culture is that complex whole whose values and practices inform the shape of social life, indeed, the very atmosphere one virtually *breathes*. Whatever else we say about spirit, it is that which in a person gets partially formed and informed by culture. We can therefore get a better handle on what spiritual formation forms by asking, What does culture cultivate?

Beyond the nature/nurture divide: Evolutionary cultural studies. Human development involves nature and nurture. However, according to the new academic discipline of cultural evolutionary studies, evolutionary processes are at work in culture and biology alike.[40] Humans are a combination of biological genes *and* cultural memes (i.e., inherited packets of culture), and the ability to transmit culture is one of the most distinctive things about the human species. We learn to think and act in large part from the communities of which we are members. And, just as certain genetic pathologies can adversely affect our bodies, so some culturally transmitted diseases can have a deleterious effect on our souls, especially when they go viral (e.g., the ice bucket challenge, dancing babies, or "the most interesting man in the world").[41]

Warren S. Brown and Brad D. Strawn critique dualism precisely for overlooking the role of social relations in spiritual formation: "We are formed

---

[40]See further Nicole Creanza, Oren Kolodny, and Marcus W. Feldman, "Cultural Evolutionary Theory: How Culture Evolves and Why It Matters," *Proceedings of the National Academy of Sciences of the United States of America*, 114, no. 30 (July 25, 2017): 7782-89.

[41]See further Robert Aunger, *The Electric Meme: A New Theory of How We Think* (New York: Free Press, 2002).

into mature, virtuous, and wise persons, not by some disembodied mystical process, but by life together in a body of persons."[42] The cultural company we keep is perhaps the single most important formative factor in what I am calling general human pneumatology.

Shapes of freedom. Culture cultivates, grows things, and what culture grows is the "spirit of an age" or Zeitgeist. Think of culture as the petri dish of the human spirit. The philosopher Hegel examines the development of civilization as *Geist's* progressive realization of freedom in the laboratory of human history. *Shapes of freedom* is the operative concept.[43] Hegel says why: "Just as gravity is the substance of matter, so . . . freedom is the substance of spirit."[44] The natural sciences explain physical events by causal laws; the human sciences strive to understand shapes of freedom. Hegel views the history of human civilization as evidence of Spirit's progress: ancient civilizations had limited notions of freedom, whereas democracy only flowered in modern times. We don't need to buy into either cultural evolution or Hegel, however, to appreciate the central point that communities and civilizations cultivate spirits, that is, specific shapes of individual and communal freedom.[45]

To the extent we are modern, we have probably been formed, at least to some extent, by the prevailing secular Zeitgeist. Modern culture trades on a particular "coming of age" story. The spirit of modernity throws off the shackles of tradition and authority in order to reason for itself. If modernity had a bio, it would surely be an emancipation narrative. To be modern is to have a liberated spirit whose aim is to liberate those who are still captive to various forms of oppression. Modern culture forms autonomous individuals: consumerist, self-entitled shapes of freedom. This, too, is spiritual formation.

"Special" human pneumatology: Christian psychology and spiritual formation. What do Christian counselors and spiritual directors assume about the human spirit? Is it significant that the term "psychology" derives from

---

[42]Warren S. Brown and Brad D. Strawn, *The Physical Nature of Christian Life: Neuroscience, Psychology, and the Church* (New York: Cambridge University Press, 2012), 87.

[43]My discussion is indebted to that of Peter C. Hodgson, *God in History: Shapes of Freedom* (Nashville: Abingdon Press, 1989).

[44]G. W. F. Hegel, *Lectures on the Philosophy of World History*, trans H. B. Nisbet (Cambridge: Cambridge University Press, 1975), 47.

[45]James K. A. Smith's concept of cultural liturgies expresses a similar phenomenon: culture forms specific shapes of worship or habits of the heart. See his *You Are What You Love: The Spiritual Power of Habit* (Grand Rapids: Brazos Press, 2016).

psyche ("soul"), not spirit? Assuming both groups accept some form of dualistic holism, what place, if any, does the notion of the human spirit play in their respective theological anthropologies?

Christian psychology. John Coe and Todd Hall build on Kierkegaard's understanding of human being as spirit ("a relation that relates itself to itself"[46]) and call for a retrieval of "a psychology that is grounded in the [Holy] Spirit and a radically relational view of the person."[47] The Christian's most important relation is with the Holy Spirit: "the ultimate end of human existence is union of the human spirit with God's Spirit."[48]

Coe and Hall highlight the Bible's use of *spirit* "to represent the core or innermost elements of the person."[49] They describe human persons as "subsisting spirits . . . which are embodied or joined as spirit-body holistic organisms and centers of motion."[50] The human spirit has a nature that is common to other human persons (Coe and Hall call this "spirit-as-nature"), but is also a unique entity as the core of personal identity ("spirit-as-agent"). Spirit is a relation because there is a dialectic between the observed-I (spirit-nature) and the observing-I (spirit-agent). The self is only fully itself, however, "when in absolute union with God in the core of the self."[51] Coe and Hall go so far as to say that a self that is not indwelt by God is "not a fully realized self, but a sort of half-person."[52]

Spiritual formation. Dallas Willard defines spiritual formation as "the process of transforming the person into Christlikeness through transforming *the essential parts* of the person."[53] What are these parts? The body is one of them: "You are a nonphysical reality with a physical body."[54] As to the nonphysical part, Willard defines the heart as "the will or the spirit . . . the executive center of the self"[55] and the soul as "the deepest part of the

---

[46]Soren Kierkegaard, *The Sickness unto Death: A Christian Psychological Exposition for Upbuilding and Awakening* (Princeton, NJ: Princeton University Press, 1983), 13.

[47]John Coe and Todd W. Hall, *Psychology in the Spirit: Contours of a Transformational Psychology* (Downers Grove, IL: IVP Academic, 2010), 37.

[48]Coe and Hall, *Psychology in the Spirit,* 84.

[49]Coe and Hall, *Psychology in the Spirit,* 220.

[50]Coe and Hall, *Psychology in the Spirit,* 222.

[51]Coe and Hall, *Psychology in the Spirit,* 264.

[52]Coe and Hall, *Psychology in the Spirit,* 264.

[53]Dallas Willard, *Living in Christ's Presence: Final Words on Heaven and the Kingdom of God* (Downers Grove, IL: InterVarsity Press, 2014), 13-14 (my emphasis).

[54]Willard, *Living in Christ's Presence,* 117.

[55]Willard, *Living in Christ's Presence,* 118.

self."[56] Christian spiritual formation *"is the process through which the embodied/reflective will or 'spirit' of the human being takes on the character of Christ's will."*[57] The main reason that spiritual transformation does not automatically accompany preaching and teaching is that these means do not involve the body in the process of transformation: "Spiritual formation is never *merely* inward."[58]

J. P. Moreland is broadly sympathetic with Willard's approach but wants to "tweak" his understanding of the human person. When Willard speaks of "parts" of persons, he doesn't really mean it. He sees the body and soul as internally related, such that the soul could exist without a body, while a body without the soul is just a corpse. Although Willard is technically a substance dualist, he takes the *person* as "the fundamental unit of analysis in that the person is a substance and the other [faculties] are seated in or dependent upon the person."[59] Accordingly, *spirit* is not a part but an aspect of a person, as is the body. This is crucial because, for Moreland, Willard's "treatment of the nature of the body and its role in spiritual formation may well have been his most important contribution."[60] Willard states that "a person *is* his or her body,"[61] and goes on to compare ingrained personal habits to "grooves" in one's body.

Evan Howard helpfully distinguishes the *aims* of spiritual formation (Paul's "until Christ is formed in you"—Gal 4:19) from its principal *agents*: the Holy Spirit, ourselves, and those who provide spiritual direction. As to human *spirit*, it refers to our heart, "the core of our own human personality," which implies that "a transformation of spirit is not merely a change of a few habits but a renovation of our character."[62] We experience ourselves as embodied souls, and we play an active role in our own formation, enabled by

---

[56]Willard, *Living in Christ's Presence*, 121.

[57]Willard, "Spiritual Formation and the Warfare Between the Flesh and the Human Spirit," *Journal of Spiritual Formation and Soul Care* 6, no. 2 (2013): 157 (emphasis original).

[58]Willard, "Spiritual Formation and the Warfare," 158.

[59]J. P. Moreland, "Body and Soul: Tweaking Dallas Willard's Understanding of the Human Person," in *Until Christ Is Formed in You: Dallas Willard and Spiritual Formation*, ed. Steven L. Porter, Gary W. Moon, and J. P. Moreland (Abilene, TX: Abilene Christian University Press, 2018), 61.

[60]Moreland, "Body and Soul," 62.

[61]Dallas Willard, *The Spirit of the Disciplines: Understanding How God Changes Lives* (New York: Harper Collins, 1988), 76.

[62]Evan Howard, *A Guide to Christian Spiritual Formation: How Scripture, Spirit, Community, and Mission Shape Our Souls* (Grand Rapids: Baker Academic, 2018), 12.

the Holy Spirit to form our lives into shapes of finite freedom that display the mind of Christ.[63]

Christian spiritual formation ultimately concerns the human spirit's participation in the Holy Spirit's work of cultivating finite shapes of freedom that display the mind of Christ and thereby glorify God. It is the process of being formed into the particular freedom for which Christ has set us free: free to be mature in Christ (Col 1:28) and more like Christ (Phil 2:5).[64] The Holy Spirit is the primary agent of new life in Christ, *a communicative agent* able to share or "make common" God's own light and life, which is to say, Jesus Christ (Jn 8:12; 11:25).

A DOGMATIC PROPOSAL: HUMAN SPIRIT AS AGENT, CENTER, AND PATTERN OF COMMUNICATION

To this point, we have established that Scripture speaks of human persons as ensouled bodies or embodied souls in a variety of ways, so much so that we had to ask, in connection with biblical studies and Christian psychology alike, Whatever happened to the human spirit? We now move from exegetical to dogmatic reasoning in our attempt to provide a conceptual representation of what we have learned from following the way the biblical words go.[65]

The human spirit and the Holy Spirit. Spiritual formation involves the testimony of the Holy Spirit to our spirit, "that aspect of the human person that relates directly to God."[66] Spirit is that aspect of the human person with which the Holy Spirit communicates: "the Spirit himself testifies with our spirit that we are God's children" (Rom 8:16).

While generic spirituality may indeed be a matter of the cultural company we keep—the other persons to whom we are in close relation—genuine Christian spirituality is a matter of our relationship to one person, even Jesus Christ, a relation enabled and deepened by the Holy Spirit. Christian spirituality is *"the study and experience of what happens when the Holy Spirit*

---

[63]See Howard, *Guide to Christian Spiritual Formation*, 74.

[64]As to the question, *what* does spiritual formation form, Howard believes it is whole persons and communities (*Guide to Christian Spiritual Formation*, 18-19).

[65]On the distinction between exegetical and dogmatic reasoning, see John Webster, "Biblical Reasoning," in *The Domain of the Word: Scripture and Theological Reason* (New York: T&T Clark International, 2012), 130.

[66]Rosner, *Known by God*, 72. Cf. Staley: "The Pauline usage of spirit [is] for the godward side of man" (*The Pauline View of Man*, 137).

meets the human spirit."[67] The Holy Spirit lives for this: to witness to Christ, conform people to Christ, and in all things to glorify Jesus Christ. Today, however, many confuse true spirituality—conformity to Christ by the Holy Spirit—with "excited" religious experience.

What spiritual formation forms: Four theses on human spirituality. Spiritual formation does not form human parts, but aspects of human persons. Can we be more precise? The following four theses set out exactly what spiritual formation forms. The first two specify the nature of human persons, the third defines human spirit, and the fourth draws out implications for spiritual formation.

1. A human person is a subject of communication, one able to call (on) others and to be called (on) by others. To be in personal relation is to enjoy "the gift and return of dialogue."[68] In Hans Urs von Balthasar's words, "Man was created to be a hearer of the word, and it is in responding to the word that he attains his true dignity. His innermost constitution has been designed for dialogue"[69]—especially dialogue with the triune God. God's address to human beings "determines the structure of human being as response."[70] Our "personhood is fostered . . . through relations which take dialogical form."[71]

2. A human person is neither an autonomous individual nor a cog in a collectivist system but a center of communication, a psychosomatic unity where dialogues unfold and about whom a story may be told. Personhood is dialogical and narratival: "We are called into being persons by the expectations others have of us."[72] Our identity is a function of our relations to others; the shape of our freedom is a function of the history of our responding to them. The human body is in this view "a field of communication." Of course, the communicative relation that constitutes our identity is the one we have with God: human persons are beings "addressed as Thou by God's I."[73]

---

[67]Edith M. Humphrey, *Ecstasy and Intimacy: When the Holy Spirit Meets the Human Spirit* (Grand Rapids: Eerdmans, 2006), 17 (emphasis original).

[68]Alistair I. McFayden, *Called to Personhood: A Christian Theory of the Individual in Social Relationships* (Cambridge: Cambridge University Press, 1990), 19.

[69]Hans Urs von Balthasar, *Prayer*, trans. Graham Harrison (San Francisco: Ignatius, 1986), 22.

[70]McFayden, *Called to Personhood*, 22.

[71]McFayden, *Called to Personhood*, 65.

[72]McFayden, *Called to Personhood*, 116.

[73]McFayden's *Called to Personhood*, 19. Both Brian Rosner and Susan Eastman acknowledge the importance for Paul of understanding personal identity in terms of *being known by God*.

3. The human spirit is a person's characteristic communicative posture and pattern. Everything we say and do with our bodies communicates something about us, bears witness to the relations that constitute us, to the way we are with others, to our loves. The human spirit is the core character of a person's psychosomatic unity, the shape a person's freedom takes in its communicative relations toward others, especially God. If a person were a ship, the spirit would be the trim of the sail, either open to receiving the wind of the Holy Spirit or not. If persons in their psychosomatic unity continue to respond defiantly to God's communicative overtures, they eventually display a "fleshly" spirit. Character is *course*: "We carry the effects of the communication we have received and the response we have made in the past forward with us into every new situation and relationship."[74] It follows that every human being is spiritual and has been spiritually formed. The question is, How have they trimmed their sails? What form does their spirit—their pattern of responding to communications from God and others; the narrative shape of finite freedom—take?

4. Spiritual formation is the process of the Holy Spirit testifying to and transforming our "spirit." John Webster describes spiritual formation as the process by which the Holy Spirit works on our spirits to *put on Christ* and *put to death* anything that does not belong to Christ's new humanity.[75] The opposite of fleshly existence is not disembodied spirituality, but rather an orientation of our human spirit—the characteristic way we communicate to God and others as ensouled bodies—toward the Holy Spirit (Rom 8:6). Christian spirituality is a matter of participating in the body of Christ, and progressively embodying the mind of Christ: "To be '*spiritual*' is not to draw on an innate 'higher' capacity of the human soul; it is to be moved, activated, and transformed by the Holy Spirit of God."[76] Christ is the form and content of God's call to us. Christ's life and light is what the Holy Spirit communicates to human spirits, particularly in and through Holy Scripture. The Holy Spirit speaks Christ, the whole Christ, and nothing but the Christ.

---

[74]McFayden, *Called to Personhood*, 7.
[75]John Webster, *Holiness* (London: SCM Press, 2003), 89.
[76]Anthony C. Thiselton, *First Corinthians: A Shorter Exegetical and Pastoral Commentary* (Grand Rapids: Eerdmans, 2006), 53.

CONCLUSION: WHOSE CITIZENSHIP? WHICH SHAPE OF FREEDOM?

What does formation form? Christians are not the only ones asking this question.

Cultivating humanity: Moral formation. Martha Nussbaum does philosophy for the sake of moral formation, and has for years looked both to the ancient Greeks, and imaginative fiction, as resources for her pleas to contemporary society to strive for greater virtue, justice, and human flourishing. All her gifts are on display in her book, *Cultivating Humanity.*[77]

Liberal education shapes and informs human freedom, and Nussbaum believes that education has the power to form adults who can function as citizens not just of their own region or group but "as citizens of a complex interlocking world."[78] It's an admirable vision: to use the humanities—especially literary works that, in stretching our imagination, helps us to identify with and relate to others who are different from ourselves—to cultivate humanity.

Cultivating new humanity: Spiritual formation. While the university may be a good place to pursue the liberal arts and cultivate liberal humanity, the local church is the best place to cultivate the new humanity that is in Jesus Christ. James Loder describes the Spirit's work as "humanizing humanity according to the nature of Christ."[79] Narrative fiction may be helpful in sensitizing world citizens to those who are culturally different, but Christian spiritual formation relies on one narrative in particular, the gospel of Jesus Christ. As the truth about how things are in Christ, the gospel is "the fundamental context of formation."[80] The Spirit bears witness to our spirit that Jesus' story is the template for our own formation. It is to this story about being made new in Christ that the word-ministering Holy Spirit conforms Christian spirits, forming them into citizens not of the world, but into citizens of the gospel.

Spiritual formation is the process of aligning our everyday life and experience to the reality of who and what we are in Jesus Christ: members of his new humanity. It is the process of coming to live in conformity to the truth of the gospel: "I have been crucified with Christ and I no longer live, but Christ lives

---

[77]Martha Nussbaum, *Cultivating Humanity: A Classical Defense of Reform in Liberal Education* (Cambridge, MA: Harvard University Press, 1997).

[78]Nussbaum, *Cultivating Humanity*, 6.

[79]James E. Loder, *The Transforming Moment*, 2nd ed. (Colorado Springs, CO: Helmers & Howard, 1992), 17.

[80]Howard, *Guide to Christian Spiritual Formation*, 34.

in me" (Gal 2:20). The gospel is essentially "a story of formation"[81]—the formation, in Christ, of a new humanity and holy nation. Spiritual formation is the Holy Spirit's work to conform our spirits to that of Jesus Christ. The result is a series of shapes of evangelical freedom—the disciple's freedom to live out the life of Christ everywhere, always, and in relation to all persons. It is for cultivating such shapes of Christian freedom that Christ has set us free (Gal 5:1).

The practices of spiritual formation (call them core exercises) reinforce who and what God says we are in Christ—who and what the Spirit is conforming our spirits to be. They're bodily exercises too, for as we have seen, persons are psychosomatic unities. Even the Desert Fathers never bracketed out the body in their quest to become more spiritual. Rather, as Peter Brown says, "[the body] was, rather, grippingly present to the monk: he was to speak of it as 'this body, that God has afforded me, as a field to cultivate, where I might work and become rich.' . . . In the desert tradition, the body was allowed to become the discreet mentor of the proud soul."[82] Our bodies are themselves "spiritualized"—permeated by and in perfect harmony with the Holy Spirit—to the extent we live *in sync with Christ* (1 Cor 15:42-44). The concentration required for both prayer and fasting, for example, involve the whole person: will, beliefs, emotions, attitudes, and physical discipline.

Our spirituality is that particular shape of freedom that communicates who we are at our core. Spiritual formation is the process of becoming more like Christ in our human spirits. It is the great privilege and responsibility of pastors to form human spirits: finite shapes of freedom that display the light and life of God in everyday experience. Theology without spiritual formation and discipleship is empty; spiritual formation without theology and the gospel is blind. Pastor-theologians preach and teach our new humanity in Christ. That's theology, and it's good, but it's not enough. The goal is not simply to fill heads—that is, to impart information and inform belief— but to transform a person's characteristic pattern of responding to the calls and cries of others and, above all, to the living and active voice of God. Calvin's word for this is *piety*: "the pattern by which we shape our lives before God in grateful obedience to what God has done for us."[83] *That's* the spirit!

---

[81]Howard, *Guide to Christian Spiritual Formation*, 36.
[82]Peter Brown, *The Body and Society: Men, Women and Sexual Renunciation in Early Christianity* (New York: Columbia University Press, 1988), 236-37.
[83]Howard L. Rice, *Reformed Spirituality: An Introduction for Believers* (Louisville, KY: Westminster John Knox, 1991), 46.

5

Jonathan Edwards on Sanctification

RACHEL STAHLE

A S WE APPROACH JONATHAN EDWARDS'S VIEW on Christian spirituality, it's important to lay a groundwork comprising the assumptions we make. Edwards's writings are so voluminous and his theology so
complex that giving this topic a thorough treatment is beyond the scope of
this chapter. Even so, we can lay out the basics and come to an understanding
of what Edwards described as genuine religion—that which is distinctly
Christian, God-honoring, humble, loving, and reliant on the Lord's grace.[1]

The assumptions that form our groundwork start with a beautiful, holy,
trinitarian God who is supremely just and supremely loving, as described in
the totality of the Scriptures. The Father, Son, and Holy Spirit exist as one in
perfect community and essence. All persons are equally divine and glorious,
but God the Father is the fountain of the Godhead, the head of all godly affairs.[2] God the Son is the perfect representation of the Father, the ideal
example of goodness.[3] By the Father's will, the Son reigns as the governor
of the moral world. As the third person of the Trinity, the Holy Spirit is the
power and love of God in act and energy. The Holy Spirit implements the

---

[1]See *The Things That Belong to True Religion*, in *Works of Jonathan Edwards Online*, vol. 25, *Sermons and Discourses, 1743–1758*, ed. Wilson H. Kimnach (New Haven, CT: Yale University Press, 2006).

[2]*The Works of Jonathan Edwards*, vol. 20, *The "Miscellanies," Entry Nos. 833–1152*, ed. Amy Plantinga Pauw (New Haven, CT: Yale University Press, 2002), 433-36.

[3]*Concerning the End for Which God Created the World*, in *Works of Jonathan Edwards*, vol. 8, *Ethical Writings*, ed. Paul Ramsey (New Haven, CT: Yale University Press, 1989), 474.

plans of the Godhead, and expedites the mutual love and glorification that are constantly overflowing among the three persons.[4] So the Son is eternally begotten as the impeccable image of the Father, while the Spirit is the eternally dynamic movement of God.

This portrait of the Trinity will be especially important for us shortly when we consider community in the body of Christ. For now, we need to place a few more pieces in our groundwork. For Edwards, Christian spiritual experience presumes the biblical concept of a historical fall into sin by Adam and Eve. Even before the world's creation, God's response to this problem of sin and evil was to formulate a plan of redemption.[5] This plan included a covenant between the Father and Son in which the Son would fulfill on humanity's behalf the covenant God originally made with Adam. Through faith in Jesus Christ, who bears the penalty of God's judgment that each deserves, sinners receive the free gift of salvation through this redemptive covenant of grace.[6] Apart from God's grace and the application of Christ's merit to their souls, no one is redeemed.

There's one more piece of groundwork to lay. Though God reveals himself to all humanity through creation, including the fact that we are created in his image, that revelation is not sufficient to teach us the depth of our sinfulness, nor to lead us to a right relationship with God. The "written word of God is this main instrument Christ has made use of to carry on his Work of Redemption in all ages since it was given."[7] Though God may choose to redeem in any manner he sees fit, the Bible's gospel message is his primary means for salvation. Once saved, only the Scriptures provide the "special revelation" needed for us to learn who God is and how he expects us to live a life of faith in Christ. Through the Bible, believers know Jesus Christ himself. He is the Word made flesh, "of whom the word written and preached is but an emanation. Christ is the sun, and the word written and preached are the rays."[8]

---

[4] *Works of Jonathan Edwards*, vol. 13, *The "Miscellanies," Entry Nos. a–z, aa–zz, 1–500*, ed. Thomas A. Schafer (New Haven, CT: Yale University Press, 1994), 260.

[5] *Works of Jonathan Edwards*, vol. 9, *A History of the Work of Redemption*, ed. John F. Wilson (New Haven, CT: Yale University Press, 1989), 309.

[6] *An Humble Inquiry into the Rules of the Word of God*, in *Works of Jonathan Edwards*, vol. 12, *Ecclesiastical Writings*, ed. David D. Hall (New Haven, CT: Yale University Press, 1994), 205.

[7] Edwards, *History of the Work of Redemption*, 182.

[8] *Christ, the Light of the World* in *Works of Jonathan Edwards*, vol. 10, *Sermons and Discourses 1720–1723*, ed. Wilson H. Kimnach (New Haven, CT: Yale University Press, 1992), 542.

With these groundwork pieces in place, we can turn to examine conversion to Christ by faith. For Edwards, this event is only possible through the activity of the Holy Spirit. Though each person's conversion differs, there is an overall pattern for how the Spirit ministers. Sinners undergo a process (varying in duration) in which they are spiritually convicted and experience "evangelical humiliation," or growing humility before God in light of the Gospel's truth. With this humility comes an increasing sense of God's love, majesty, and mercy, again imparted only by grace through the Spirit. Such humility carries on into Christian life as defining evidence of God's transformative work in one's heart.[9]

The Bible describes conversion, or what Edwards more often calls "regeneration," as resurrection from the dead, the creation of a new being, and the giving of new eyes to the blind. To Edwards, these are much more than literary devices. When a person submits to the lordship and love of God by trusting in Christ alone for salvation, she is made "legally" right with God. The relationship between Creator and creature once severed by sin is restored. But this justification also involves a real, fundamental change in one's soul, "a cleansing from moral filthiness" and a "change from a state of wickedness."[10] Edwards even calls conversion an event of "re-existence," because a soul that was as good as dead in its state of judgment for depravity is granted new, abundant life leading ultimately to eternal glory.[11] Such "re-existence" is so radical that loving Jesus and hating sin become the primary concerns, the driving forces, of the new believer. Above all, the believer is enabled by the Spirit to glimpse and adore the perfections, glory, and beauty of God.[12] They do "taste and see that the LORD is good" (Ps 34:8).

While the blessings of conversion to faith in Christ are many, Edwards notes that they're just the tip of the gracious iceberg. Because the Holy Spirit takes up residence *within* a believer, and establishes a permanent relationship *with* the believer, she is forever bonded with the trinitarian God. She becomes a participant with God in his redemptive plan for the world.

---

[9]See *Saving Faith and Christian Obedience Arise from Godly Love,* in *Works of Jonathan Edwards,* 9:25.

[10]*Works of Jonathan Edwards,* vol. 3, *Original Sin,* ed. Clyde A. Holbrook (New Haven, CT: Yale University Press, 1970), 370.

[11]Edwards, *The "Miscellanies,"* 13:324.

[12]See *Of Those Who Walk in the Light of God's Countenance,* in *Works of Jonathan Edwards,* vol. 25.

The indwelling Spirit teaches saints heavenly things, and scatters the darkness and coldness that threaten saints as they work out their salvation with fear and trembling (Phil 2:12). The Spirit also endows a believer with spiritual gifts, and develops those gifts so the saint is increasingly given to love and charity toward God, others, and self. Above all, the Holy Spirit cultivates a foundational principle of godly love, what Edwards calls "the sense of the heart," so the Christian is increasingly conformed to God's holiness and moral excellency.

This sense of the heart is the means by which "saints know both intellectually and experientially the power of God in salvation, and the presence of the Spirit in their souls."[13] Through this sense, the Spirit imparts and actuates a holy nature consistent with the mind of God. It draws together the saints' bond with the Godhead itself, truths of biblical revelation, human faculties, and the good works that are the fruit of conversion—all of this in total is what Edwards calls a "divine and supernatural light." Through this light, eyes of faith can see God at work in the world, and in one's own life. Divine beauty becomes self-evident everywhere. It is the conduit of a spiritual knowledge of holiness that is a gift of God through Christ, with the Holy Spirit acting as the "immediate efficient cause."[14]

Having said that, Edwards also placed heavy emphasis on the Christian's need to be devoted to God through consistent, godly practice. Though the Spirit is always ministering to us, we are never to be passive or negligent of our responsibility to cultivate our spiritual lives. We are to be purposeful in loving the Lord our God with all our heart, soul, mind, and strength. The Spirit's presence in us will empower us to want to live in a Christlike manner, to know our Lord, and to desire to turn away from sin. In other words, the fruit of the Spirit described in the New Testament will be evident in us, for all to see.

Our part is to make the most of the opportunities for spiritual growth the Lord provides for us day in and day out, while relying on his grace to do so. "All that men do in real religion is entirely their own act, and yet every tittle

---

[13] *Works of Jonathan Edwards*, vol. 2, *Religious Affections*, ed. John E. Smith (New Haven, CT: Yale University Press, 1959), 141.

[14] *Works of Jonathan Edwards*, vol. 14, *Sermons and Discourses 1723–1729*, ed. Kenneth P. Minkema (New Haven, CT: Yale University Press, 1997), 251.

is wrought by the Spirit of God."[15] Spiritual growth is applied to the soul by the Holy Spirit, who as the giver of life is "the spiritual heavenly food with which God feeds the saints."[16] This doesn't mean we will be sinless in this life. Sanctification is inherently a purification process, which has its setbacks at times and great strides in holiness other times. "A Christian's life may be attended with many and exceedingly great imperfections, and yet be a holy life, a truly Christian life."[17] The crucial factor is that the Spirit has created a new, holy disposition through which we can make choices for good and the glory of God.

Edwards is well known for his landmark volume *Religious Affections*. He observes throughout this volume that when the Holy Spirit is about the business of making us holy, as God is holy, our faith in Christ will be manifest through good works and a desire to please and obey the Lord. "Religious affections," broadly speaking, are such manifestations of divine power. More narrowly, though, Edwards defines them as "the more vigorous and sensible [sensory] exercises of the inclination and will of the soul."[18] The Holy Spirit works through religious affections to bring about conversion to Christ, and then enables faith to express itself through the affections as the believer walks with Christ by faith. "The affections manifest the center and unity of the self; they express the whole man and give insight into the basic orientation of his life."

Spurred on by Christian books, preaching, sacraments, prayer, music, and the Word of God (the greatest producer of spiritual blossoming), the "religious affections" are personal expressions of romance to God. They originate with God, wash as a current through the Christian, then flow back to him as declarations of love, a sincere desire to be holy, and gratitude for God's work in his life so far. "The more he experiences, the more he knows this excellent, unparalleled, exquisite, and satisfying sweetness, the more earnestly he will hunger and thirst for more, till he comes to perfection [in heavenly glory]."[19]

---

[15]Edwards, *The "Miscellanies,"* 13:240.

[16]*Works of Jonathan Edwards*, vol. 15, *Notes on Scripture*, ed. Stephen J. Stein (New Haven, CT: Yale University Press, 1998), 240.

[17]Edwards, *Charity and Its Fruits*, in *Ethical Writings*, 309.

[18]Edwards, *Religious Affections*, 14.

[19]Edwards, *Religious Affections*, 379.

The capacity for religious affections is present in all people because it is a remnant of humanity's pre-fall bond of loving fellowship with God in Eden. Sin has skewed these affections to be expressed in self-centeredness, opposition to God, and worship of false gods. To Edwards, an unregenerate person is much like a demon that apprehends God's terrible majesty and power, but cannot properly love him for his beauty and holiness.[20] This explains why people may be religious and even highly moral, but do not love the Lord and do not trust in Christ for redemption.

Part of the Holy Spirit's work in regeneration and then in sanctification is to restore the affections so a believer can love and revere God as he asks and deserves. Thus, genuine religious affections abide and thrive by God's grace. They involve both rational and spiritual convictions of the certainty of the gospel's truth. While genuine affections see and affirm the truth of the Scriptures intellectually, there is a spiritual component of faith that is almost beyond description. "He that truly sees the divine, transcendent, supreme glory of those things which are divine, does as it were know their divinity intuitively; he not only argues that they are divine, but he sees that they are divine."[21] This rational and intuitive knowledge of God and his truth are the bedrock of genuine faith. It is then incumbent on the Christian to apply this "divine and supernatural light" to daily life.[22]

Doing so is the chief manner in which believers imitate the Savior. As the perfectly virtuous God-man, Jesus displayed perfect affections, perfect devotion to his Father, and perfect compassion to humanity. "The Lord Jesus Christ . . . was a person who was remarkably of a tender and affectionate heart; and his virtue was expressed very much in the exercise of holy affections. He was the greatest instance of ardency, vigor and strength of love, to both God and man, that ever was."[23]

Edwards's presumption was that as the Holy Spirit carries out sanctification, Christians will come to display Christ's tenderness in an enduring state of gracious sincerity, purity, and spirituality.[24] Through the Spirit's transforming grace, believers are clothed with Christ's qualities of righteousness,

---

[20]Edwards, *Religious Affections*, 263.
[21]Edwards, *Religious Affections*, 298.
[22]Edwards, *Religious Affections*, 99.
[23]Edwards, *Religious Affections*, 111.
[24]Edwards, *Religious Affections*, 146.

for "a Christian spirit is Christ's mark, that he sets upon the souls of his people; his seal on their foreheads, bearing his image and superscription."[25] To sum up, Edwards observes that the Christian with genuine affections "has more holy boldness, so he has less of self-confidence, . . . and more modesty. . . . He has the firmest comfort, but the softest heart: richer than others, but poorest of all in spirit: the tallest and strongest saint, but the least and tenderest child among them."[26]

By God's design, spiritual transformation cannot occur in a vacuum. Just as the Trinity is the community of God, we who are made in his image are meant to thrive in the context of God's people. While Christ and his Church are united by covenant according to the divine plan of redemption, there is also a mystical union in which human and divine joy are knit together by the Spirit "to perfect excellency and beauty in his image and in holiness, which is the proper beauty of spiritual beings."[27] The church is wholly possessed by God, but at the same time the church wholly possesses God because she is united with the ruler of all.

This union with God in human community fuels spiritual growth and is summarized by Edwards's concept of "partaking." A moment ago, I mentioned that genuine religious affections are developed when a believer takes advantage of learning from Christian books, preaching, sacraments, prayer, music, and above all, the Word of God itself. These are the nuts and bolts of daily Christian discipleship. But what's happening as we learn from those resources, and learn from our interactions with others (especially other Christians), is "partaking" of God himself. As with the indwelling of the Holy Spirit, partaking of God does not mean that we share in divine *essence*. It means that we take part in and enjoy God's "spiritual beauty and happiness."[28] In everyday life, Christians experience the pleasure of God and his goodness, just as a guest might participate in conversation and dining while taking part in a feast.[29]

---

[25]Edwards, *Religious Affections*, 347. See *Christ Is to the Heart Like a River to a Tree Planted by It*, in vol. 25, *Sermons & Discourses, 1743-1758*.
[26]Edwards, *Religious Affections*, 364.
[27]Edwards, *History of the Work of Redemption*, 125.
[28]Edwards, *Religious Affections*, 203.
[29]Edwards, *Notes on Scripture*, 186.

Just to be clear, partaking of God is not just a nice feeling or a metaphor for a spiritual idea. It is a real experience of union with God in which living for Christ and loving God is the believer's very life. The saint is "invigorated with him, with his Holy Spirit which is diffused as new life all over his soul" in a refreshing shower of grace.[30] This is basically how sanctification takes place from a spiritual vantage point. God gently imposes his glorious, excellent image on the Christian's soul moment by moment as she progresses toward full perfection in heaven. Believers thus partake of God not only as we apprehend him and his beauty, but as he shares himself with us to stamp his image on our souls.

None of this is merely an individual experience, as I touched on before. The common partaking of God by his people is the reality of the kingdom of God in our hearts. By the Spirit's presence, God does rule our hearts by grace. But our union with other believers expands his rule, and thereby expands the influence of the Spirit throughout our communities, across the globe. God is growing a holy kingdom that is rooted in believers' souls, and earnestly desires the salvation of others' souls. As Paul Ramsey explains, "The kingdom of Christ building up in the souls of men should never be separated from the kingdom of Christ building up in the world among men."[31]

So we should not be surprised that to Edwards, "to be of a Christian spirit is to be public-spirited." Being a genuine Christian means that we see most clearly the great need the world has for forgiveness and redemption through Jesus. As we partake of God, we'll also share in his loving concern for souls to be redeemed. Evangelism should be as much a natural part of Christian experience as worship, fellowship, and prayer are. Caring for others' basic human needs includes their need for salvation. While Edwards did not write a formal theology of missions, he spent the latter part of his life ministering among Native Americans. He knew as well as anyone that only the Lord has the power to rescue souls from false religion and idolatry, which to Edwards were abominations. Partaking of God, especially his love for the lost, will lead believers to share the gospel and live out godly examples for the unsaved to take notice of.

---

[30]Edwards, *Living to Christ and Dying to Gain*, in *Sermons & Discourses, 1720-1723*, 570.
[31]Paul Ramsey, "Editor's Introduction," in *Ethical Writings*, 71.

Much of the thought Edwards devoted to spiritual transformation occurred in the context of the Great Awakening that swept through Britain and
the American colonies in the 1730s and 1740s. The theologian was intent on
discerning biblical principles by which he could both lead and participate in
this Spirit-driven revival of Christian faith. Edwards turned to the Scriptures
for his answers, and developed a framework for understanding the ways God
works to transform sinners into saints, particularly in times of revival.

In essence, a revival occurs when the Holy Spirit carries out extraordinary
and heightened activity to stir devotion and dramatically increase holiness
in Christians. Revival is a "special season of mercy" in which Christ's church
lives out her faith with special vibrancy, shares the gospel ardently, and sees
evidence of the love of God in unusually lively fashion.[32] As a result, society
in general is positively impacted, and nonbelievers are stirred to take interest
in the gospel. There are widespread conversions to Christ, and the fruits of
the Spirit are abundantly evident. From God's perspective, revival is an ac-
celerated advancement of his kingdom, and a foretaste of heavenly glory in
which faith and love abound in community.

Implied so far is the fact that such revivals are entirely carried out through
the power and ministry of God. They are not humanly planned or manufac-
tured, though we can and should pray for the Lord to bless us with them.
While new converts tend to be the most dramatic aspect of revivals, they
typically start when those who already believe are markedly refreshed in
their faith. They may be spiritually lackadaisical or slumping Christians, or
those who've held steady as disciples. Whatever the case, there is abundant
evidence that the Holy Spirit is bringing about awakening—a renewed, intense, sustained awareness of our need to be humble, to repent, to adore, to
praise, and to serve Almighty God.

When thinking of spiritual growth and transformation, the theology Edwards developed during the Great Awakening was intended to help people
understand the work of God in their hearts. It was also intended to highlight
why some unusual behaviors that occurred—fainting, laughing, or crying
hysterically, for example—may have been genuine human responses to overwhelming grace. Edwards also didn't want people to be deceived, or deceive

---

[32]Edwards, *History of the Work of Redemption*, 143.

themselves, about whether they were truly redeemed. Spiritual transformation in some ways is a beautiful mystery, but God's Word has revealed the Spirit's workings in that same mystery.

When we read of the dramatic excesses that happened during the Great Awakening, we can see why people would be skeptical that groaning, shouting, uncontrolled zeal, and outlandish indecency could actually be evidence of the Holy Spirit's work. Edwards pointed out that some of these same behaviors occurred in the early church, and were answered by corrections from the apostle Paul, in particular. For Edwards, spiritual renewal will involve some influence of sin simply because it occurs in the fallen realm of depraved humanity. The great love of God may lead to great sin if zealous people do what they believe is pleasing to God, yet are mistaken. Believers may react unwisely to an overwhelming sense of God's presence and power, and even sin in ways they'd never struggled with. Whether for converts or established disciples, times of revival can be like the growth of a tree: "the fruit of it, though it be very sweet and good when it is ripe, yet before it has had time to ripen, has a mixture of poison."[33] In fact, God may permit sin and excess during revivals to teach his church lessons he will use later for her benefit. "Our follies and sins that we mix, do in some respects manifest the glory of it: the glory of divine power and grace is set off with the greater luster by what appears at the same time of the weakness of the earthen vessel."[34]

So as we look with Edwards to the mindset of an individual who is being greatly impacted by the Holy Spirit (during times of revival or otherwise), what do we see? Fundamentally, we see God's workmanship in transforming needy, feeble sinners into the likeness of Christ. Through faithful preaching and reading God's Word, God turns their weakness into holy strength, for their sanctification and his glory. Godly examples encourage others to take faith seriously. Edwards urged the avid discussion of religion and doctrine so all could learn about their need for redemption.

Above all, we see a sincere, ardent love for Jesus Christ, a desire to know him and treasure him, and a heart for loving others as he did. "The love that

---

[33]Edwards, *Some Thoughts Concerning the Present Revival of Religion in New England*, in *Works of Jonathan Edwards*, vol. 4, *The Great Awakening*, ed. C. C. Goen (New Haven, CT: Yale University Press, 1972), 318.
[34]Edwards, *Some Thoughts*, 347.

appeared in the Lamb of God, was not only a love to friends, but to enemies, and a love attended with a meek and humble spirit."[35] In fact, Edwards believed that Christlike love and meekness—a sincere, unpretentious love for God and others—are wholly sufficient proof that a revival is in fact a work of God, regardless of any excesses. Only the Holy Spirit is capable of enabling people to love Christ sincerely, to hunger for and grasp the Scriptures, and to care for others selflessly.

With this love for Christ, we'll also see in mature Christians an active support for the work of the Holy Spirit in whatever shape it takes. Though the Spirit impels revivals, God expects believers to endorse his work and battle with him for the salvation of souls. Each must "look into his own heart and see to it that he be a partaker of the benefits of the work himself, and that it be promoted in his own soul."[36] Then a faithful disciple will affirm biblical orthodoxy (especially in preaching), abound in fasting and prayer, worship regularly and wholeheartedly, be kind and charitable, and teach others about true holiness. In all of this, there can be no pride, since the revival is solely from the work of the Spirit. "When we have great discoveries of God made to our souls, we should not shine bright in our own eyes."[37]

While Edwards's thoughts about Christian spiritual transformation were greatly impacted by the context of revival, there are principles that abide for any day. To him, it's all about holiness—and this shouldn't surprise us, because the believer is not only converted through the power of the Holy Spirit, but then has the Spirit take up residence within. This indwelling does not mean that a person is given new spiritual precepts that are independent of God's revelation in Scripture. There is no case in which the Spirit will override someone's personality. The Spirit will not give guidance that requires no human thought, judgment, or wisdom. The Spirit, in short, works in tandem with the Scriptures and human personality to mature a believer in the knowledge of God and the ability to discern truth. The Spirit unites mind and heart to re-create an intelligent, spiritual creature in the image of God.

As much as we've mentioned the ministry of the Holy Spirit, we should note that it's through the Spirit that Christ himself resides and reigns in the

---

[35]Edwards, *The Distinguishing Marks of a Work of the Spirit of God*, in *The Great Awakening*, 258.
[36]Edwards, *Some Thoughts*, 502.
[37]Edwards, *Distinguishing Marks*, 277.

heart of a saint. Christ bonds a believer to himself and thus the entire Godhead, and becomes upon conversion the principle of life in the soul. "The soul is united to Christ, and therefore partakes of his life: he lives in Christ and Christ lives in him, yea, not only lives in him but *is his life*. He is invigorated with him, with his Holy Spirit which is diffused as new life all over his soul."[38]

With this magnificent bond to Christ, human holiness is particularly expressed through faith, hope, and love, which together for Edwards make up "charity." Through charity, believers demonstrate saving faith and our embrace of Christ and Christianity.[39] In charity we cultivate holiness in imitation of the Savior. Through the Spirit's power and grace, our exercises then turn into habits, which yield greater virtue and holiness. Our love for God grows in strength and depth, and such habits of love overflow into love for others. These in turn grow and mature into holy wisdom, which is a spiritual acumen that can only come through the tutelage of the Holy Spirit. Holy wisdom is "the highest and most excellent gift that ever God bestows on any creature: in this the highest excellency and perfection of a rational creature exists."[40] Because every Christian has the Spirit indwelling, every Christian is empowered to be holy. The degree to which a person attains that holiness in this life depends on the openness to the Spirit's work they cultivate in their hearts and express practically in their lives.

For Jonathan Edwards, spiritual transformation is at its core a gracious, merciful work of God. More broadly, it is a work of the trinitarian community to redeem sinners from sin and brokenness and restore them to a beautiful, holy relationship with their Creator. Such transformation is denoted by humility before the Lord, by love for him and others, by opportunities for growth we must embrace, and by service within the body of Christ and evangelism beyond it. Its goal is resemblance to the Savior in holiness and tenderness, and leads ultimately to an inheritance of perfection Christians enjoy in glory, in the presence of God. All of this can be summed up in one word: grace.

---

[38]Edwards, *Living to Christ and Dying to Gain*, in *Sermons & Discourses, 1720–1723*, 570.
[39]Edwards, *Notes on Scripture*, 276.
[40]Edwards, *A Divine and Supernatural Light*, in *Works of Jonathan Edwards*, vol. 17, *Sermons and Discourses, 1730–1733*, ed. Mark Valeri (New Haven, CT: Yale University Press, 1999), 422.

What is the earnest and beginning of glory, but grace itself, especially in the more lively and clear exercises of it? 'Tis not prophecy, nor tongues, nor knowledge, but that more excellent divine thing, charity that never faileth, which is a prelibation and beginning of the light, sweetness, and blessedness of heaven, that world of love and charity. 'Tis grace that is the seed of glory, and dawning of glory in the heart, and therefore 'tis grace that is the earnest of future inheritance. What is it that is the beginning or earnest of eternal life in the soul, but spiritual life? And what is that but grace?[41]

Some may hold that Edwards's views on spiritual transformation are too cerebral for practical use in the twenty-first century. If that's true, it's more of a commentary on a modern devaluation of biblically oriented Christian thought than on Edwards. What we must take away from him starts with his concern for a thoroughly scriptural, God-revering theology that values glorifying the Lord above all. No one today would be worse for the wear if they were to share Edwards's passion for knowing the Lord, understanding his Word, and delving into the intricacies of how God's truth applies to all of life. Within Edwards's genius is a sincere, heartfelt passion for unbelievers to believe, and believers to thrive. I think it safe to state that Christ was his "all in all," truly his first love, and we would do well to follow suit.

---

[41]Edwards, *Religious Affections*, 236.

6

Spiritual Misformation

Dietrich Bonhoeffer on Human Sin

JOEL D. LAWRENCE

INTRODUCTION: FORMATION AND MISFORMATION

Over the past four decades, the evangelical church has had an intense engagement with the process of spiritual formation. Arising from a sense that evangelical approaches to discipleship have been overly reliant on rationalist approaches,[1] this engagement has spawned deep reflections on the formative nature of Christian discipleship, generating a spiritual formation industry of publishing, retreats, and spiritual guidance. This emphasis has encouraged evangelicalism to employ a wide variety of formative practices whose purpose is to heal that which has gone awry in the human soul.

But are we clear about what has gone awry? Have our approaches to spiritual formation given adequate attention to spiritual misformation? To make a point that is perhaps too obvious, in order to speak about spiritual formation we must speak about spiritual misformation; or, to say it another way, to engage in a process of forming we have to be aware of what has been misformed. In my view, the evangelical church has not fully grasped the nature of human misformation as described in Genesis 3, and so our vision of spiritual formation is lacking.

My purpose in this essay is to encourage the church to reflect on spiritual misformation that we might better understand the process of formation. To

---

[1]See James K. A. Smith, *You Are What You Love* (Grand Rapids: Brazos Press, 2016), 1-4.

do this, I will explore Dietrich Bonhoeffer's theology of human misformation. Bonhoeffer, whose best-known works, *Discipleship* and *Life Together*, are viewed as spiritual classics, has impacted the evangelical vision of discipleship and community in pursuit of spiritual formation. But this aspect of Bonhoeffer's teaching, the notion of human misformation, is underutilized in formation conversations. In his book *Creation and Fall*,[2] Bonhoeffer offers a theological exegesis of Genesis 1–3, focusing through this engagement with the first chapters of the Bible on the creation intention of God for humanity.[3] In so doing, Bonhoeffer lays out an anthropological vision in which he explores what it means that humans are created in the image of God and called to live in the freedom of obedience to the loving command of God. But the work also provides insight into human misformation, into what happened when Adam and Eve chose to rebel against God's Word and eat from the tree of the knowledge of good and evil. I suggest that Bonhoeffer's vision of human misformation can add valuable understanding to the church's conception of formation, and so can help us as we continue to reflect on the nature of God's work in the human soul to restore and renew those reconciled to him.

The plan for this essay is as follows: In the first part, I will explore Bonhoeffer's vision of human formation, focusing on his notion of freedom, which is at the heart of his vision of what it means to be human. Following this, in the second section, the bulk of this essay, we will analyze Bonhoeffer's understanding of the narrative of Genesis 3, the fall of humanity. In this narrative, Bonhoeffer describes the effects of humanity taking the knowledge of good and evil for ourselves, and the impact that this has on our being human. I will then conclude with some reflections on how Bonhoeffer's conception of human misformation can provide valuable insights into the evangelical conception of spiritual formation.

---

[2]Dietrich Bonhoeffer, *Creation and Fall*, Dietrich Bonhoeffer Works, vol. 3, trans. Stephen Bax (Minneapolis: Fortress Press, 1997).

[3]Bonhoeffer wrote this book in the vein of Karl Barth's *Römerbrief,* a style that, while not ignoring the issues of historical-critical exegesis, was not dominated by those forms, and so sought to break free from the dominance of academic scholarship in the German liberal tradition, instead approaching Scripture from within the convictions of Christian creedal faith. As such, Bonhoeffer, who was not a trained Old Testament scholar, was not attempting a work that met the criteria of the academic guild, but rather one that was a faith-filled reading of Genesis 1–3.

THE FORMATION OF HUMANITY: FREEDOM

Creation and Fall was originally a series of lectures given at the University of Berlin in the winter semester of 1932–1933.[4] Those familiar with German history will recognize that this was a tumultuous time. On January 30th, 1933, Adolf Hitler was elevated to the position of chancellor of Germany and, in the weeks that followed, quickly moved to consolidate his power.[5] These events were taking place literally down the street from where Bonhoeffer was lecturing on Genesis,[6] reflecting on the nature of creation, history, human rebellion against God, and God's mission to restore humanity to himself. In Bonhoeffer's lecture theater, the Word of God's grace was expounded even as the great evil revealed in that Word was beginning to take power over Germany.

At the heart of Bonhoeffer's reflections on humanity in *Creation and Fall* is his emphasis on human freedom. When God created humanity, he created us to be free. But this freedom must be theologically defined.[7] For Bonhoeffer, the starting point for the idea of human freedom is divine freedom. As those created in God's image, our freedom can only be understood as a reflection of God's Trinity union. The Godhead, in the unity of Father, Son, and Holy Spirit, lives in free relation to the other, sharing life as one God in three persons. The unity of the Trinity is a oneness in the freedom of self-giving love and relationality. Therefore, when we speak of God's creation intent for humanity, we are speaking of his desire to have the image of the triune freedom reflected on earth. Bonhoeffer writes, "To say that in humankind God creates the image of God on earth means that humankind is

---

[4] The original title was *Schöpfung und Sünde* (Creation and sin), but another book was published with this title before Bonhoeffer's went to the presses. For more on the historical context, see John DeGruchy, "Editor's Introduction to the English Edition," in Bonhoeffer, *Creation and Fall*, 1-17.

[5] For an excellent recent work on the rise of Hitler, I commend Benjamin Carter Hett, *The Death of Democracy: Hitler's Rise to Power and the Downfall of the Weimar Republic* (New York: Henry Holt and Company, 2018).

[6] The University of Berlin is just under a mile from the Reichstag, down the Unter Den Linden Strasse.

[7] In his earlier work, *Act and Being*, Bonhoeffer works to distinguish between philosophical concepts of freedom, which operate on a largely individualistic vision of freedom, and theological concepts of freedom, which are located in the church community. See Bonhoeffer, *Act and Being: Transcendental Philosophy and Ontology in Systematic Theology*, Dietrich Bonhoeffer Works, vol. 2, ed. Wayne Whitson Floyd Jr., trans. H. Martin Rumscheidt (Minneapolis: Fortress Press, 1996).

like the Creator in that it is free."[8] He continues by stating that this freedom
has a very specific cause and purpose: "To be sure, it is free only through
God's creation, through the word of God; it is free for the worship of the
Creator."[9] Human freedom is a reflection of the divine freedom, the
purpose of which is to draw humanity into the free worship of the Creator
for the sake of God's glory on earth.

Following his description of the meaning of human freedom, Bonhoeffer
turns his attention to the difficulty of describing how something that is
created can be free. He asks, "But how can what is created be free? What is
created is determined, bound by law, conditioned, not free."[10] Approaching
the question of freedom philosophically bogs us down in the mire of as-
serting human freedom while also acknowledging the inherently limited
nature of human existence. But theologically, this is not a problem, but is, in
fact, the heart of what it means for humans to be free. Bonhoeffer acknowledges the limitation of being a creature, but in doing so, recognizes that,
according to Genesis, this very limitation *is* our freedom. The command of
God given in the prohibition of eating from the tree of the knowledge of
good and evil is the means by which humanity is free; the prohibition is not
a temptation, but rather is God's grace, the sign of our creaturely limitation
through which we discover our freedom and the way that our freedom reflects the freedom of the triune life.

Bonhoeffer is here making the claim that humans, as creatures, reflect
God's freedom but are not free as God is free. God's freedom is an unlimited
freedom; human freedom is limited. As such, humans are only free when we
are limited by the Word of the Lord and acknowledge his Word as that which
binds us to himself in a relationship of obedience. As such, the tree of the
knowledge of good and evil is God's Word that limits the creature. Because
of this, humanity is free only in obedience to this Word, and only when we
are bound to God in a relationship of reverence and worship. Similarly, Eve
is given to Adam in order to fulfill the image of God on earth and as a limit
to Adam, as the means by which freedom can occur in relation to the other.[11]

---

[8]Bonhoeffer, *Creation and Fall*, 62.
[9]Bonhoeffer, *Creation and Fall*, 62.
[10]Bonhoeffer, *Creation and Fall*, 61.
[11]Bonhoeffer, *Creation and Fall*, 94-95.

As Bonhoeffer says, "Freedom is not a quality that can be uncovered; it is not a possession . . . instead it is a relation and nothing else. To be more precise, freedom is a relation between two persons. Being free means 'being-free-for-the-other,' because I am bound to the other. Only by being in relation with the other am I free."[12] Freedom is not to be understood individually, but communally. To be free is to be free for others, and human thriving can only be what God intended when the human is free to give her life to others.

From this we can summarize Bonhoeffer's vision of God's creation intent for humanity: God creates humanity to be his image on earth, reflecting the life of the triune God in an existence of self-giving love. This existence is a freedom for others, a freedom that is only true freedom when lived as a life of obedience to God's guiding Word and dwelling in his loving presence. As such, we can say that, for Bonhoeffer, humans are only free when living in total dependence on God's command, and so are only free when bound, limited, and obedient.

THE MISFORMATION OF HUMANITY

Humanity did not long persist in obedience to God's Word, and so humanity did not long remain free. Rather, Genesis 3 describes the event of human misformation, in which Adam and Eve's rebellion against the Creator results in the loss of freedom as given by God. For Bonhoeffer, human misformation is rooted in the act of humanity to take the knowledge of good and evil for ourselves. In his reading, humanity was not intended to know good and evil but was meant to be in immediate relationship with God through his Word. In knowing God, we are called to obey God's Word as those who rely on his Word, not questioning or judging his Word. As creatures, we are in no position to scrutinize God's Word, but are called to trust God and obey him. The freedom given to us by God was meant to be unencumbered by the burden of knowing good and evil. In knowing God, we know all we need to know. Let's now turn to explore Bonhoeffer's vision of human misformation more closely.

The offer. Bonhoeffer's reading of Genesis 3 centers on the offer made by the serpent. In coming to Eve, the tempter engages her in what Bonhoeffer

---

[12]Bonhoeffer, *Creation and Fall*, 63.

calls "the first conversation *about* God, the first religious, theological conversation."[13] The nature of this conversation is important for Bonhoeffer because it reveals the danger in which the human now finds herself: dialogue at a distance from God, dialogue *about* God, places Eve in the position of being the evaluator of God. Being the evaluator means taking a place humans were never intended to occupy, that of judging God. Already, at the beginning of the conversation, the serpent is manipulating Eve through a dialogue that will position her, no longer under God's Word, but over it, a position that changes the essential relationship of humanity to God. Bonhoeffer writes that now, "it is not a common worship, a common calling on God, but a speaking about God, about God in a way that passes over, and reaches beyond, God. Inasmuch as Eve has let herself become involved in this conversation, the serpent can now risk the real attack."[14] By engaging the conversation with the serpent, Eve has allowed herself to be placed in a position of distance from God, a place that exposes her to the vulnerability of the serpent's chief attack, which can now commence.

What is this temptation, the principal attack the serpent now mounts? The true attack begins when the serpent asks the question, "Did God really say . . . ?"[15] With this question, the serpent places Eve into a position not simply of questioning God, but of doubting God: doubting his motives, doubting his reliability, doubting his Word. Bonhoeffer summarizes the scene as follows: "*Did* God really say . . . ? Yes, God *did* say . . . But *why* did God say it . . . ? God is not a good but an evil, cruel God; be clever, be cleverer than your God and take what God begrudges you."[16] By making this claim, the serpent is saying that God is a liar, and must not be trusted, and, according to Bonhoeffer, "That is the ultimate possible rebellion, that the lie portrays the truth as a lie."[17] Evil is rooted in the word of the deceiver that masks itself as the truth and so calls the truth a lie.

---

[13]Bonhoeffer, *Creation and Fall*, 111. Inherent in this comment is a warning from Bonhoeffer about the danger of "doing theology." While we must risk the theological venture, we must always be aware that it is, in fact, a risk. Talking about God is a dangerous activity, putting those who reflect on God in the hazardous position of potentially assuming the role of evaluator and judge of God, the very danger in which Eve finds herself in the conversation with the serpent.

[14]Bonhoeffer, *Creation and Fall*, 111-12.

[15]Bonhoeffer, *Creation and Fall*, 112.

[16]Bonhoeffer, *Creation and Fall*, 112.

[17]Bonhoeffer, *Creation and Fall*, 112.

The serpent has mounted the attack and now goes in for the kill. In placing Eve in the position of questioning God, the serpent can now offer a vision of the life that God has been withholding from her: "You will not die at all. Instead God knows that on the day you eat from it your eyes will be opened, and you will be like God and know what good and evil is."[18] Bonhoeffer declares that standing before this offer "We stand . . . at the last point to which the Biblical author brings humankind, before the abyss comes and the inconceivable, infinite chasm opens,"[19] the chasm that separates humanity from life, freedom, each other, and God. Eve now hears the serpent's offer of life and "truth," the offer to become *sicut deus*, "like God." In making this offer, the serpent places an alternate existence before humanity with the promise that it will be better.

This promise tempts and traps Adam and Eve, but how can they understand the trap? How can Adam and Eve, in their innocence not knowing evil, understand what is happening, what is at stake? Bonhoeffer believes that they can't, and that, for Adam, the offer "can only mean a new, deeper kind of creaturely being. *This* is how he is bound to understand the serpent."[20] And yet this is not what the serpent is offering, and it is not what Adam and Eve will receive if they take and eat the fruit of the tree. Though they may not have grasped the depths of the events overwhelming them in this moment, Adam and Eve are still, knowingly, disobeying the Word of God and failing to trust him. Though they may not have understood the offer, they knew God's Word. Now, trusting the word of the serpent rather than the Word of the Lord, Adam and Eve take and eat, an act of disobedience that fundamentally misforms humanity in tragic ways.

Misformation: Knowing good and evil. What is the nature of human misformation? What happened to humanity in this act of disobedience? According to Bonhoeffer, the first thing that happened is that humanity has now moved to the center, taking the place of God in our own lives. Humans were created to live outside the center, oriented toward God and his Word, ever revolving around the center as our affections and desires are focused outside of ourselves toward God. He, his Word and his life, were to be the

---

[18]Bonhoeffer, *Creation and Fall*, 112.
[19]Bonhoeffer, *Creation and Fall*, 112.
[20]Bonhoeffer, *Creation and Fall*, 113.

center of our life. Humans were not created to live with our life at the center of our world, but with God's life at the center. This centrality of God is symbolized by the other tree in the garden, the tree of life. Bonhoeffer writes, "The life that comes from God is at the center; that is to say, God, who gives life, is at the center. At the center of the world . . . is not Adam himself but the tree of Divine life. Adam's life comes from the center which is not Adam but God; it revolves around this center constantly, without ever trying to take possession of this center of existence."[21] In doing so, Adam would live in the creaturely freedom that we explored above, the freedom of obedience to God and his Word that gives life. Life is not to be in Adam's possession but is always to be received as a gift from outside. Adam, to live as God intended, is to remain oriented to, but not in possession of, life. "It is characteristic of humankind that human life constantly revolves around its own center, but that it never takes possession of it."[22]

But now, Adam and Eve have transgressed, storming the center and taking the place of God, and the consequences of this disobedience are dire. Created to live as those who receive life from God, from the tree at the center of the garden, Adam and Eve have how taken the central place. Believing that they could find a new and better existence, trusting the serpent that they could become like God, Adam and Eve have taken from the tree of the knowledge of good and evil and have become, as the serpent said they would, like God. But it is here that the promise of the serpent is exposed as a lie for, in becoming like God, Adam and Eve lose God. In becoming like God, Adam and Eve lose each other. In becoming like God, Adam and Eve lose the limit of God's Word and grace, and so lose their creatureliness. In becoming like God, Adam and Eve *die.* The tree of the knowledge of good evil, according to Bonhoeffer, is the tree of death: "It stands immediately next to the tree of life, and *the tree of life is* untouchable. . . . Whoever grasps at life must die."[23]

Adam and Eve have grasped at life, and in so doing have died. Bonhoeffer declares that death for Adam and Eve is a living death in which they must now "live" according to their own resources: "Standing in the middle means living from its own resources and no longer from the center."[24] Adam and

---

[21]Bonhoeffer, *Creation and Fall*, 84.
[22]Bonhoeffer, *Creation and Fall*, 84.
[23]Bonhoeffer, *Creation and Fall*, 89.
[24]Bonhoeffer, *Creation and Fall*, 115.

Eve are now no longer vitally connected to the life of God and living according to his resources. Rather, they are dead in having to live by their own resources. And the primary resource that Adam and Eve must now depend on is the resource inherited from taking the fruit of the tree: the knowledge of good and evil.[25] Bonhoeffer is here making the claim that humanity was never meant to possess the knowledge of good and evil. This knowledge belongs to God, who is the Good, and whose command would direct humanity to walk with him in paths of goodness. Had humanity remained oriented to God at the center, we would have lived in the goodness of God's Word, allowing him to possess the knowledge of good and evil and trusting his guidance for us. But now, humanity, in becoming *sicut deus*, have rejected fellowship with God and replaced his Word with the knowledge of good and evil. Expanding on this, Jacques Ellul, whose reflections on Genesis 3 are influenced by Bonhoeffer, writes the following:

> As Genesis shows us, the origin of sin in the world is the knowledge of good and evil. In this context knowledge means decision. What is not acceptable to God is that we should decide on our own what is good and what is evil. Biblically, the good is the will of God. That is all. What God decides, whatever it may be, is the good. If, then, we decide what the good is, we substitute our own will for God's.[26]

In substituting our own will for God's, humanity initiates an existence in rebellion against God, turning from a life oriented to God to a life oriented to the self.

Following Luther, Bonhoeffer describes the sinful condition of knowing good and evil as the *cor curvum in se*, the heart turned in on itself.[27] Rather than a life directed toward God at the center, in taking on the knowledge of good and evil and living in reliance on our own resources, humanity has become curved in on ourselves. In this condition, we are no longer able to live outwardly in love

---

[25]Bonhoeffer writes, "Humankind now lives out of its own resources, by its knowledge of good and evil, and thus is dead." *Creation and Fall*, 91.

[26]Jacques Ellul, *The Subversion of Christianity* (Eugene, OR: Wipf and Stock, 2001), 70. See Andrew Goddard, *Living the Word, Resisting the World: The Life and Thought of Jacques Ellul* (London: Paternoster Press, 2002), 73n50.

[27]This notion is developed by Bonhoeffer theologically in *Act and Being*, but its evidence and impact on humanity is seen in his description of fallen humanity in *Creation and Fall*. See *Act and Being*, 41-44.

of God and neighbor, but are now, truly, self-centered and reliant on our own decision and affirmation of good and evil rather than on God's Word.

The creation of conscience. Bonhoeffer now turns his attention to another result of human rebellion: the inward curve of humanity results in the creation of conscience. In much Christian ethical teaching, the conscience is depicted as a capacity given by God to humanity as a component of our created nature and is the means by which we navigate the moral challenges of life and choose to obey God. But this is not how Bonhoeffer understands the conscience. For him, human sinfulness has left Adam separated from God, but also separated from himself. In the flight from God seen in Adam's hiding, we see the human divided against himself.[28] And it is the fallen division of humankind with the self that creates the conscience. Bonhoeffer writes, "This flight, Adam's hiding away from God, we call conscience. Before the fall there was no conscience."[29] For Bonhoeffer, the conscience is the sign that humanity in sin is hiding from God, is in flight from him. In this flight from God that is the conscience, humanity has moved from being a God-referential being to a self-referential being.

As such, Bonhoeffer rejects the notion that the conscience is the inner voice of God guiding the human in our moral life. In fact, "conscience is not the voice of God within sinful human beings; instead, it is precisely their defense against this voice."[30] Conscience as a defense against God is the idea that now, in taking on godlikeness and resisting God's Word, humanity will persist in this rebellion by trusting in our own word of truth, our conscience, and so resisting God's Word of truth. In other words, conscience for the fallen human creature, rather than being the voice of God within, is instead the conversation that the *cor curvum in se* has with itself regarding the decisions we are to make in light of our knowledge of good and evil. This dialogue is the result of our fallenness because it has replaced the immediacy of fellowship with God and obedience to his Word. Humans now rely on conscience, our decision about good and evil, as that which will guide us through life.

And so, for Bonhoeffer, the misformation of the human soul is the devastation of humanity's rejection of God's life-giving presence and Word.

---

[28]Bonhoeffer, *Creation and Fall*, 128.
[29]Bonhoeffer, *Creation and Fall*, 128.
[30]Bonhoeffer, *Creation and Fall*, 128.

Having been promised that they will become like God, humanity has reaped the whirlwind of this promise: a life bent in on the self, enclosed in our inner dialogue of conscience, living but dead. As Bonhoeffer states it starkly, "For humankind to become-sicut-deus as the serpent promises can mean nothing but what the Creator calls death."[31] Now, as the narrative of Genesis 1–3 comes to its tragic conclusion, Adam and Eve are now cast out of the garden, out of proximity to the tree of life. Bonhoeffer believes that Adam and Eve's expulsion from the garden reveals the true point of the story: "The whole story moves toward its end in these verses. The significance of the tree of life . . . becomes really clear at last. Indeed it becomes clear that the whole story has really been about this tree."[32] The story has been about the desire of God to create the image of his life on earth through the creation of Adam and Eve. Had Adam and Eve trusted in God, living in his presence and according to his Word, they would have known the fullness of life and freedom in God's world. But Adam and Eve, trusting in the promise of the serpent that they could become like God, have taken on the knowledge of good and evil, being curved in on themselves in the inner dialogue of the conscience, and so separated from God and his life-generating Word.

CONCLUSION: MISFORMATION AND SPIRITUAL FORMATION

In the introduction to this essay, I stated a rather obvious point: to talk about spiritual formation is to talk about spiritual misformation. As I conclude this essay, I want to reflect on a particular aspect of Bonhoeffer's vision of misformation that we have explored that I propose can shape a vision of spiritual formation: his reframing of the way Christian spirituality approaches the conscience and its relation to knowing good and evil.

Gordon Fee has written about the tendency in evangelical approaches to formation to use the word *spirit* to refer to the human spirit rather than the Holy Spirit.[33] In doing so, I believe that a subtle expectation is present in evangelical approaches to formation that humans are responsible for the formation of our own spirits. This expectation brings with it an emphasis on

---

[31]Bonhoeffer, *Creation and Fall*, 112.
[32]Bonhoeffer, *Creation and Fall*, 141.
[33]Gordon Fee, "On Getting the Spirit Back into Spirituality," in *Life in the Spirit: Spiritual Formation in Theological Perspective*, ed. Jeffrey P. Greenman and George Kalantzis (Downers Grove, IL: InterVarsity Press, 2010), 36-44.

the conscience as a guide to the moral formation that we must do to form our spirit.[34] But, if Bonhoeffer's reframing of the conscience as the result of sin is correct, then this means that approaches to formation that focus on the conscience end up immersing us more deeply into our fallen condition rather than freeing us from it. I propose that Bonhoeffer's vision of misformation helps us avoid this danger by making clear the dynamic of the human soul in sin. As we have seen, the heart of Bonhoeffer's theology of sin is the inversion of the human soul bent in on itself as the result of humanity taking possession of the knowledge of good and evil, which replaces God's Word and results in the creation of the conscience. If the conscience is, as Bonhoeffer claims, a product of human fallenness, then it must follow that we cannot have an emphasis on the conscience as a component of spiritual formation. Bonhoeffer shows us that the conscience must be understood to be the opposite of the Spirit, and so any formative process must be conceived of as replacing the conscience with the Spirit. When this is done, we see clearly that the referent of the word *spirit* is not the human spirit but the Holy Spirit, who decenters us and calls us to no longer listen to our conscience and its knowledge of good and evil, but once again to attend to God and his guiding Word as it is mediated to us by the Spirit.

Therefore, the work of the Spirit to form misformed humans is the work of freeing us from our knowledge of good and evil and the conscience this knowledge creates. When we come to faith in Christ, the Spirit opens us up once again to the dialogue with God we were created to have, and so we are freed from the inner dialogue with ourselves regarding the knowledge of good and evil. When this happens, the Spirit of God truly takes up residence in our lives, and we see clearly that the work of formation is not ours to do, but is the Spirit's work, a work that overcomes our self-reliance and inward curvature. Bonhoeffer's emphasis on misformation helps correct a false emphasis on the human spirit and its reliance on the conscience evident in evangelical approaches to spiritual formation. And his vision of human misformation enables us to better understand the dynamics at work in the fallen human soul and so better attend to the work of the Spirit in our lives and churches, as he works to turn our bent selves outward once again, that we might be image bearers of God in the power of the Spirit who conforms us to Christ.

---

[34]How many of us were taught as children to "let your conscience be your guide"?

7

Drawing from the Well

Learning from African American Christian Formation

VINCENT BACOTE

O N OCCASION I ENTERTAIN THIS thought experiment: What if Rod Dreher looked to those who didn't have the conditions to make some of the choices assumed by the Benedict Option?[1] What if he looked to those who had experience dealing with being in a clear disadvantage in society? What if it was called "The African American Option"? Alas this is a fantasy, but it raises the question of why this tradition was not among the resources to which Dreher turned. Jemar Tisby gives an answer:

> In offering the Benedict Option, Dreher almost completely overlooks the wisdom of Christians, especially people of color, who have always endured marginalization. The absence of the influence or perspective of people of African descent is particularly noticeable. The Benedict Option takes a running leap over the black church and lands on another continent in another millennium. Dreher goes back 1,500 years to find the Rule of St. Benedict when he could have gazed back over the past 400 years and looked across the street to the black church for guidance. . . . Dreher didn't feel he had the "moral authority" to talk about the black church. That's probably true, but it's not difficult to gain information about the black church. He could have asked black Christians for input during the editorial process. He could have spent time reading the dozens of books about the black church in America. Or he

---

[1]Rod Dreher, *The Benedict Option: A Strategy for Christians in a Post-Christian Nation* (New York: Sentinel, 2017).

could have even had a co-author write it with him. Instead, he just leaves out the black church.[2]

While Dreher may have left out this tradition, here we have opportunity ask, "What can we learn from the African American church tradition, in this case in reference to spiritual formation?" In what follows I highlight only a few dimensions; it is very important to state that this tradition is far from monolithic and there is not space for anything near comprehensiveness. Perhaps we can consider this the beginning of drawing on a deep well where wisdom can be found. I begin with a few current observations about African Americans and faith.

DIFFERENCES IN APPROACH TO DISCIPLESHIP

Before directing our attention to specific contributions, it will be helpful to note some distinctions that emerged in a recent Barna survey on approaches to discipleship between African American and white Christians.

> When both groups define "discipleship," white believers are more likely to refer to it as a "process of learning to follow Jesus Christ as Savior and Lord, seeking to observe all that Jesus commanded, by the power of the Holy Spirit and to his glory." Black Christians instead commonly refer to it as "The process of transformation that changes us to be increasingly more like Christ through the Word, the Spirit, and circumstance."[3]

While there may be shared spiritual aspirations with white Christians, black Christians emphasize life experience and developing Christian character, rather than simply achieving spiritual goals. This stress on spiritual growth through weathering life's storms affects the motivations of black Christians as well: "black Christians are more likely to say they have been through tough times in life, and that growing spiritually will help them (34% compared to 27%)." But these experiences do not always facilitate or catalyze deep spiritual growth; the opposite can occur. The survey observed that "black pastors are more likely than white pastors to state that 'guilt about things in the past' poses a major obstacle for their congregation's spiritual maturation (64% compared to 42%)."[4]

---

[2]Jemar Tisby, "The Real Reason the Benedict Option Leaves Out the Black Church," *The Witness*, March 29, 2017, https://thewitnessbcc.com/benedict-option-leaves-out-black-church/.

[3]Barna Group, "Racial Divides in Spiritual Practice," *Research Releases in Culture and Media*, January 12, 2017, www.barna.com/research/racial-divides-spiritual-practice/.

[4]Barna Group, "Racial Divides."

The survey also observes that black believers are more likely to position their growth in Christ in the context of community and fellowship, while white Christians take a more individualized approach:

A crucial part of fellowship for black Christians is mentorship. They are more likely to currently be mentored and discipled by another Christian (38% compared to 19%) and to be discipling others themselves (28% compared to 17%). White Christians are more likely than black Christians to prefer being discipled on their own (39% compared to 31%), whereas black Christians show a greater preference for group-based discipleship (32% compared to 22%). Black Christians are also more likely to list large group study or discussion groups (18% compared to 4%) and family members (71% compared to 61%) as "very important" in aiding spiritual development.[5]

A further dimension of this divide between communal and individualistic emphases in spiritual development is the way black and white Christians view their spiritual lives:

It is unsurprising therefore that white Christians are more likely to view their spiritual life as "entirely private" (42% compared to 32%). Black Christians, on the other hand, are much more likely to believe their personal spiritual life has an impact on others—whether they are relatives, friends, community or society at large. For instance, black Christians are much more likely to believe that their personal spiritual lives have an impact on broader society (46% compared to 27%).[6]

A dimension that may be a surprise to some with minimal exposure to the black church is the emphasis on studying the Bible and the stronger devotion black Christians show toward it.[7] "They are more likely to believe that the Bible is 'totally accurate in all of the principles it teaches' (59% compared to 48%), a belief that translates into more consistent and frequent study of the Bible (63% compared to 45%) and memorization of Scriptures (46% compared to 16%)." The study further observed that African American Christians place a higher premium on the spiritual impact of Bible study than white Christians do, a view that goes from the top down: "this starts

---

[5]Barna Group, "Racial Divides."

[6]Barna Group, "Racial Divides."

[7]I make this claim in light of the view held by some that African American churches are characterized by an emphasis on emotion to the exclusion of deep spiritual formation.

with leadership; black church leaders are also more likely than their white counterparts to believe that 'teaching the Word in weekly services' (90% compared to 80%) and 'memorizing Scripture' (75% compared to 63%) will have a 'significant impact on developing disciples.'"[8]

As Cristena Cleveland notes, this corporate emphasis has its roots in both historical and current racial tensions and systemic injustice. The primary reason we have African American churches and denominations is that white congregrations excluded black Christians. In view of the fact that the segregation of Sunday morning remains a reality, as Martin Luther King Jr. famously noted, African American Christians still find safety and resources for resistance in their churches:

> There's something powerful about being together. It reminds me of a Henri Nouwen quote about the ministry of presence that suggests we underestimate just what being together means. . . . Often we want to preach eloquent sermons or produce some sort of amazing artistic expression to touch people's hearts, and that's great . . . but a lot of it is laughing and knowing that we're not alone.[9]

While some of these dimensions of African American spirituality may seem familiar, this is not the only part of the story. In spite of the greater tendency for African American Christians to see a relationship between their personal spiritual lives and having an impact on society, the common problem of disconnection is also present. Nilwona Nowlin's interview with Almeda Wright, the author of *The Spiritual Lives of Young African Americans*, provides a helpful picture, one not viewed as merely a problem as revealed in this series of quotes:

> Young African Americans . . . are facing all kinds of challenges. But in the midst of those challenges, they have something to teach Christians and the world at large: a way of being Christian that requires us to rethink some of the disconnects between our love of God and our love of justice, or our ability to talk about personal spirituality without also talking about social transformation. . . . Spiritual fragmentation is not necessarily a new concept. It's discussed as early as 1903 by W. E. B. DuBois and 1909 by William James. DuBois's idea of "double consciousness" is one example of this fragmentation.

---

[8]Barna Group, "Racial Divides."

[9]Cristena Cleveland, "The Black Church: A Necessary Refuge," *Christianity Today*, September 17, 2015, www.christianitytoday.com/ct/2015/september/black-church-necessary-refuge.html.

James talks about the "sick soul" and the "divided self," which is another example. . . . The hardest thing to hear about spirituality among young African Americans is that they're getting exactly what we teach them. Fragmentation isn't something that they're inventing. In some ways, we're modeling for them this kind of compartmentalized life.[10]

The important point here is that this disconnection between spirituality and commitments to justice or other "real life" issues reveals the challenge to cultivate forms of spiritual formation that facilitate holistic discipleship.

In another extensive quote, Wright shares observations about excavating theology in creative spaces like spoken word events, which invite serious consideration:

I'm both surprised and encouraged by the extent to which young African Americans are doing creative art in community. I've noticed that the arts have become another source of communal life and spiritual formation that I think churches and even youth groups have lost. In a different generation, youth group or sports teams might have played that role. I remember listening to some of the kids talking about their writing groups and poetry troupes and saying, "If it wasn't for this group, I don't know if I would've survived." That's powerful and scary at the same time. They are searching for spiritual formation and communal belonging and finding them in places that church folks might consider unlikely. . . .

How do we tap into that? How do we honor the creative arts and the ways they bring people together? It's amazing to think about providing young people with the form of a lament or a prayer and then inviting them to create their own the way they do in poetry circles. Can we do this instead of expecting them to learn through rote memorization? . . .

Creative arts are also essential just for wholeness and well-being, especially for people who historically have been marginalized and oppressed. They can function as catharsis and healing, and I see that with these young people and the poems they're writing. It's given me fresh insight into their theology.[11]

The disconnect between artists and the church is not new, but Wright's observations suggest that there may be organic forms of community in creative

---

[10]Nilwona Nowlin, "How Young African Americans Are Fusing Faith and Activism," *Christianity Today*, February 1, 2018, www.christianitytoday.com/ct/2018/january-web-only/how-young-african -americans-are-fusing-faith-and-activism.html.

[11]Nowlin, "How Young African Americans."

spaces that could be connected to the contexts of spiritual formation more typically associated with church life.

Now we turn from these descriptions and give attention to some of the historical dimensions of the African American church that help reveal some of the helpful spiritual formation resources for churches of all kinds.

THE EMERGENCE OF AFRICAN AMERICAN CHRISTIANITY AMID DISTORTION

As Judith Wiesenfeld writes, under chattel slavery, African Americans

> produced distinctive religious forms of spirituality that aided individuals and communities in persevering under the dehumanization of slavery and op-pression. As African Americans embraced Christianity . . . they gathered in independent church communities and eventually created larger denomina-tional structures such as the African Methodist Episcopal Church, the African Methodist Episcopal Zion Church, and the National Baptist Convention.[12]

Amid the history of slavery and Jim Crow, Matthew Johnson in *The Tragic Vision of African American Religion* helps us see the experience of African Americans as one of calculated disintegration, fragmentation, disorientation, and a threat of nothingness and meaninglessness (apart from being property suitable for slave labor). He compares it to a crucifixion experience. While this horrific experience occurred (amid slavery and beyond after the eman-cipation), there was also the development of Christianity among the slaves, and African American Christianity developed a mode of formation that in part was characterized by hopefulness:

> This hopefulness, which is always at once a longing, is not to be confused with the cheeriness of a blanket reassurance free of doubt and ambiguity. At root, the hopefulness that we encounter when we review the experience is a funda-mental existential affirmation that manifests itself in an aspiration or longing born of lack, disparity, and the "Sturm und Drang" of the peculiar institution and its sociocultural, mutant offspring. It is a state of being, a very different experience from that which we commonly refer to as hopeful. It is an affir-mation that lends to life the existential impact of hope. One presses on. This

---

[12]Judith Wiesenfeld, "Religion in African American History" *Oxford Research Encyclopedia*, http://americanhistory.oxfordre.com/view/10.1093/acrefore/9780199329175.001.0001/acrefore-978019 9329175-e-24.

level is reached only after "hopes" have been challenged and the fundamental stabilities of a person's or a group's existence have been disturbed. This experience is the result of a decision about how to respond to the implied question inherent in the existentially ambiguous position of all human beings at the "limits," "To be or not to be?" It is the presence of the power to do so, that is, to say "to be," that is commonly referred to as joy or celebration. But here again I must press the point that this must be understood in the living context of what it is to be of African descent in America.[13]

Here we could say that this is hope in the face of strategic dehumanization. Johnson continues,

> The African American lives under circumstances that facilitate frequent and intense encounters with the limits of life. The sociocultural context of the African American fostered and continues to foster profound and disturbing ambiguity. The African American community is a traumatized community in which the traumatizing forces are institutionalized and embedded in daily linguistic and social practices, making the experience an intersubjective field and, therefore, chronic. As a result of the initial trauma, wherein the common frames of meaning and interpersonal relations were permanently disrupted, destroyed, or subject to arbitrary destruction, the African in America had to live with and somehow cope with profound uncertainty and ambiguity. . . . Even the best of the experience amounted mostly to relief from its most menacing aspects.[14]

This kind of hope has a constant companion in lament because of the undeniable experience of oppression. Johnson later elaborates,

> The African American religious imagination possessed a psychic value and reality that helped maintain spiritual, emotional, and psychological equilibrium in the face of forces that fostered fragmentation as well as psychic and spiritual disintegration. The African American appropriation of Christian symbolism, the production of religious ritual using all available resources, was a creative response to the "loss" endured during and sustained after transplantation. It was a response to the structured marginalization and the chronic melancholia that ensued.[15]

---

[13]Matthew V. Johnson, *The Tragic Vision of African American Religion* (New York: Palgrave Macmillan, 2010), 91-92.
[14]Johnson, *Tragic Vision*, 91-92.
[15]Johnson, *Tragic Vision*, 112-13.

The spiritual formation in the African American church cultivated hope, even amid the tragic irony of a white Christianity hostile to their flourishing. This can be especially seen in the music and in preaching that emphasizes hope. One can observe this today in many African American churches that emphasize telling the story of Christ being raised each week. The emphasis on Christ's resurrection victory makes considerable sense when one thinks about a faith forged in the face of despair. A personal observation: I did not understand this when I was growing up, and could not understand why hearing this story each week was so powerful for many members of the congregation I attended as a child. The scales have now fallen from my eyes.

Regarding the context in which African American faith emerged, it is also interesting to consider the effect of Darwin's *Origin of Species* (note the full title—*On the Origin of Species by Means of Natural Selection, or the Preservation of Favoured Races in the Struggle for Life*) on white Christians in 1859 and onward on both sides of the higher criticism debate: progressives now had further scientific basis to believe those of African descent weren't as "developed," and conservatives, even if resistant to Darwin, had another basis for believing in the inferiority of black people. Even though there was emancipation in 1865, there was not massive transformation of the beliefs about African Americans. Emancipation didn't equate to a belief in equality.[16]

In African American life post–Civil War, there was an explosive growth of churches, particularly in the South (e.g., the National Baptist Conventions had 3 million members by 1895). This was actually a matter of necessity: there was no employment, no land, no police protection, limited access to education, and the church became the center of everything in the small towns that emerged. Even with denominational differences among black Christians, the church was consistently the center of the community and the pastor the main community leader. As far back as the eighteenth century, "these churches and denominations became significant arenas for spiritual support, educational opportunity, economic development, and political activism. Black religious institutions served as contexts in which African Americans made meaning of the experience of enslavement, interpreted

---

[16]Carl Jeffrey Wright, CEO of Urban Ministries, Inc., brought this insight to my attention, as well as some of the subsequent dimensions about the postemancipation African American church.

their relationship to Africa, and charted a vision for a collective future."[17] The attention to the broad sweep of life helps us see that the spiritual formation of the people had an emphasis on what we could call a Matthew 25 ethic (focused on attending to "the least of these") and a Luke 4 gospel (an emphasis on addressing circumstances of distress—this is not to the exclusion of a Matthew 28 gospel, but "saving souls" alone was not an option when survival was at stake).

What does this mean regarding spiritual formation? There are two important areas of insight: (1) it is notable that there was a disposition of Christian hope attended by lament in the midst of a living hell (an aspect of formation that is real and necessary because of experiences of suffering); and (2) once African Americans were emancipated from slavery, spiritual formation included a whole-life emphasis as a matter of necessity; while they did not have something like a dense theology of public life, church and the rest of life had to be connected out of necessity.

This kind of spiritual formation still exists today, though some observe that the church is not the center of community life like it was, and at least some young people are wondering where to find the explicit connection between faith and public concerns.[18]

It is important to observe that when we think about matters of Christian formation, it is helpful to consider the assumptions that we have about what is normal or possible for life. The following quote from the late womanist theologian Katie Cannon is very illuminating. She is speaking about ethics, but it is appropriate to conversations about spiritual formation:

> When I turned specifically to readings in theological ethics, I discovered that
> the assumptions of the dominant ethical systems implied that the doing of
> Christian ethics in the Black community was either immoral or amoral. The
> cherished ethical ideas predicated upon the existence of freedom and a wide
> range of choices proved null and void in situations of oppression. The real-
> lived texture of Black life requires moral agency that may run contrary to the
> ethical boundaries of mainline Protestantism. Blacks may use action guides
> which have never been considered within the scope of traditional codes of

---

[17]Wiesenfeld, "Religion in African American History."
[18]The reasons for this are debated, with culprits ranging from the prosperity gospel to the success of civil rights to a diminished prophetic voice.

faithful living. Racism, gender discrimination, and economic exploitation, as inherited, age-long complexes, require the Black community to create and cultivate values and virtues in their own terms so that they can prevail against the odds with moral integrity. For example, dominant ethics makes a virtue of qualities that lead to economic success—self-reliance, frugality and industry. These qualities are based on an assumption that success is possible for anyone who tries. . . .

Dominant ethics also assumes that a moral agent is to a considerable degree free and self-directing. Each person possesses self-determining power. For instance, one is free to choose whether or not she/he wants to suffer and make sacrifices as a principle of action or as a voluntary vocational pledge of crossbearing. In dominant ethics a person is free to make suffering a desirable moral norm. This is not so for Blacks. For the masses of Black people, suffering is the normal state of affairs. Mental anguish, physical abuse and emotional agony are all part of the lived truth of Black people's straitened circumstances. Due to the extraneous forces and the entrenched bulwark of white supremacy and male superiority which pervade this society, Blacks and whites, women and men are forced to live with very different ranges of freedom. As long as the white-male experience continues to be established as the ethical norm, Black women, black men and others will suffer unequivocal oppression. The range of freedom has been restricted by those who cannot hear and will not hear voices expressing pleasure and pain, joy and rage as others experience them.[19]

If there is to be anything learned from the spiritual formation of African Americans, it will require the cultivation of a listening ear, as well as a genuine desire to learn about the lived experiences of those often not truly seen or known.

What do I hope readers will learn from these dimensions of African American spiritual formation? Four items:

There can be spiritual formation that occurs that is orthodox in confession, while there are cultural norms that contradict that confession at the same time (this is as general as consumerism and as specific as assumed racial hierarchy). We have to be ready to learn from what has gone wrong as well as what is exemplary.

---

[19]Katie G. Cannon, *Black Womanist Ethics* (Atlanta: Scholars Press, 1988), 2-3.

Spiritual formation requires attention to integration and embodiment. Our spiritual formation is not an individualistic, disembodied intellectual exercise that has nothing to do with being embodied persons who are in relationship with other embodied persons (including culture, class, race, etc.). We can pay attention to the embodied particularity of others and learn from them, as they can provide insights into the pursuit of Christlikeness that we would not otherwise consider because of the limits of our own contexts.

Spiritual formation can cultivate resilience amid traumatic, horrific experiences. While Christians hear texts about persecution that is sure to come with pursuing fidelity to Christ, the comfort of our modern lives can act as a drug that leads us to think that life with God is normally a matter of safety and blessing. Because the kingdom of God has not yet arrived in fullness, our formation ought to account for the ways the horrific aspects of the "not yet" are part of our normal life experience.

Spiritual formation can cultivate the courage to love our neighbors in new ways we have never considered. Love of neighbor is opportunity and challenge.

CONCLUSION: IS THERE A REAL DESIRE TO LEARN FROM THIS TRADITION?

Jemar Tisby again:

> The reality for many white believers is that Christians of color may provide inspiring stories of resistance and are certainly nice to have on display in the congregation, but they are not a true source of wisdom for the white church. To some white Christians, the faith traditions of racial minorities may offer great aesthetics like preaching or musical style, but they don't have the legitimacy to lead the way into the future. The constant refusal to learn from the black church can only be termed ecclesiastical arrogance.[20]

If Tisby is to be proved wrong, what needs to happen? I ask the reader, Will you be an example of ecclesiastical humility and curiosity?

I will end with another thought experiment, one that turns my above suggestions into several questions:

What if African American Christian formation helped us to acquire a necessary resilience? Are we willing to acquire the resilience we need if we

---

[20]Tisby, "The Real Reason."

are to pursue lives of discipleship that include an orientation toward addressing the distressing past and frustrating present of issues related to race and justice? This is a path of discipleship that is hopeful but also laments the horror.

What would it look like to form Christians with a faith more connected to the entirety of life and that expressed love of neighbor by first expressing the courage to look for the cultural distortions and idolatries in our own faith, as well as the courage to truly look at the horror of racialized society? Put another way, does the spiritual formation in our congregations include an openness to God where Jesus can interrogate our beliefs and expose idols, including idols of nation, race, and culture?

Are you, the reader, willing to pursue and cultivate an approach of Christian formation that includes love of neighbor, expressed as embracing the darkness of our racialized past?

How does your approach to formation diagnose and address versions of cultural blindness?

How do you help people connect their faith to all of their life, especially when they are fairly comfortable?

Does your catechesis inform what people say when others are not around?

As you practice a more integrated faith, are you willing to learn from pastors of a different race or class—are you willing to get know them and be known by them, learning from them?

My hope is that at least some who read this are willing to consider these questions and to have the courage to answer yes.

Part Two

PRACTICAL
WISDOM

8

The Integrated Pastor

Toward an Embodied and Embedded Spiritual Formation

TODD WILSON

T HIS IS PARTLY AN OBSERVATION, partly a confession. I'd like to call it *a disquieting observation from a middle-aged pastor.* After more than two and a half decades as a Christian, and a decade and a half as a pastor, I have come to this conclusion: *pastors can be godly and yet dysfunctional at the same time.* They can be both holy and not whole. They can be both biblically faithful and yet psychologically maladjusted. They can be both spiritually mature and emotionally immature.

Pastors can love evangelism yet fear those of a different race or the opposite sex. They can be "prayer warriors" and "control freaks," powerful preachers and domineering spouses, faithful shepherds and disengaged or overbearing parents. They can love Jesus and be addicted to food, pornography, or pain medication.

While these are unsettling juxtapositions, they are, sadly enough, empirically verifiable. This is why we must learn to swallow the sobering truth that pastors can possess real spiritual depth and yet live lives that are riddled by psychological compulsions and emotional reactivity.

Perhaps you followed the recent revelations of pastor Bill Hybels of Willow Creek Community Church in South Barrington, Illinois. Of course, we did because we live in Chicago and couldn't help but follow the story. It was on our evening news. Following the story was a gut-wrenching experience, as more and more sordid details came to light. It felt like watching a car accident in slow motion. I grieved for everyone involved: the women he victimized, the leaders he deceived, the congregation he devastated, and not least his own family, who were left to put all the pieces back together.

The Reverend Bill Hybels is one of America's most famous pastors, and I have no reason to doubt that he sincerely loves Jesus, treasures the gospel, believes in justification by faith alone, prays and reads his Bible on a regular basis, loves and serves his wife and family, and has a big heart for reaching the lost with the life-giving message of the risen Christ. And yet, he is also one who was engaged in a decades-long pattern of deeply dysfunctional sexual misconduct, deceit, and manipulation.

What do we make of this? How do we explain this combination of deep Christian commitment and psychological and behavioral dysfunction? Many of us, I suspect, are tempted to go all Manichean on Hybels and conclude that he is either good or bad, real or fake, saint or sinner, godly or charlatan. But I think it's a bit more complicated than that.

Consider another example. You may recall in August of 2014 when news broke that another one of America's most famous pastors, Mark Driscoll, resigned as pastor of Mars Hill Church in Seattle. What emerged and led to Driscoll's resignation was a deep pattern of anger, pride, intimidation, and abuse of power on his part. His overly muscular version of Christianity wasn't just for Larry King or the ladies on *The View*; evidently, it was his modus operandi, and has had profoundly painful repercussions on countless lives.

But, as with Bill Hybels, I have little reason to doubt that Mark Driscoll sincerely loves Jesus, treasures the gospel, believes in justification by faith alone, prays and reads his Bible on a regular basis, loves and serves his wife and family, and has a big heart for reaching the lost with the life-giving message of the risen Christ. And yet, he is also one who was engaged in protracted and persistent abuses of power, people, and position.

To reiterate: pastors can be both godly and dysfunctional—holy and not whole, spiritually mature and emotionally repressed, biblically faithful and psychologically maladjusted.

I know this to be true from observation. But I also know this to be true from experience—personal experience. My own experience. I told you this was partly observation, partly confession. Now is time for the confession.

For many years of my ministry I would say that *I* was godly and dysfunctional. I have no doubt that if you lived with us for a week, slept on our couch, observed me throughout my day, you would come away thinking, "He's a pretty godly guy. He loves Jesus. He loves the Bible. He loves the church. He cares about his wife and children and making a difference in the world for Christ."

But if you came and lived with me in the early weeks of January 2015, you would also see that I was fairly dysfunctional. At least, that's when I came to confront the reality of it for the first time.

I was granted a three-month sabbatical from my regular church responsibilities—a delicious season of pastoral bliss with no sermons, no meetings, no counseling sessions, no leadership decisions, no management difficulties, no long-range planning or goal setting, not even any compulsory reading or studying or writing.

To be sure, I had big plans for my sabbatical: I was going to finish one contracted book manuscript and start working on another; I was going to reread all fifteen hundred pages of Calvin's *Institutes*; I was going to memorize the book of James; I was going to plow through a three-foot high stack of books; and I was going to brush up on Hebrew.

When I shared these plans with my elders, one of them wryly said, "Are you going to do anything else?" Clearly, my compulsions had already gotten the better of me, but I was perhaps the only person at the table who couldn't recognize it. So I doubled down on the insanity and reassured them that all would be well and that this three-month season of ostensible rest was going to be what I called, ironically enough, a "working sabbatical."

But rather than dive right into all the work I had planned, I figured it would behoove a godly pastor like me to exercise a little self-restraint and Christian character by taking the *first week* to simply do nothing. It was a sabbatical, after all!

So that is what I did.

But I must confess, it didn't go well. My strategy of rest worked for about two days. By Wednesday of week one I was starting to unravel.

Perhaps you've known someone with a serious substance abuse problem, or you may have come alongside that person as he was trying to kick the addiction. It's not a pleasant experience. Without their chemical of choice people start to unravel, mentally and emotionally. They get irritable, edgy, panicked, overwhelmed with persistent cravings.

That was me by the middle of week one of my sabbatical. I was a godly
pastor going through withdrawal. I was an addict who needed a hit—not of
whiskey or meth but of accomplishment and achievement. Christian psychiatrist Gerald May defines addiction as "a state of compulsion, obsession,
or preoccupation that enslaves a person's will and desire."[1] That, sadly, was
me. I was irritable, edgy, panicked, overwhelmed with persistent cravings
for getting things done—and I was driving my dear wife insane!

"Todd, you've got to do something about this!" she admonished.

And so I did. I knew just what to do.

I went back to work.

On Monday morning of week two of my sabbatical I returned to my
normal routine: I got out of bed at 5:00 a.m. and into the pool at the YMCA
by 5:30 a.m. I swam two thousand yards, showered, and got to my study at
church by 7. There I read my Bible and prayed until around 8, at which point
I transitioned to begin the day's work. I wrapped up around 5:30 p.m. and
was home for dinner by 6.

And I can tell you, I felt better instantly! I felt the chemical surge of satis-
faction in my brain, like I had just taken a hit of my favorite narcotic—or at
least a double espresso. My irritability was gone. So too was my edginess,
panic, sense of desperation. I was back to my old self—a godly pastor feeding
his compulsions with a working sabbatical!

Everything was going swimmingly. But then a friend had the nerve to text
me sometime during week three. His text read, "Hey man, isn't that you're
car in the church parking lot? Aren't you on sabbatical?"

Do you remember that scene in 2 Samuel 12:7 when the prophet Nathan
says to David, "You are the man!" That was how this friend's text message
struck me. A stinging rebuke. *Todd, you are the man!* Godly, yes, but dysfunctional, broken, perhaps even addicted. There are powerful subterranean
forces at work in your life, controlling you.

A few weeks later, to my own surprise, I found myself in a therapist's office.
I didn't know exactly why I was there. I had never sat with a therapist before.

"Why are you here?" he asked.

"I think I'm addicted to achievement," I said somewhat sheepishly.

---

[1]Gerald G. May, *Addiction & Grace: Love and Spirituality in the Healing of Addictions* (New York:
HarperCollins, 1988), 14.

"Okay. Why don't you tell me a little bit about your family background," he said.

Thus began a conversation, and a therapeutic relationship, that continued for many months—one that helped me to see that I was both godly and dysfunctional. I discovered that twenty-five years of growth as a Christian had successfully added layer on layer of spiritual formation on top of some deep-seated compulsions that were still profoundly influencing my life.

The Problem with Evangelical Spiritual Formation: A Lack of Integration

Bill Hybels, Mark Driscoll, and Todd Wilson. Different people with different scenarios, and different outcomes. And yet our stories are more alike than I would care to admit. We're all godly and also dysfunctional pastors. What do we make of this?

At the risk of oversimplification, all three stories hinge on one word: *integration*. Or more accurately, four words: *a lack of integration*. What unites Hybels and Driscoll and Wilson and a thousand other godly and dysfunctional pastors? *A lack of integration*.

Integration. From the Latin *integrare*, which means "to make whole." To integrate is to bring together different elements of a single system into a coordinated, unified whole. To be *dis*-integrated is the failure to bring together different elements of a single system into a coordinated, unified whole. So for the purpose of this conversation, integration is to bring together the different elements of the human person into a coordinate, unified whole, and to be *dis*-integrated is to fall short of that purpose.

It is my conviction that most forms of evangelical spirituality fail to foster integration. We prioritize doctrinal instruction and moral development. But we neglect psychological healing. We emphasize the cultivation of character. But we overlook our deep-seated psychological compulsions, fixations, and emotional reactivity.

You might say that evangelical approaches to spiritual formation often fail to promote integration. Sadly, this means that, if left to itself, evangelical spirituality will breed not integrated but dis-integrated pastors whose ministries may sooner or later disintegrate all around them.

Dis-integration isn't a problem just for pastors. It's a condition that afflicts many Christians. We have dis-integrated pastors, but we also have dis-integrated *Christians*—sincere followers of Jesus who live with deep (albeit well-managed) psychological dysfunctions.

At the risk of sounding like a grumpy old man, may I say that we see evidence of dis-integrated Christians all around us.

Let me ask this question: Why is it that good Christians don't always make good human beings? They're faithful to their families, consistent in church attendance, read their Bibles and pray for the lost. But they can be, at the same time, rigid, self-righteous, xenophobic, racist, sexist, controlling, narrow minded, emotionally repressed, sexually dysfunctional, bitter, impulsive, angry. In a word, *unChristian*.[2]

Or why is it that non-Christians can be more Christian than Christians? Haven't you had that experience, or had someone say something like that to you? It's as though those without knowledge of the gospel can achieve a measure of psychological health and healing that outstrips even what some professing Christians have attained.

Or consider this: Why is it that evangelicals are notoriously clumsy when it comes to dealing with issues like race, sex, and gender? Could it be that all three of these issues—race, sex, and gender—are *body issues*. They concern the body—the very thing that much of evangelical spirituality conditions us to downplay or overlook. Is it any wonder, then, that we struggle to speak thoughtfully and winsomely about these body issues when we spend so little time cultivating a spirituality that concerns our own bodies?

Where am I going with all of this? We need to rethink our approach to spiritual formation. We need an approach to spiritual formation that *fosters integration*—that brings together doctrinal instruction and moral development *with* psychological healing.

In short, I'm appealing for an approach that—by the grace of God, through the Spirit of God, grounded in the Word of God—engenders *not only holiness but wholeness.*

In saying this I'm sounding a note similar to the one Dallas Willard sounded several decades ago. Willard's concern was that Christians weren't

---

[2]Gabe Lyons and David Kinnaman, *unChristian: What a New Generation Really Thinks About Christianity* (Grand Rapids: Baker Books, 2007).

attaining Christlikeness. Why not? Not because of a lack of effort, he concluded. No, everywhere he looked he saw sincere Christians doing the very best they could.

Instead, according to Willard the problem is our deficient theological anthropology. He explains,

> For serious churchgoing Christians, the hindrance to true spiritual growth is not unwillingness. While they are far from perfect, no one who knows such people can fail to appreciate their willingness and goodness of heart. For my part, at least, I could no longer deny the fact. I finally decided their problem was a theological deficiency, a lack in teaching, understanding, and practical direction. . . . As I now see it, . . . the gospel preached and the instruction and example given these faithful ones simply do not do justice to the *nature of human personality, as embodied, incarnate.* And this fact has far reaching implications for the development of human health and excellence.[3]

We have a deficient theological anthropology, a failure to do justice to the true nature of the human personality, to take seriously that we are not just souls inhabiting bodies, or minds connected to brains. Rather, we are embodied and even incarnate creatures. To put it bluntly, we don't *have* bodies— we *are* bodies. Yes, we have a mind and soul too (or at least soulish capacities), but they are far better *integrated* with our bodies than we've been led to believe.

What, then, would a better theological vision of spiritual formation look like? It would be one that takes seriously the nature of the human person as a psychosomatic unity, that does justice to our embodied, incarnate nature, and that promotes integration of the doctrinal and moral with the psychological and even neurological.

To develop a more integrated approach to spiritual formation would require that we take at least the following three steps: (1) we will need to take the *body* more seriously, (2) we will need to take the *brain* more seriously, and (3) we will need to take *interpersonal communion* more seriously.

---

[3]Dallas Willard, *The Spirit of the Disciplines: Understanding How God Changes Lives* (San Francisco: HarperCollins, 1988), 18 (emphasis original).

STEP #1—TAKE THE BODY MORE SERIOUSLY

Not long ago I listened to a well-known pastor deliver a powerful message in the chapel service of a well-known seminary. The message was about how to make the most of one's seminary experience. And the pastor's approach was to focus on the essence of the Christian life, or you might say, the essence of spirituality and spiritual formation.

It was an excellent message about glorifying God with your education, delighting in God through seminary, finding joy in Greek and Hebrew syntax, developing your mind by carefully tracing the argument of great books, and so on. And this pastor spoke with characteristic passion and insight. It was moving, insightful, inspirational, challenging.

But at the end of the message the thought suddenly occurred to me: "This is a great vision of spiritual formation, but *you don't need a body for any of it.* An angel could just as easily embrace the content of this message as an embodied person. You don't have to be a human being to do anything he just advocated. In fact, it could have been a chapel message just for angels and archangels rather than seminarians and faculty!"

Here is something we often and easily forget. Every approach to spiritual formation presupposes some understanding of the human person—a theological anthropology.

And what is the dominant theological anthropology of evangelicalism? It is *a dualism of mind-body, inner-outer, spiritual-physical*—a dualistic anthropology that is, as best as I can tell, indebted to the monumental influence of the great St. Augustine.

As Christian philosopher Nancy Murphy says, "It is in fact the case that most Christians, throughout most of their history, have been dualists of one sort or another."[4] Most Christians have assumed that the person has two parts—soul or mind, on the one hand, and body, on the other; or, inner and outer, or spiritual and physical parts.

We owe this dualism, as Murphy notes, to the fourth-century bishop and theologian Augustine.

> Augustine (354–430) has been the most influential teacher on these matters [of mind-body dualism] because of his legacy in both Protestant and Catholic theology and because of his importance in the development of Christian spirituality.

---

[4]Nancey Murphy, *Bodies and Souls, or Spirited Bodies* (New York: Cambridge University Press, 2006), 37.

Augustine's conception of the person is a modified Platonic view: a human being is an immortal (not eternal) soul using (not imprisoned in) a mortal body.[5]

She adds, "From Augustine to the present we have had a conception of the self that distinguishes the inner life from the outer, and *spirituality has been associated largely with the inner.*"[6]

Or as the esteemed Canadian philosopher Charles Taylor argues in his *Source of the Self,*

> On the way from Plato to Descartes stands Augustine. Augustine's whole outlook was influenced by Plato's doctrines as they were transmitted to him through Plotinus. . . . He could liberate himself from the last shackles of the false Manichaean view when he finally came to see God and the soul as immaterial. Henceforth, for Augustine, the Christian opposition between spirit and flesh was to be understood with the aid of *the Platonic distinction between the bodily and the non-bodily.*[7]

Consequently, Augustine's modified Platonic dualism merged with Paul's way of talking about flesh and s/Spirit. Western Christianity hasn't been the same since. At least, our understanding of spirituality and spiritual formation hasn't been the same. As Taylor says, "Augustine is always calling us within."[8]

Let me try to summarize it this way. Augustine's dualistic anthropology leads very naturally to a dis-integrated spirituality, an approach to spiritual formation that focuses on the mind or soul and not on the body, on the inner person and not the outer, or on the spiritual and not the physical.

But if we want to move toward a spiritual formation that promotes integration, then we need to scrutinize our dualistic anthropology. We need to ask ourselves whether it is the most biblically faithful, theologically sound way of understanding what it means to be human. Or are there not better ways to conceive of the person that are more in line with Christian commitments to embodiment?[9]

---

[5]Murphy, *Bodies and Souls*, 14.
[6]Murphy, *Bodies and Souls*, 30 (emphasis added).
[7]Charles Taylor, *Sources of the Self: The Making of the Modern Identity* (New York: Cambridge University Press, 1989), 127 (emphasis added).
[8]Taylor, *Sources of the Self*, 129.
[9]For extended reflections on this question in line with the overall direction of this essay, see Warren S. Brown and Brad D. Strawn, *The Physical Nature of the Christian Life: Neuroscience, Psychology, & the Church* (New York: Cambridge University Press, 2012).

Step #2—Take the Brain More Seriously

By taking the body more seriously (step #1) we are led naturally to take a second step. We need to take the *brain* more seriously. Of course, we won't take the brain seriously if we don't first take the body seriously. But once we begin to appreciate the significance of our embodiment for spiritual formation, then we will be better positioned to think more specifically and concretely about what it means to take seriously this corporeal body of ours—which will inevitably lead one to take the brain more seriously.

If evangelicals want a more integrated approach to spiritual formation, then we need to take brains more seriously, so that spiritual formation is viewed, in a very real sense, as *brain formation*—or brain re-formation!

And yet, how many of us think "brain" when we hear the words *spiritual formation*? It's like those SAT questions that ask you to identify which doesn't belong: "prayer, Bible study, fasting, and neural networks." For evangelicals the brain is hardly even a category of spiritual formation.

But it should be. The reality is that the brain underwrites everything about our spiritual formation—our thoughts, our feelings, our actions. As cultural biologists Steven R. Quartz and Terrence J. Sejnowski nicely put it, "Every nuance of yourself, the fabric of your experience, ultimately arises from the machinations of your brain. The brain houses your humanity."[10] Perhaps I can put it a tad bit more provocatively: *there is no spiritual formation without brain formation or re-formation.*

I recently came across an illustration that drives home this very point. Let me give you an advanced warning: It's an awkward and troubling story. But it's powerful and to the point.

Back in 2000, a forty-year-old man, a Virginia high school teacher, was arrested for making sexual advances toward his stepdaughter. His wife called police to come and arrest him. When the police arrived, they found he had been, for some time, collecting pornographic magazines and visiting pornographic websites. He was convicted and required to attend a mandatory twelve-step recovery program for sexual addicts.

But he failed the program because he couldn't stop making advances at the other women in the program. So the judge was going to sentence him to

---

[10]Steven R. Quartz and Terrence J. Sejnowski, *Liars, Lovers, and Heroes: What the New Brain Science Reveals About How We Become Who We Are* (New York: HarperCollins, 2002), 3.

jail time. But the day before his sentencing, he drove himself to an emergency room, complaining of a raging headache. Doctors did an MRI and discovered that he had an egg-sized tumor on the right frontal lobe of his brain. So they operated on him to remove the tumor. And to everyone's surprise, the lewd behavior and pedophilia went away with the removal of the tumor.

However, a year later the tumor started to grow again. And, remarkably, so too did the inappropriate sexual behavior. So the medical staff decided to operate once again. And, stunningly, when they removed the tumor for a second time, so too did the illicit sexual desires dissipate, for a second time.[11]

A fascinatingly true story. It tells us something about what it means to be a human being. We are morally and spiritually dependent, so to speak, not only our bodies, but on our brains. Consider how closely linked morality and personality are in this story—*how a damaged brain can bend behavior*, or how an otherwise moral guy can do some really immoral things if his brain isn't working right.

My wife Katie and I have seven children, three biological and four adopted from Ethiopia. The two youngest, twin boys, we adopted when they were just six months old. The other two we adopted when they were ages six and eight. The twins are now ten, and the older two are eleven and thirteen.

Having seven children is a wild ride! But having four adopted has definitely added to the adventure. We've learned a lot about parenting and families and adoption and, not least, ourselves. But we've also learned a lot about the brain.

Renowned psychiatrist Bessel van der Kolk has written a highly acclaimed study of trauma and healing so aptly titled *The Body Keeps the Score*.[12] Over the last decade of parenting four adopted children, Katie and I have learned that the body does indeed keep the score. The traumatic events in a child's life—things like abandonment, emotional or physical abuse, and neglect—often scar the body by doing things to the brain, affecting its wiring and firing and, ultimately, its integration.

---

[11] The story is told in Malcolm Jeeves and Warren S. Brown, *Neuroscience, Psychology and Religion: Illusions, Delusions, and Realities About Human Nature* (West Conshohocken, PA: Templeton Press, 2009), 63-65.

[12] Bessel van der Kolk, *The Body Keeps the Score: Brain, Mind, and Body in the Healing of Trauma* (New York: Penguin, 2014).

Neuroscientists now tell us that brains can be scarred, that the body does keep the score—or, to be more precise, that the brain keeps the score. The brain holds onto the trauma of the past. The experience is embedded in the circuitry of the brain—perhaps not as explicit memory, the kind you can recall like looking at a photo album. But it will be stored as *implicit* memory, the kind you *re-experience emotionally* even though there may be no "memories" or visual images coming to mind.[13]

So, the child who has experienced trauma in his or her life carries those memories—bears those scars—in their bodies, in their brains. And those memories, whether explicit or implicit, affect everything about that child— the child's attitudes, actions, emotions, reactions, mood, and all the rest.

But there is another layer of complexity to the situation. Human beings have developed an ingenious yet costly way of coping with trauma. We disconnect our minds from our bodies, so that we can live up in our heads, not down in our bodies, as it were. As a defense mechanism, we disconnect our minds from our bodies, so as to distance ourselves from the painful memories stored in our bodies (i.e., in our brains). In other word, we *dis-integrate* in order to survive.[14]

Think about the spiritual formation of a child who has suffered significant trauma. We realize that to form our children spiritually, especially our adopted children, we cannot simply put pressure on their wills to compel them to "do what Jesus would do." Nor can we simply "shepherd the child's heart" without attending to the child's brain. Instead, we have had to step back and take not just their bodies but also their brains seriously. We have had to come to terms with the fact that there will be no lasting spiritual formation without deep psychological healing—the healing of brains, new neural networks created through kindness, care, compassion.

My wife Katie and I have come to another important realization—in this fallen world we've all been traumatized in different ways and to varying degrees. We've all been roughed-up by this abusive world. Each of us has

[13]See Daniel J. Siegel, *Mindsight: The New Science of Personal Transformation* (New York: Bantam, 2010), 145-65; Curt Thompson, *Anatomy of the Soul: Surprising Connections Between Neuroscience and Spiritual Practices That Can Transform Your Life and Relationships* (Wheaton, IL: Tyndale, 2010), 63-87.

[14]See Siegel, *Mindsight*, especially chapter 7, "Cut Off from the Neck Down: Reconnecting the Mind and the Body," 120-44.

had to endure a certain kind of abuse, neglect, or trauma. All of us have had damage done to our bodies, to our brains, so that none of us is entirely whole. We've all been dis-integrated through the ravages of sin, personal, social, cosmic. For each of us, the body does keep the score.

We may not see obvious effects of trauma in our lives because we have added layer on layer of moral and spiritual development on top of our psychological brokenness in a way that effectively muffles its impact. But if we attend to our lives more carefully and probe beneath the surface, we will no doubt discover the subterranean reality of our own psychological brokenness.

What does this brokenness look like? It looks like the compulsions we cannot seem to control, even with our best moral efforts. This brokenness can look like strong involuntary urges, the fixations, the obsessions, the emotional reactivity to persons or situations that we cannot quite explain and that seem to emerge from out of nowhere. These intractable features of our lives are telltale signs that all is not well in our body, that is, with our brain.

We are familiar with that famous passage in Romans 12:2 where Scripture calls the Christian not be conformed to the pattern of this world but to "be transformed by the renewal of your mind [*nous*]." I wonder if healing the brain is at least part of what Scripture has in mind in this verse: the renewal of the *nous*—not in a dualistic sense as that which is fundamentally distinct from the body, but as the whole psychosomatic unity we call the person.

Step #3—Take Interpersonal Communion More Seriously

There is a third and final step we need to take if we are going to move toward a more integrated approach to spiritual formation. We need to take more seriously *interpersonal communion*.[15]

When we take bodies seriously, we will take brains seriously—as the concrete focus of our embodiment. And when we take brains seriously as embodied and indeed socially embedded realities, then we will naturally take interpersonal communion seriously.

---

[15]My emphasis on interpersonal communion draws on the work of Daniel Siegel's approach. He refers to it as "interpersonal neurobiology" but attempts to frame it in explicitly Christian terms of communion of persons with other persons and with God. For a similar approach, see Thompson, *Anatomy of the Soul*.

By "interpersonal communion" I mean the communion of persons, or as we sometimes say, "the meeting of minds." Perhaps we should talk about it as the "bonding of brains." It is deeply mutual, personal, reciprocal. Christian Smith defines communion as "the mutual giving of personal selves as gifts of fellowship and love for the good of each person concerned."[16] It is the experience of not just *knowing* another person but *being known* by that person.[17]

If you have a dualistic understanding of the person, then you will naturally prioritize the mind over the body. You will also inevitably put the emphasis on knowing rather than being known. In fact, "knowing rather than being known" would be a fair description of so much of evangelical spiritual formation, in which the focus is almost exclusively on learning and education and instruction.[18]

For centuries ordinary Christians have understood that profound personal and spiritual transformation happens not as much from knowing as from being known. A new generation of neuroscientists is helping us to see this more clearly.

Why is Alcoholics Anonymous far and away the most successful behavioral change program to have ever existed? Because every meeting begins the same way. "Hi, I'm Todd. I'm an alcoholic." "Hi, Todd." It's a place where many people, often for the first time in their life, are *known by other people for who they are.*

What AA has discovered—and what we as the church sometimes struggle to grasp—is the transformative power of interpersonal communion.

Something miraculous happens when two minds, empathetically, meet one another. We know this to be true from experience. But now neuroscientists have the data to back this up. Something literally happens inside of you (i.e., your brain) when you know that you are known by someone else— new neural networks are created, new synapses fire and wire, and your brain is changed, for the better.

---

[16]Christian Smith, *What Is a Person? Rethinking Humanity, Social Life, and the Moral Good from the Person Up* (Chicago: University of Chicago Press, 2010), 68.

[17]Thompson, *Anatomy of the Soul*, 11-20.

[18]Similarly, Brad S. Strawn and Warren S. Brown, "Christian Education as Embodied and Embedded Virtue Formation," in *Neuroscience and Christian Formation*, ed. Mark A. Maddix and Dean G. Blevins (Charlotte, NC: Information Age Publishing, 2016), 87-97.

Psychiatrist Dan Siegel calls this the experience of "feeling felt."[19] It happens when you sense that another person has entered into your internal world and shares with you in the experience of what is going on inside of you. This is what we call empathy, which is at the heart of interpersonal communion. But it is also the ignition key to personal and spiritual transformation—being known, not just knowing. And not just by another human being, but ultimately, and most importantly, by God himself.

Christian psychiatrist Curt Thompson puts it very well: "The process of being known is the vessel in which our lives are kneaded and molded, lanced and sutured, confronted and comforted, bringing God's new creation closer to its fullness in preparation for the return of the King."[20]

CONCLUSION

When we talk about spiritual formation, we are talking about the process whereby a person moves toward maturity in Christ by the power of the Spirit. Spiritual formation is, as Paul puts it in Colossians, about becoming complete in Christ. "He is the one we proclaim," the apostle writes, "admonishing everyone and teaching everyone with all wisdom, so that we may present everyone fully mature [*teleios*] in Christ. To this end I strenuously contend with all the energy Christ so powerfully works in me" (Col 1:28-29). We could say that the telos or goal of spiritual formation is to be *teleios* or complete in Christ.

The burden of this essay has been to say that we will have a very hard time getting to this telos without taking more seriously the body, the brain, and interpersonal communion. We will not become "complete in Christ" without being known—not only by one another, but by our Lord and Maker himself.

And so we take heart, learn to walk by faith, lean into the communion of saints, the forgiveness of sins, and the power of God's Spirit. "For now we see only a reflection as in a mirror," Scripture says, but "then we shall see face to face. Now [we] know in part; then [we] shall know fully, *even as [we] are] fully known*" (1 Cor 13:12).

---

[19]Siegel, *Mindsight*, 10-11.
[20]Thompson, *Anatomy of the Soul*, 13.

9

Practice Resurrection, Live Like Jesus

CHERITH FEE NORDLING

"PRACTICE RESURRECTION"

On a gray day in Oxford at a conference almost twenty years ago, I listened to a woman press Eugene Peterson for a definition of "spirituality" or of the Christian life that, in her words, "would fit on a T-shirt." Not surprisingly, Eugene didn't want to play: "No, I don't have such a definition, and I'm not sure I'd trust a T-shirt-sized message." As the awkward laughter in the hall quieted, the woman piped up again, "But if you *did,* what would you say?" Once more he answered, "I wouldn't." "But," she insisted a third time, "if you *did*!" Perhaps to relieve the awkwardness in the room, or perhaps by the leading of the Spirit, Eugene paused, waited, and then answered, "Practice resurrection."

Yes, I thought. Practice resurrection. In other words, enact the life of our future human glory now in the power and character of the same Spirit by whom the Father raised Jesus from the dead. The same Spirit by whom Jesus was given—and still lives—his incarnate human life. The same Spirit who empowered Jesus to do the will and work of the Father on earth as in heaven, so that Jesus could say, "Anyone who has seen me has seen the Father" (Jn 14:9). If ever there was a description of what it means to be human, and thus to bear the image of God, it is this: that we look like our Father in heaven because we look like our incarnate Lord and elder brother, Jesus of Nazareth. This is formation by the Holy Spirit.

Biblical spirituality knows only one source—the Holy Spirit. We are not the agents of our "spiritual formation," nor are "spiritual practices" something we do to try to get the Spirit to draw near to us. Such practices merely posture us in readiness. As beloved children of our Father and coheirs with Christ our brother, we are to be readied for radical obedience through the Holy Spirit to participate in God's triune life and love among us. Such practices can help us attend to the Spirit and to embody habits that strengthen our "muscle memory" as we enact our final calling and destiny in Jesus Christ.

Already our future human life is "hid with Christ in God." And that future determines our present. Hid in the wonder of the resurrected Jesus, "the firstborn of a new creation," and his outpoured, recreating Spirit, we live and move and have our being on the earth as his image-bearing siblings. As we participate with him, living by the Spirit as he did, we manifest life and hope until death has died and all things are renewed. As those who live between Christ's two advents, we actively await the hope of our salvation, "the redemption of our bodies," or our glorious human restoration as God's children. All of creation waits with us because what happens to us happens to everything. And unless it does, we have no hope at all (Rom 8; 1 Cor 15). But in Jesus, it already has happened, and nothing can separate us from the Father's love for us human children. That love is on display in the resurrected, embodied life of his Son.

This is the gospel and the hope for which we have been saved. Were the resurrected Jesus not our ascended King and mediating High Priest, we would not be saved. Or, to put it another way, we would have been saved for nothing. To be saved from sin and death without being saved for eternal *human* life leaves us unmoored and disconnected from Jesus, the Word made—and stayed—flesh. Jesus' ongoing life makes it abundantly clear that we were not saved to go to heaven as disembodied souls. (Just try finding that in the New Testament!) Rather, we were made to bear the image of God in our humanity, and nothing can stop God's loving fulfillment of our telos (Eph 1:3-14). In and with Jesus, "the firstborn from among the dead," we finally get to be who we were meant to be—healed, glorified, purpose-filled stewards of God's new creation. Forever. Looking at Jesus, we see our own human transformation in its "ever-increasing glory, which comes from the Lord, who is the Spirit" (2 Cor 3:18).

As our new Adam, Jesus has finally done what we were made to do: he has lived a truly human, Spirit-empowered life in full alignment with God, in God's "image and likeness." Hence Jesus' life is *our* life, given to us at first creation by the Spirit who breathed life into us as human children of God, and then again as "children of the resurrection" (to use Jesus' words in Luke 20:36), empowered by the same Spirit who breathed new creation life into Jesus. To practice resurrection is to live as children submitted to God, empowered by God, and conformed to the image of God manifested through his Son. To practice resurrection is to practice our future life with Jesus. Now.

SPIRIT-FILLED IMAGE BEARERS CONFORMED TO THE IMAGE OF THE SON

As God's human children, we are creaturely ministers of God's life and love on the earth.[1] We are viceregents in the divine image and likeness. Our being, identity, and calling are made manifest as we manifest God's presence, character, power, and *shalom*. In its context as an ancient Near East creation narrative, Genesis places human beings as the communal image of God in creation's temple-palace-garden to function as God's royal suzerain, mediating within creation the immanence of the transcendent Creator. As humanity's embodied existence testifies to YHWH's kingship, God's creative act of making human beings "'in our image, in our likeness' . . . male and female" (Gen 1:26-27), asserts the destiny and vocation of humanity to be God's representatives on the earth. The biblical language indicates that all human beings, in our embodied maleness and femaleness, individually and communally, are intended to be living pictograms of YHWH our Creator, enlivened by his breath and his indwelling Spirit.[2]

Because the original creation narrative gives no specifics as to what this vocation actually looks like, the biblical quest leads to Jesus Christ. As God's true image and ours, Jesus is the divine agent and redeeming Lord of all

---

[1]This essay is a revised and abbreviated version of Cherith Fee Nordling, "'Living as Jesus Did': Practicing an Embodied Future in the Present," in *Revisioning, Renewing, Rediscovering the Triune Center: Essays in Honor of Stanley J. Grenz*, ed. Derek J. Tidball, Brian S. Harris, and Jason S. Sexton (Eugene, OR; Wipf & Stock, 2014). Permission granted. Scripture quotations are from the NIV. (The above-mentioned volume can be found at Wipfandstock.com.)

[2]See Rikk E. Watts, "The New Exodus/New Creational Restoration of the Image of God," in *What Does It Mean to Be Saved?*, ed. John Stackhouse (Grand Rapids: Baker, 2002), 15-41.

creation who has been moving all things to their final destiny with the Father and the Spirit. As Athanasius saw so clearly, "[*T*]*he renewal of creation has been wrought by the Self-same Word Who made it in the beginning.* There is thus no inconsistency between creation and salvation. . . . It was He alone, the *Image of the Father*, Who could recreate man made *after the Image.*"[3] In the Word made flesh, Jesus Christ, the reality and meaning of the *imago Dei* have been reordered forever.

> The *imago Dei* is the divinely intended vocation of all humankind and the shared goal of our existence. This vocation, in turn, defines our very being. God's intention is that we might experience eschatological transformation after the pattern of the resurrected Christ, who is the Second Adam. Or, viewing our destiny from another perspective, God desires that we find our being as we are caught up in the narrative of the Son. In this manner, the *imago Dei* emerges as the christologically focused and eschatologically oriented, universal human vocation.[4]

Although Jesus is the center of the biblical narrative, he is not its end per se; rather, Jesus' story opens to include all those born into his family by the resurrecting, eschatological Spirit, who receive his life and story as their own and come to be conformed ultimately to his likeness. In Paul's "final exegesis" of Genesis 1:26-27, he indicates that the divine intention is for women and men who are in Christ to participate in his destiny and thereby replicate his glorious image: "For those God foreknew he also predestined *to be conformed to the image of his Son*, that he might be the firstborn among many brothers and sisters" (Rom 8:29).

Stan Grenz regularly asserts that the New Testament "imperative is always bound up with the indicative": those who are destined to be the new humanity carry the responsibility to live out that reality in the present. Precisely as those who see "our present life in the light of God's future," the question that orients us, says Grenz, is "how we as the church of Jesus Christ ought to understand ourselves and our mission in the present age."[5]

---

[3]Athanasius, *On the Incarnation: The Treatise* De Incarnatione Verbi Dei (Crestwood, NY: St. Vladimir's Press, 1996), 26, 44. Original emphasis.
[4]Stanley J. Grenz, *The Named God and the Question of Being: A Trinitarian Theo-Ontology*, The Matrix of Christian Theology (Louisville, KY: Westminster John Knox Press, 2005), 360-61.
[5]Stanley J. Grenz, *Theology for the Community of God*, 1st ed. (Vancouver, BC: Broadman & Holman and Regent College Publishing, 2000), 854.

The New Testament answer to that question regarding our present life is both eschatological (orienting us toward our human future and destiny) and pneumatological (given and enabled by God the Spirit). The Christian life in God's already/not yet kingdom is not abstractly or even generally ethical. It is reordered in precise conformity to Christ and his Spirit-lived life of empowered, costly love in submission to the Father.

The first letter of John sums it up rather matter-of-factly; "in this world *we are like Jesus*" (1 Jn 4:17; cf. 2:6). This ad hoc summary or description assumes the following: (1) we have received the indwelling presence of God, the Spirit, who has been "poured out" from the Father and the Son; (2) our conformity to the image of the risen Jesus, our "Spirit-ual formation," has already begun; and thus (3) we are to enact our vocation and final destiny together as women and men, bearing the power, authority, and character of God, even now. And that looks like the self-giving love of our obedient, suffering, risen, and reigning Lord Jesus. Look at Jesus. Look hard. He is the image of the invisible God. He is also the image of God's resurrection children, the living prototype of new creation.

JESUS, THE INDICATIVE OF OUR SPIRIT-FILLED IMPERATIVE

> The eschatological destiny of bearing the divine image is present in the here and now as the Spirit is at work transforming those who are in Christ into the image that Christ bears. In this process humans are becoming the new humanity in accordance with God's intent from the beginning. New Testament writers, however, repeatedly declare that an imperative is always bound up with the indicative. Those who are destined to be the new humanity and as such to reflect the divine image, and therefore are already in the process of being transformed into that image, carry the ethical responsibility to live out that reality in the present.[6]

"An imperative is always bound up with the indicative." The Spirit is transforming God's people "into the image that Christ bears," to enact the life of his kingdom with him. Such is the witness of the New Testament. Period. It

---

[6]Stanley J. Grenz, *The Social God and the Relational Self: A Trinitarian Theology of the Imago Dei*, The Matrix of Christian Theology (Louisville, KY: Westminster John Knox, 2001), 251.

assumes that we see Jesus' anointed life the same way his disciples did. As Peter explained at Pentecost,

> Jesus of Nazareth *was a man accredited by God to you* by miracles, wonders and signs, *which God did among you through him,* as you yourselves know. This man was handed over to you by God's deliberate plan and foreknowledge; and you, with the help of wicked men, put him to death by nailing him to the cross. But God raised him from the dead, freeing him from the agony of death, because it was impossible for death to keep its hold on him. . . . God has raised this Jesus to life, and we are all witnesses of it. Exalted to the right hand of God, he has received from the Father the promised Holy Spirit and has poured out what you now see and hear. (Acts 2:21-24, 32-33)

Peter saw, up close and personal, the temptations, challenges, weakness, power, and faithful obedience unto death of his precious friend, this man through whom God did wonders. And after the resurrection, Peter came to know him as risen Messiah and Lord. The Jesus Peter knew did not raise himself. Nor did he run around doing wonders in his own power, like a Superman in Galilean disguise. Peter testified to what he saw: by the anointing of the Spirit, God was with and on Jesus throughout his ministry and death; God then vindicated Jesus by raising him to life and exalting, or coronating him, as King on God's throne. Together with his enthroned, incarnate Son, the Father gave to his disciples—and has given us—God the Spirit, the giver of Jesus' own life.

Unlike Peter, however, the closer many Christians get to Jesus Christ, our true indicative, "a man accredited by God," the less seriously we take the fundamental imperative of being like him. This is because we don't take Jesus seriously, or rather the fact that he was, and is, truly like us. We frequently skirt around Jesus himself, and replace our call to be like him with a call to live some version of the New Testament church's early life (however idealized or watered down) or a simplistic version of the great love command (e.g., niceness to our neighbor). We seldom recognize how the heresies of Gnosticism (rejection of the body and creation for immortality of the soul) and Docetism (that Jesus only appeared in human form without really becoming human in nature) consistently frame an evangelical "gospel" in which Jesus is no longer, and maybe never was, truly human. These heresies, both of which make Jesus only *seem* to be human, or certainly less human than we are, significantly change the content of the good news. The heart and flesh of the gospel, however, is found in the resurrected Son from heaven and Nazareth, who presently embodies and mediates the hope of an embodied, broken world. Without the incarnate Son for and with us, and us with and for him, we are left wondering what salvation really means.

Yet Jesus was, and will forever remain, incarnate precisely to give us our human lives back. Forever. Hence our hope of salvation, as Paul reiterates, is "the redemption of our bodies." This is the good news for which we have been set free—free from sin and free for resurrection life as God's renewed people. To be saved is to experience through the Spirit what Jesus experienced, to participate with Jesus in what he is currently doing, and to become like him in the process.

When social justice, outreach/activism, or even Spirit-gifting for its own sake become our indicatives instead of Jesus, the ensuing imperatives quickly lead us to an overrealized eschatology (with or without the Spirit) in this world. Alternatively, when being saved out of this world becomes our indicative, then the imperative may manifest as an underrealized eschatology, as a kind of "quietism." Here *agape* is reduced to "niceness" toward our neighbor while we await a disembodied life in heaven. Mission is misunderstood as saving souls out of creation rather than manifesting true humanity together with Jesus *as* new creation. As we shift away from Jesus, our lack of focus makes us aimless, purposeless, and caught up in other narratives that compete with the truth of our life in the kingdom and our call to manifest that kingdom on earth.

Lack of attention to the integrity of the *homoousion*—that the incarnate Son is not only "of one being with the Father" but also forever "of one being with us"—can lead us heretically to think that Jesus could do what he did (and perhaps now does *without* a body), because he is the divine Son. This thinking assumes that Jesus' body was a temporary shell discarded at the ascension, useful only until his earthly mission was completed in his own divine power.

From this perspective Jesus seems wholly unrelated to our present humanity. It is difficult to see his authentic human life lived by the Spirit, let alone to see who Jesus *still is* and what he is *presently doing*. Yet, the climax of the gospel is that the Word not only took on flesh and lived in the power of the Spirit, but (also) has remained flesh in glory and exaltation! In short, Jesus' incarnate life is a permanent reality. As ours will be. To dismiss Jesus' humanity is to dismiss our own. And to dismiss the Spirit as the power of God present within our human experience, and that of Jesus, is to turn Jesus' human life, and ours, into a sham.

When we tacitly perpetuate the christological heresies that overemphasize Jesus' divinity (giving him a pass to do all that he did because he was God), we also end up perpetuating heresies that undermine the person and work of God the Holy Spirit. Despite the Nicene Creed's trinitarian insistence that the Spirit is "worshiped and glorified" with the Father and Son as "the Lord, the Giver of Life," from Genesis 1 to Revelation 22, we domesticate the Holy Spirit with cessationist-like claims, or our own inattentiveness and lack of expectation. In so doing, we fail to recognize the Spirit of God as present and active on the earth today just as he was throughout the Old Testament, in the life of Jesus, and in the church throughout history.

As Jesus ushered in and continues to extend the kingdom of God, he has manifested the life of God on the earth precisely as God's divinely human image bearer. Uniquely born of the Spirit and of a young woman from Galilee, he became like us in every way so that we could become like him as human children of God. In his union with us, Jesus did not consider his divine prerogatives as the Son to be used to his advantage (Phil 2:6-11). Instead, he exercised the power of God in the same way that every other image bearer does and must do—by the Spirit (loudly signaled at his baptism in the Jordan River). Jesus embodied the call of true humanity, and the Scriptures are adamant that we recognize the pattern of his life for what it was— *obedience* to God his Father in the Spirit's power (Is 52–53; Acts 10:38; Phil 2:6-11; Heb 2:17-18; 4:15).

Jesus' Spirit-empowered life is what the *imago Dei* has always been intended to be—the human, embodied presence of God on the earth. Jesus' life in the Spirit is not to be misunderstood as unique *to* Jesus, however uniquely the Spirit ministered in and *through* Jesus.[7] Rather, from Genesis forward the biblical assumption is that where God's image and likeness is, so, too, is God in all divine power and authority.

---

[7]Gerald F. Hawthorne, *The Presence & the Power: The Significance of the Holy Spirit in the Life and Ministry of Jesus* (Dallas: Word, 1991), 227-43.

JESUS' LIFE IN THE KINGDOM—AND OURS

Jesus' story is that of the true, Spirit-enlivened image bearer. In light of the older story of Israel's genesis and eschatological hope, and in contrast to her long history of rejecting her identity in favor of falsehood and idolatry, Jesus ushers in Israel's new exodus/new creation return from final exile as God's true "image" or *eikōn*. John the Baptist proclaims Isaiah's promised messianic deliverer and baptizer in the Holy Spirit (Lk 3:16, 21-22). Jesus' baptism and temptation recapitulate Israel's passing through the waters. He is declared God's "beloved Son" and receives the anointing of God the Spirit (a dove over the waters of new creation) to enact his divine-human calling.

Just as Jesus' anointing for ministry is utterly dependent on the Spirit, his expectation is that those who follow him will receive that same anointing to enact the loving power and character of God through their lives. His twelve disciples reconstitute a new community of Israel. He demonstrates the "new command" of love (Mt 22:37-39) among them and, through his self-giving obedience, summons them also to become a cruciform community of love in word and action. In a kind of early Spirit baptism (as is his privilege), Jesus partially confers on the twelve and then the seventy-two disciples the anointing he eventually opens up for all humanity through his death, resurrection, and exaltation: "he gave them power and authority to drive out all demons and to cure diseases, and he sent them out to proclaim the kingdom of God and to heal the sick" (Lk 9:1-2; cf. Acts 2:32-33). The parallels to the Synoptic descriptions of Jesus' Spirit-filled life are unmistakable: "Jesus went throughout Galilee, teaching in their synagogues, proclaiming the good news of the kingdom, and healing every disease and sickness among the people" (Mt 4:23; cf. Mk 1:32-34; Lk 4:40-43).

Both groups of disciples return to testify that this is precisely what happened (Lk 9:1-10; 10:1, 10). Jesus, who sees the eschatological picture in full, reminds them that their true cause for rejoicing is in their identity as children of God—their names are already "written in heaven" (Lk 10:20)—rather than in the accompanying evidence of that fact itself. Spirit-empowered actions flow from Spirit-birthed identity. Jesus' followers, like servants in training, or in formation "to be like their master," will do what Jesus does, acting out of love and power in his name as fellow children of the Father (Mt 10:25; cf. Jn 13:15-17).

In short, *they will be like Jesus*. John's Gospel reiterates that as those who belong to Jesus are united to him and the Father in love, they will be led by the Spirit to live out their eternal life in the present in Jesus' name and will thus see "greater things than these" (Jn 14:12, 16-17, 26; 15:17; 16:7, 13)! In Acts, Luke presents this as the "new normal" for those who follow Jesus and bear witness to the resurrected Lord. Those who bear Jesus' name will manifest the evidence of the Spirit's power and presence among them both in signs and wonders *and* in the fellowship of his suffering (Acts 4:30; Rom 8:16-17). Throughout the remainder of the New Testament, God's new community is called to participate (whether in suffering or glory or both) in the life of God's true living image, the resurrected Lord. They are imperatively joined to their indicative—Jesus Christ.

TAKING JESUS' HUMANITY SERIOUSLY WITH THE APOSTLE JOHN

If Jesus was never really like us, then it seems futile to take seriously a mandate to be like him. Because he was and still is like us, however, we must take his entire life—past, present, and future—with the utmost seriousness. Our life is a participation "in Christ." Our hope is active, attentive, oriented to our living King Jesus. We trust, follow, and worship him as "the faithful witness, the firstborn from the dead, and the ruler of the kings of the earth" (Rev 1:5). United to this "faithful witness" (who embodies the truth about God and human being), we practice resurrection, or eternal life, already through the power of his Spirit. In the context of divine and human community we are a living testimony: "And this is the testimony: God has given us eternal life, and this life is in his Son. . . . Those who keep his commands live in him, and he in them. And this is how we know that he lives in us: We know it by the Spirit he gave us" (1 Jn 5:11; 3:24).

Marianne Meye Thompson is among the Johannine scholars who argue for the humanity of Jesus in John. To say the "Word became flesh," states Thompson, is to say "the signs are deeds done by a human being."[8] John's Gospel emphasizes that in the flesh of Jesus *God* is revealed (Jn 1:14). The emphasis of 1 John is on Jesus' humanity as the locus of divine revelation— that *in the flesh* of Jesus God is revealed (1 Jn 4:2).[9] Whether in the Gospel or the letters, Jesus' truly human life is taken for granted, even as he displays

---

[8]*The Humanity of Jesus in the Fourth Gospel* (Philadelphia: Fortress, 1988), 117, 121.
[9]Thompson, *Humanity of Jesus*, 122.

divine power and identifies with the Father. Failure to see God's self-revelation precisely in Jesus' humanity, she argues, is to misunderstand John and the revelation of the Spirit. "Jesus repeatedly asserts that he works not by his own power and authority, but by God's, and not by his own will, but in submission to that of the Father. . . . On the one hand, the signs do not efface Jesus' humanity. . . . On the other hand, the signs underscore the claim that the works of this human being reveal God's own activity."[10]

John's first epistle is full of eschatological imperatives that stem from the one indicative—the crucified, resurrected Lord Jesus Christ—traced back to the apostolic eyewitness[11] "which we have looked at and our hands have touched—this we proclaim concerning the Word of life. The life appeared; we have seen it and testify to it, and we proclaim to you the eternal life, which was with the Father and has appeared to us. . . . Our fellowship is with the Father and with his Son, Jesus Christ" (1 Jn 1:1-3). The community's fellowship is given through the life-giving Spirit, whose most dramatic sign of anointing on them is God's *agape* among them, which gives them eschatological confidence in Jesus, who guarantees their eternal life: "This is how love is made complete among us so that we will have confidence on the day of judgment: In this world we are like Jesus" (1 Jn 4:17).

Precisely because this is so we are called to be like him (1 Jn 2:6; 4:17). As he was anointed by the Father and received the empowerment of God the Spirit to live out his identity and vocation "in this world," so it is with us. In this world we are like "that one" (1 Jn 3:3, 5, 7, 16; 4:17). Those who are "in God" are shaped by the character and behavior of God's righteousness, truth and love. It is to bear the image of Christ, the *eikōn* of the invisible God, in obedience to and fellowship with the Father by the power of the Spirit.

In a wonderful wordplay, John's epistle describes the Johannine community as having "an anointing" (*chrisma*; 1 Jn 2:20); they know and live *en Christō* in contrast to *antichristos*, false teachers who point away from Jesus. Only the anointing Spirit makes it possible for the *chrisma* to see Jesus as the Son of God and to reveal Jesus' crucifixion as a sign of God's glory rather than "of this world." They bear the family likeness in contrast to the idolaters or false image bearers who have sought to influence them by bearing false witness

---

[10]Thompson, *Humanity of Jesus*, 121.

[11]Just how direct is a matter of extensive Johannine scholarship not taken up here.

through the claim that there is life apart from God and his Son, Jesus of Nazareth. These Spirit-breathed, empowered, beloved children walk in the light, keep God's commands as Jesus did, and love one another as an expression of love for God (1 Jn 3:24; 4:7-8, 13, 20-21). They can discern truth from falsehood, test the spirits, and recognize idolatry, which defames the name and character of God. There is no sin or deceit in them. In their life together, they manifest their life in God by caring for one another's basic needs (1 Jn 3:16-18).

What the community knows to be true is inextricably linked to *how* they know it, specifically in their life together. To borrow Grenz's language, their God-given, Spirit-revealed indicative is enacted as a visible imperative: "*This is how we know* that we love the children of God: by loving God and carrying out his commands" (1 Jn 5:2); "This is how we know what love is: Jesus Christ laid down his life for us. And we ought to lay down our lives for one another" (1 Jn 3:16); "This is how we know that we live in him and he in us: He has given us of his Spirit" (1 Jn 4:13); "This is how we know who the children of God are" (1 Jn 3:10); and so on.

As John's epistle exclaims, "See what great love the Father has lavished on us, that we should be called children of God! And that is what we are! . . . Dear friends, now we are children of God, and what we will be has not yet been made known. But we know that when Christ appears, we shall be like him, for we shall see him as he is" (1 Jn 3:1-2). Although we haven't yet seen our own final glory, Jesus has revealed that we will look like him.

CONCLUSION

As we practice resurrection, praying and living our vocational identity every day, we practice the life to come, offering a partial preview of the holy future in the midst of God's broken, beloved world. We ask, as Jesus instructed us, for the Holy Spirit (Lk 11:13) so that we might authentically participate in the life of his kingdom and join in the work of new creation through cruciform love that looks like Jesus. We participate in the fellowship of Jesus' signs and wonders, and in his suffering, until we hear his final "it is finished" spoken over creation's suffering. In sum, we become who we already are and will be in the manner and likeness of our Lord. It could not be more explicit: "This is how we know we are in him: Whoever claims to live in him must live as Jesus did. . . . This is how love is made complete among us . . . in this world we are like Jesus" (1 Jn 2:5-6; 4:17).

10

Friendship

The Lost Spiritual Discipline

PAMELA BAKER POWELL

T HOMAS MERTON, A TRAPPIST MONK and a prominent voice in
Christian spirituality, made an important observation for spiritual formation. He wrote, "The spiritual life is first of all a life. It is not merely
something to be known and studied, it is to be lived."[1]

We do well to never forget that when we are considering *spiritual formation, its art and science,* and how we address this in our own lives and the
lives of those in our congregations and ministries—that when all is said and
done, in all our academics and pastoral ministry and all those in the various
endeavors of work, the spiritual life is—first of all—a life. We live it. People
in our ministries are living it. It isn't esoteric or for the select few. It is a real
human experience available to all. Embodied. Lived. Merton was highlighting the reality that the spiritual life extends beyond quiet meditation
and heroic missionary efforts. In fact, the spiritual life ranges throughout
daily life's most quotidian activities, most ordinary tasks, to the soul's most
elevated spiritual experiences. It moves from morning prayers to evening
baths—from reading the newspaper to reading the Scripture, from going to
work, to going to church, from taking out the garbage, to taking in the
stranger, from walking the dog to walking the Camino, from looking for
God's guidance in prayer to looking for one's keys—from the joyful miracle

---

[1]Thomas Merton, *Thoughts in Solitude* (New York: Ferrar, Straus and Cudahy, 1958), 37.

of bearing a child to the grief of burying a parent. The spiritual life is a life—a whole, entire, real, human life.

While many pastors, theologians, scholars, and committed laypersons of various vocations have had profound personal spiritual experiences inspired through the Holy Spirit, and many have experienced deep personal insights in meditation and study of Scripture and prayer, yet, each of us, the youngs and the middles and the olds, has to function as a human being living in our physical skin, situated in the community we inhabit, planted on this earth. Everyone has to, or should, care for their bodies; everyone has to, or should, care for their living arrangements; everyone has to, or should, enter into or care for their relationships. It is here, in the everyday living of life, in the natural development of life from infancy to that great step into eternity, that we see the importance of our embodied and ensouled selves. There is no point when it stops. The truth is, we take us with us wherever we go—in this life or the next. We do not divest ourselves of our selves. As we consider the art and science of spiritual formation, I will emphasize that it is precisely at the intersection of each one's human life and each one's soul's yearning that true spiritual formation takes place. Spiritual formation develops as the daily practice of the Great Commandments, to love God and love our neighbor as ourselves, is observed. It is in relationship that human beings are formed from conception to eternity into the persons that God has created us to be. I am proposing in this writing that we, as human beings, are formed in character and in soul strength in two key ways: the Holy Spirit at work in our lives as we engage with Scripture, prayer, worship and sacraments, and the Holy Spirit at work in our relational connections to others, especially our Christian friendships. In friendship, especially Christian friendship, the human soul finds the most formative crucible for growing into a mature human being who is conformed to Christ.

The key to life as God intends us to live, in this world and the next, is love in relationality, and the key to love in relationality begins on this side of eternity in Christian friendship, which often includes spouses and other family members. Merton's observation remains true. The spiritual life is a life, a life lived with others. Certainly, it is true, when thinking about spiritual formation and the art and the science of it, that there is one glaring omission of significant importance. It is the emphasis on the great value of friendship. Friendship in our current culture is an overlooked, undervalued, unacknowledged key formative aspect of the spiritual life. It is, in fact, what I would call, the lost spiritual practice or discipline.

Addressing the two topics before us, the art and the science of spiritual formation, I will first address the current *science* of spiritual formation by highlighting the cultural evidence of concern regarding, what I am calling, "relationality." Our daily lives are taking place in the midst of a culture that is displaying the strains evidenced from widespread signs of crisis in relationships, and from how that affects our human bodies.

The science of spiritual formation has to be addressed with the recognition of the current cultural milieu of loneliness. Life in our current Western culture is a complex intersection of many factors that constitute concern. One of the key aspects of concern is the diminishing of personal relationships, especially friendships, and I would add, Christian friendships.

On November 25, 2016, the *Wall Street Journal* published an article by Will Schwalbe intended to promote reading literature in an internet age. Here are a few sentences from that article that describe today's cultural experience.

> We overschedule our days and complain constantly about being too busy. We shop endlessly for stuff we don't need and then feel oppressed by the clutter that surrounds us. We rarely sleep well or enough. We compare our bodies to the artificial ones we see in magazines and our lives to the exaggerated ones we see on television. We watch cooking shows and then eat fast food. We worry ourselves sick and join gyms we don't visit. We keep up with hundreds of acquaintances but rarely see our best friends. We bombard ourselves with video clips and emails and instant messages. We even interrupt our interruptions.[2]

One psychosocial study after another in the current literature emphasizes this. One study reports that "on this side of the Atlantic, researchers believe as many as 60 million Americans are lonely" (with millennials feeling the least connected). It goes on to say, "That's no surprise given an aging population, later marriage, more divorce, and our addiction to social media. . . . Add in smart devices that ironically obviate the need to talk to anyone, bigger houses that keep neighbors at bay, declining civic participation, automated tellers, and online shopping. . . . Human interaction is at an all-time low."[3]

---

[2]Will Schwalbe, "The Need to Read," *Wall Street Journal*, November 25, 2016, C1.
[3]Juliana Chan Erikson, "Cruel Summer," *World Magazine*, June 30, 2018, 40.

What can we draw from this? People are lonely. Loneliness, it turns out, is related to psychological pain and stress, as well as to physiological stress effects. Researchers have discovered that "the bodies of lonely people are markedly different from the bodies of non-lonely people. . . . The cardiovascular effects are frequently attributed to cortisol, the 'stress hormone,'" which is elevated in lonely people. Lonely people are more susceptible to illness, and they consistently have the lowest antibody response. "When people felt lonesome, they had significantly higher levels of norepinephrine, the hormone that shuts down viral defense." Loneliness, with its increasing heart rates and blood pressure, "is bad for both your figurative heart and your literal one."[4]

Research results abound from experts studying this cultural malaise. The research of Sarah Pressman, of UC Irvine, is cited in a *Harvard Business Review* article: "While obesity reduces longevity by 20%, drinking by 30%, and smoking by 50%, loneliness reduces it by a whopping 70%. In fact, one study suggests that loneliness increases your chance of stroke or coronary heart disease—the leading cause of death in developed countries—by 30%."[5] "A UCLA Berkeley study published last year found that even though adults between 21 and 30 had larger social networks, they reported twice as many days spent feeling lonely or socially isolated than adults between 50 and 70." The author was also reporting on the need to teach how to be a good friend in K–12.[6]

In fact, while twenty years ago, the average adult in the Western world reported having three (and sometimes more) close friends to whom they could tell anything and their friends would be supportive and understanding, now, adults are reporting that their close friends have decreased from three or more to two close friends whom they can really, truly trust. This is a reduction by 33.3 percent.[7]

That is a big hit to the human psyche. So, all this is to say, people today, across the age spectrum, are just plain lonely. If the statistics are correct, as you look out on your own congregation or your ministry or your business

---

[4]Ashley Fetters, "What Loneliness Does to the Human Body," *The Cut*, January 22, 2018, www.thecut.com/2018/01/the-health-effects-of-loneliness.html.

[5]Emma Seppälä and Marissa King, "Burnout at Work Isn't Just About Exhaustion. It's Also About Loneliness," *Harvard Business Review*, June 29, 2017.

[6]Fetters, "What Loneliness Does."

[7]Janet Kornblum, "Study: 25% of Americans Have No One to Confide In," *USA Today*, June 22, 2006. This particular study reports that 25 percent of adults reporting having no friends at all.

or your neighborhood, you can pretty much assume that 40 percent—almost 50—of those folks are lonely. The truth is that we've all been fed a cultural myth that the two most important things in life, the two goals that give life its meaning, are wealth and bold independence. And what's the result of all this materialistic striving and extreme social independence? Loneliness. Deep personal, heartbreaking loneliness. It's distressing to consider that these are some of the prominent influences forming secular America in character and in soul.

In contrast to our culture's message of isolating independence, we have the biblical message of love in relationality. We are called to love God and love our neighbor as ourselves. There is no place for loneliness in this calling. It is all interdependence. It is all about love. It is here that we find the way and the truth of Christian spiritual formation. It is here that we find life in abundance.

Jesus, Emmanuel, God with us, is our model in this communal connectivity. From his incarnation, Jesus lived this out publicly from the beginning of his earthly ministry. The humanity of Jesus sought human companionship. For the three years of his itinerant ministry, the twelve were with him. The night before his death, he told them he was no longer calling them servants, but friends, and he gave them a new commandment to love one another as he had loved them.

In fact, this loving one another is the sign that the world would know that they were his disciples. After the crucifixion, and in the resurrection appearance on the beach, Jesus asks Peter one question—one question—of all the questions Jesus might have asked. Jesus asked Peter, "Do you love me?" (Jn 21:17).

Life, as it turns out, is all about love. Life, as it turns out, is relational. We are buying a myth when we ignore this and think that we are being faithful to the Lord in pursuing all sorts of other primary outward goals. Relationality is our key calling—to love God and to love one another. Everything of any meaning and eternal value issues from this. It is always about a pure dedicated love. Ultimately, it is always about friendship love—love for God in Christ as our friend, and love for our neighbor as a friend as close as ourselves.

When the time is taken to trace the historical, philosophical, and theological writings about Christian friendship throughout the ages, we are soon struck with the overwhelming contribution made by one man. Augustine of Hippo, who lived from AD 354 to 430, is considered by many as the key prominent Christian theologian of the first thousand years of Christianity and beyond. A great mind and a great believer, he came to faith under the ministry of Bishop Ambrose of Milan. Augustine wrote and preached voluminously, and he did not neglect the topic of friendship. Friendship, as Augustine defined it, is "agreement in things human and divine, with benevolence and love, in Jesus Christ our Lord, our most true peace."[8] Augustine saw the Trinity—Father, Son and Holy Spirit—and the love within the Trinity as the source from which all friendship begins. He observed that the bond and center of true friendship is the Spirit who unites friends. It is through that love that comes from the Spirit that friends are transformed.

Augustine continues with the astonishing claim that God is the end as he is the beginning of all true friendship.[9] This causes us all to consider the friendships we have cherished in our own lives. The perspective of considering that these particular friends are God-sent adds a dimension to our personal understanding that enhances our lives and our soul's formation as it directs us to a deeper appreciation and love for our friends. God is love, Augustine asserts with 1 John 4:16, and the foundation and essence of Christian friendship is love (*caritas*).[10] Here we see that Augustine holds true to Jesus' teaching of the Great Commandment—to love one's neighbor as oneself. Finally, Augustine offers a significant insight for our topic today as we think about spiritual formation. "Friendships," he writes, "are a means of redemption. They are not peripheral to the Christian life, but are relationships of conversion, in which Christians move to God by being transfigured in their love for God."[11] In Christ, friendships are eternal, and death brings no permanent loss.[12] Augustine asks this question: "Who does not long for that city, from which no friend leaves?"[13] Here is introduced into prominent Christian theology the emphasis that friendships are eternal.

---

[8]Augustine, *The Works of Saint Augustine: A Translation for the Twenty-First Century*, vol. 4., ed. Boniface Ramsey (New York: New City Press, 2005), 195.

[9]Marie Aquinas McNamara, OP, *Friendship in Saint Augustine* (Fribourg: University Press, 1958), 196.

[10]Augustine, *De Trinitate* 6.vi.7, (NPNF 3:100).

[11]Paul J. Wadell, *Friendship and the Moral Life* (Notre Dame, IN: University of Notre Dame Press, 1994), 100.

[12]Liz Carmichael, *Friendship: Interpreting Christian Love* (New York: T&T Clark, 2004), 61.

[13]Augustine, *Ennarat. Ps.* 85.7 (NPNF 8:407).

Many have read the biblical chapter 12 of Hebrews and wondered over the portrayal of the great cloud of witnesses. Perhaps these are people to meet some day in eternity. They haven't been dissolved into some sort of spiritual vapor. They are still distinct souls, observable in the bleachers of that great coliseum, recognizable somehow in the great community of heaven. Nevertheless, it was only a few years ago that I began to consider it true that the specific friendships in Christ that one has on this earth will continue in eternity. To have that thought—to hold that truth—expands one's perspective, one's hopes, as well as one's joy in the Lord.

As meaningful as Augustine's contribution to Christian thought is, no serious consideration of the topic of friendship can continue without valuing the contribution that Cicero made to the understanding of the value of friendship in human life. Cicero's writings had a strong influence on Augustine himself.

Roman philosopher and statesman Marcus Tullius Cicero, 106–43 BC was born a century before Christ. We Christians owe a debt to him because his dialogue on friendship, *Laelius, De amicitia* (On friendship), and its wisdom and popularity for centuries, eventually brought it into the hands of perhaps the most significant Christian writer to ever address friendship, Aelred of Rievaulx of the twelfth century. It was Cicero who valued friendship as the highest value next to goodness, and who gave us a definition that has directed thinkers and theologians through the millennia. He defined friendship as "nothing else than accord in all things, human and divine, conjoined with mutual goodwill and affection."[14] Does this sound familiar? Does it sound like Augustine without the Christian ascription? We remember Augustine's definition of friendship: "Agreement in things human and divine, with benevolence and love, with Jesus Christ our Lord, our most true peace."[15]

Cicero believed friendship to be of the highest value next to goodness. When he refers to those who suggest friendship should be for profit, he replies, "People who propound this sort of theory seem to me to be doing nothing less than tearing the very sun out of the heavens. For they are, in

---

[14]Cicero, *De amicitia*, trans. W. A. Falconer, Loeb Classical Library, vol. 154 (Cambridge, MA: Harvard University Press, 1923), 131.
[15]Carmichael, *Friendship*, 58.

fact, depriving life of friendship."[16] He also says the following about friendship: "The only thing in the whole of human life which everyone, without exception, agrees to be worthwhile is friendship."[17] "Without friendship, life does not deserve the name."[18] "If you are lonely, every pleasure loses its savor."[19] "For any human being the best support of all is a good friend."[20] "Next to goodness itself, I entreat you to regard friendship as the finest thing in all the world."[21] "Real friendships are eternal."[22]

Perhaps the most important Christian theologian and leader to seriously address the topic of friendship was Aelred of Rievaulx, who lived in twelfth century England. Aelred was a Cisterian monk and abbot of Rievaulx Abbey in the hill country northwest of York, who wrote the book *Spiritual Friendship*, the insights of which are still reverberating today! Aelred's writings were important to emphasize the accessibility and the great spiritual value of Christian friendship—especially in the twelfth century. It seems that from about AD 500 AD to 1000, emphasis on Christian friendship had been reserved and faded, and in some circles, become suspect. It was maintained that *philia*, friendship, was too exclusive, and Christians were called to express *agape*, God's love for all.[23] This clouded the emphasis on Christian friendship, which did not emerge from this cloud until after the millennium, AD 1000.[24] When Aelred began to write, he had two sources on hand that influenced his writing—one from Cicero and one from Ambrose of Milan. We have discussed Cicero's writing *On Friendship*; I will quickly reference here Ambrose.

When Ambrose (AD 339–397) was the bishop of Milan, and a mentor to Augustine, he composed *De officiis* (*On Duties of the Clergy*), a three-volume work for priests and other clerics in Milan. Ambrose was the first to collect together, in one place, the obvious biblical material on friendship, while

---

[16]Cicero, *On the Good Life*, trans. Michael Grant (New York: Penguin Classics, 1974), 201.
[17]Cicero, *Good Life*, 218.
[18]Cicero, *Good Life*, 219.
[19]Cicero, *Good Life*, 219.
[20]Cicero, *Good Life*, 220.
[21]Cicero, *Good Life*, 227.
[22]Carmichael, *Friendship*, 61.
[23]Paul J. Wadell, CP, *Friendship and the Moral Life* (Notre Dame, IN: University of Notre Dame Press, 1989), 71.
[24]Aelred of Rievaulx, *Spiritual Friendship*, trans. Mary Eugenia Laker, SSND, introduction by Douglass Roby (Kalamazoo, MI: Cistercian Publications, 1977), 71.

referencing Cicero. Ambrose became an important resource for Aelred of Rievaulx.[25] For Ambrose the hallmark of Christian friendship is intimate sharing on the pattern of John 15:15, where Jesus calls his disciples "friends." It was Ambrose who wrote, "A faithful friend is the medicine of life, the charm of immortality."[26] Aelred, having read Ambrose and Cicero, began a labor of some years as he sought to express the greatest wisdom on Christian spiritual friendship. Aelred's book *Spiritual Friendship* is written as a conversation among friends on the model of Cicero's writing, maintaining that friendship is "mutual harmony in affairs human and divine coupled with benevolence and charity [love]."[27] However, from there, Aelred goes beyond. Aelred's more forthright definition of Christian friendship is, "Two people together with Christ as their bond."[28] Thus Aelred establishes an explicitly trinitarian definition of friendship. This is the key foundation of Aelred, a triad of relationship in friendship.

Aelred saw friendship as beginning in Christ, being preserved in the Spirit of Christ—and in completion returning to Christ.[29] For Aelred, Christian friendship, selective and personal, thrives in Christ. Each friend not only encourages the other in growth in Christ, but is encouraged himself or herself to grow in Christ. This is spiritual formation, each friend seeking to grow in Christ and receiving the emotional support and encouragement of the other. Aelred would say that friends are of one mind and one heart seeking to serve one another and Christ, and believed that friendships between Christians are eternal.[30] They are a gift from God.

In conclusion, returning to our current cultural climate, there is the looming concern of loneliness for clergy, ministry workers, as well as most in the busy population today. Ambrose in his *On Duties of the Clergy* exhorted his clergy to be friends to one another. He made it clear that friendship is integral to the lifestyle of the Christian minister.[31] Of course, this is true of those in many professions today due to our frantic lifestyles,

---

[25] Ambrose, *Off.* 3.128 (NPNF 10:88).
[26] Ambrose, *Off.* 2:37 (NPNF 10:49).
[27] Aelred, *Spiritual Friendship*, 54.
[28] Aelred, *Spiritual Friendship*, 52.
[29] Aelred, *Spiritual Friendship*, 53.
[30] Aelred, *Spiritual Friendship*, 71.
[31] Carmichael, *Friendship*, 46.

but this is particularly true of clergy. Ministers of one kind or another are usually surrounded with people—so many people and so many ministry or work efforts that they almost don't notice that close friendships are missing. It feels as if there is no time. It feels as if taking time for friendship is a personal indulgence.

I have surveyed several clergy and taught in two theological seminaries, and the issues seem to be the same with each generation. Clergy training emphasizes boundaries in personal life and boundaries with one's parishioners. Yet clergy are immersed in living life among the members of their congregation in almost a boundary-less environment. Clergy have wide access to much of their parishioners' lives. They are the only remaining professionals in our culture who can go to a congregant's home, work, kids' soccer game—anywhere they are invited. This is a wonderful privilege for pastors and benefit to the ministry, but it does come at a personal cost. There is little time or energy to step outside that world and develop close friendships.

Some thirty-plus years ago now, a few friends from seminary put together an idea of inviting a group of forty pastors of the same mind theologically who would meet together yearly for three to four days in worship, prayer, and fellowship. I have done this, along with my husband, John, all but one of those years. It has been an encouragement to be with others who are in kingdom work and seeking to have a supportive friendship base. Meeting just once a year, it takes a few years to know people, and of course, it works out that people seem to gather in certain friendship groups after a while. It has been a confidential place to share about feelings, to discuss theology, to enjoy one another and to worship together.

At Trinity School for Ministry, where I was on the faculty, I would speak about this in my classes, and I noticed a few months ago in the school publication that a group of former students had been gathering for some years now, practicing Christian friendship and supporting one another in their various congregations.

So why is there reluctance to form friendships with other clergy? There are many factors that contribute to hesitance and disengagement among and between clergy, but a few are professional competition, vulnerability, fear of personal exposure of weakness, an experience of friend betrayal in the past, a secular culture of individualism versus a biblical culture of covenant relationship, and finally a lack of expectation of having friends, which contributes to a lack of seeking and building friendship. And of course, the overriding excuse for everything not done in our culture is—no time.

It is my hope that exploring the depths of Christian friendship and its personal spiritual formation will be an encouragement to all, as pastors, ministry leaders, and laypeople to pursue Christian friendship. Christian friendship begins here on earth but exists eternally in heaven.

Reviewing what I have presented here, there is so much more that could be unpacked on the theology of friendship. In talking about Cicero, the Roman, we did not mention the Greeks: Socrates, Plato, or Aristotle. We skipped Philo of Alexandria, Anselm of Canterbury, Abelard, Thomas Aquinas, Luther, Calvin—not to mention those in our own time such as Merton or Moltmann. It feels to me a bit like the end of Hebrews 11, when the author of the epistle writes that there are so many others not here named. In conclusion, the reading of one stanza of an old hymn touches the subject as well as touching the heart. It's titled "For the Beauty of the Earth."[32]

> For the joy of human love,
> brother, sister, parent, child,
> friends on earth, and friends above
> for all gentle thoughts and mild,
> Christ, our Lord, to you we raise,
> this, our hymn of grateful praise.

---

[32]Folliot S. Pierpoint, "For the Beauty of the Earth," tune by Conrad Kocher, https://hymnary.org/text/for_the_beauty_of_the_earth#tune.

11

Shepherding Survivors of Sexual Abuse

ANDREW J. SCHMUTZER

WHEN IT COMES TO ADDRESSING sexual abuse today, we crave data more than dialogue. But if we're going to tackle the pandemic of sexual abuse, particularly in communities of faith, we need clearer conversations, not simply more of them. Society's romance with intersectionality is a functional distraction to the church's calling to help heal wounds, regardless of their etiology. While the causes of sexual abuse are multifactorial, most wounded are not "coming home." They have their reasons. At present, there are some key challenges we face.

ADDRESSING SEXUAL ABUSE REMAINS A FORMIDABLE CHALLENGE

Healing is even harder in a time of context collapse. There is no connected social milieu or agreed assumptions. Instead, what is determinative are one's subjective "internal" claims. Reality has become self-referential. What one can validate from history or science no longer matters; an existential passion is largely what matters now.

Society is infatuated with "victim Olympics." Older commitments of honor, shame, and virtue have given way a culture of victimization. In this culture, the personal has become the political. We need to replace the word *power* with *courage*, because the contemporary agenda for power does not bring healing.

The #MeToo campaign has blown off course. While the voice granted to female victims and the demand for greater accountability has been helpful, its mode of discourse has become a toxic war on men. The movement is not interested in aid for all victims, just those of one gender. In fact, gender has become weaponized. Today masculinity is overwhelmingly something to destroy. Reconciliation between the genders is now hopelessly out of reach.

What do these challenges reveal? It is not knowledge or even resources we lack but, rather, the collective will to shepherd survivors in a holistic manner. The truth is that the church lacks nothing that survivors need. So using cultural assessment, pastoral appeal, and some personal experience, I want to offer pastors, mentors, and survivors some challenges and insights that can help shepherd survivors of sexual abuse. Before we can nurture survivors, we should understand some common barriers that still stand in the way of healing in the church environment.

SOME BARRIERS IN THE CHURCH THAT THWART HEALING

The barrier of "sacred silence." The barrier of "sacred silence" must be exchanged for *timely honesty*. It is not about talking more loudly or slowly, but honestly.[1] Survivors have waited long enough for someone to speak out *for* them. Faith communities—regardless of their stripe—selectively discuss the social ills they want to face. Ironically, this can be accompanied by an avoidance of preaching and teaching of biblical passages that directly address incest, rape, and sexual betrayal. This barrier forces the frightened victim to out their story first because the leadership refuses to break the silence for them.

The barrier of minimization. The barrier of minimization must become a *hermeneutic of empathy*. Claiming that "all sin is the same at the foot of the cross" is a PC mantra that actually trivializes the complex evils like sexual abuse. Those who make such statements are unwilling to admit that *not all sin is equally devastating.*[2] This minimizes the complex consequences of abuse. For that matter, "not all evil is chosen, for, while evil can

---

[1] This section is developed further in my "Sexual Abuse: Suffering from a Host of Betrayals," in *Between Pain & Grace: A Biblical Theology of Suffering,* coauthor Gerald W. Peterman (Chicago: Moody Publishers, 2016), 209-35.

[2] The *Second Helvetic Confession* (chap. 8) reads, "We . . . confess that sins are not equal; although they arise from the same fountain of corruption and unbelief, some are more serious than others. As the Lord said, it will be more tolerable for Sodom than for the city that rejects the word of the Gospel (Matt 10:15; 11:20-24)."

subtly seduce, it can also brutally enforce its will."[3] Such messages are particularly painful to hear when the nonabused tell the abused how they should feel and respond. Would civilians tell a returning soldier how to deal with their phantom limb? Yet abuse survivors often endure spontaneous and insensitive critique.

The barrier of forgiveness. The barrier of mandated forgiveness must learn to *prioritize the needs of the victim.* While it sounds spiritual, this call to forgive the abuser is a revictimization for survivors that stems from not understanding the layers of trauma surrounding sexual abuse. Additionally, this is the common mistake of equating forgiveness with reconciliation. It is time to let the needs of the abused, and their healing, set the agenda. For example, while a jewel thief may be forgiven, should that person return to work for the shop owner? For the abused, forgiveness is not an event to be logged, but a process to be nurtured. The late Ray Anderson is correct: "In the end, reconciliation as well as forgiveness is a divine gift of grace that we receive bit by bit and grow into."[4]

Among a host of things people can do are some things that should never be said. Telling a victim, "All things are new in Christ Jesus," "Just submit to the Holy Spirit," "Why didn't you speak up earlier," or the ever-pious "All things work together for good" is further traumatizing and actually functions to divert rather than embrace another's pain. Victims need to hear, "Thank you for telling me. How can I help?" If the abused can risk speaking, the nonabused can risk an empathetic silence.

The barrier of "victory" theologies. The barrier of "victory" theologies that declare "In Christ we overcome everything" must be exchanged for a *theology of brokenness.* Victory theologies are not capable of addressing horrendous evil, such as the betrayals of incest or sex trafficking. In fact, such theologies have little patience for healing as an extensive *process* and often blame too much on the devil. Suffering is more complex.

---

[3]Ralph C. Wood, *The Gospel According to Tolkien: Visions of the Kingdom in Middle-Earth* (Louisville, KY: Westminster John Knox, 2001), 70.

[4]Ray S. Anderson, *The Shape of Practical Theology: Empowering Ministry with Theological Praxis* (Downers Grove, IL: InterVarsity Press, 2001), 300. Forgiveness has wrongly become associated with weakness, especially for counselors with little theological integration. See the helpful discussion of Jim Sells and Emily G. Hervey, "Forgiveness in Sexual Abuse: Defining Our Identity in the Journey Toward Wholeness," in *The Long Journey Home: Understanding and Ministering to the Sexually Abused,* ed. Andrew J. Schmutzer (Eugene, OR: Wipf & Stock, 2011), 169-85.

Victory theologies commonly ignore or dismiss the candor of lament theology. Such theologies also lack adequate integration with the disciplines of psychology and medicine, which also speak into the spectrum of abuse trauma. Is there no room for a *Christus Dolor* theology alongside the *Christus Victor*? Paul states, "He was crucified in weakness, yet he lives by God's power. . . . Likewise, we are weak in him" (2 Cor 13:4). Behind these victory expressions is often a misunderstanding of how abuse lives on within the relational ecosystem of the victim's life.

The barrier of isolated suffering. The barrier of isolated suffering must be replaced with *collective grief.* The believer's new identity in Christ stems from their union with Christ, which provides a new citizenship and a new corporate solidarity. The Christian community is morally preserving when it also learns to demonstrate a collective grief for its sexually broken brothers and sisters. Evil is always stronger than isolated individuals.[5]

To heal a survivor is to restore a community. Relationships in the believing community are to be characterized by a quality of love that signifies the eschatological work of God in their hearts. Regardless of profound isolating experiences, "Christians are part of the eschatologically restored people of God," the fulfillment of Jeremiah 31:31-34, with God's law now written on their hearts.[6] This is the foundation of the new citizenship in Christ for believers, regardless of our isolating wounds.

SHEPHERDING SURVIVORS IN THE FAMILY OF GOD

Like standing amid the broken glass and twisted metal of a car wreck while arguing over how the accident happened, contemporary talk of abuse is either too vague to explain the depth of betrayals or too politicized to offer genuine healing. Yet, with so many resources, the church actually has a unique healing role that survivors need. I want to explore the present state of timidity or misdirection that survivors can face in the church.

We cannot cure what time must heal. Speaking as a survivor myself and facilitator of abuse support groups, I've learned that healing can be a long

---

[5]Anthony C. Thiselton, *The Living Paul: An Introduction to the Apostle's Life and Thought* (Downers Grove, IL: IVP Academic, 2009), 79.

[6]Frank Thielman, *Theology of the New Testament: A Canonical and Synthetic Approach* (Grand Rapids: Zondervan, 2005), 243, 244.

journey. The abused need safety and compassion, not timetables (e.g., "You've had a year of therapy"), suspicious questions (e.g., "So, are you ever going to reconcile with that person?"), or theological adages about the sufficiency of the gospel—from the nonabused. Effectual truth still requires timely application. If the abused can risk speaking, their community can risk an empathetic silence.[7]

Because sexual abuse is an extensive breach of the interconnected realms of personhood (emotions, body, and psyche), healing can be a complex art that requires a lifetime. Healing does not remove suspicion. In particular, it is common for survivors to struggle with trust issues for the rest of their lives. The victim's psychological software may also strain to process unilateral orders, authoritarian demeanor, unanticipated touching, physical "gag" jokes, and general power differentials.[8]

Biblical counselors should prioritize comforting over confronting. The presenting problem of a survivor may mask far deeper issues they have no idea how to face. Particularly in faith communities, pastors need to be able to distinguish the "sounds" (coping mechanisms) from the "signal" (abuse itself). A forced timeframe for healing shows not only impatience with process, but honest words and broken lives. It's not about cure, it's about care. Let the needs of the survivor set the agenda, not a fixed timetable or a desire to use the Bible with apologetic fervor. Survivors need someone to walk with them in their brokenness, so spend quality time listening to their story and struggles.

Work closely with counselors in ministry. Many psychological tools are merely explaining complex relational behaviors, not justifying them. Become more aware of how triggers work in the traumatized lives of survivors. Mentors who work with survivors need to think in terms of an extended process of healing. When the inexpressibility of trauma joins with the inexpressibility of God's nature, the crisis for a survivor of faith can be profoundly acute and requires patience, not proof texts.[9] Shepherds willing to walk the healing path with survivors are capable of calling out abuse for what it really is.

---

[7]Andrew J. Schmutzer, "A Theology of Sexual Abuse: A Reflection on Creation and Devastation," *Journal of the Evangelical Theological Society* 51 (2008): 809.

[8]Schmutzer, "Theology of Sexual Abuse," 797.

[9]See my discussion in "Spiritual Formation and Sexual Abuse: Embodiment, Community, and Healing," *Journal of Spiritual Formation & Soul Care* 2 (2009): 76, quoting L. J. M. Claassens and D. G. Garber, "First Words . . . Faith Facing Trauma," *Review and Expositor* 105 (2008): 188.

We cannot heal what we will not name. We've heard politicians around the world stammer through absurd terms to describe the evil of radical Islamic terrorism. Yet the same pathology can exist in faith communities where leaders struggle to call out the evil of sexual abuse. Ignoring 20 percent of a congregation (1 in 4 women; 1 in 6 men) effectively hollows out the courage of many and certainly disregards the need of victims for advocacy, especially children who have no voice. Whether it is the spinelessness of a PC culture, a gritty protection for the powerful, or some skewed notion of religious decorum, this mutism in our churches dodges a vital principle of healing—*accurate naming.*

When shepherds name sexual abuse among their flock, it releases a holy disgust for the betrayal of trust, develops a redemptive patience for the healing journey, and ignites a collective empathy that sanctifies profound relational wounds. It is hard to improve on Volf's observation: "If no one remembers a misdeed or *names it publicly*, it remains invisible. To the observer, its victim is not a victim and its perpetrator is not a perpetrator; both are misperceived because the suffering of the one and the violence of the other go unseen. A double injustice occurs—the first when the original deed is done and the second when it disappears."[10]

This kind of naming is not stigmatizing or labeling—the motive and tone are different. Labeling confuses sociology with theology, ideology with science, and is not interested in accuracy or applying Christ's mission to a broken world. Healing requires right names, not safe terms. Right names are well suited to the nature of psychological, relational, and spiritual triage. Both the abused and nonabused need the tutoring of healing names.

Sexual abuse is radical internal terrorism—sound familiar? It is a comprehensive wounding, capable of clawing at the soul. Naming is empowering, because it is reality-depicting. Abuse does not need the hollow support of gender stereotypes or the nervous hush of family members who are desperate for image management. The horrors of abuse reach beyond hashtags into the complex systems of power capable of shaping both faith and family.

Leaders must give victims the gift of words. A wise shepherd knows that at any moment they are speaking for an abused child frozen in confusion, a

---

[10]Miroslav Volf, *The End of Memory: Remembering Rightly in a Violent World* (Grand Rapids: Eerdmans, 2006), 29; emphasis added.

muted adult locked in denial, a molesting father-in-law or two in ten marriages that are suffering the effects of childhood sexual abuse.[11] Naming promotes the meaning and compassion that victims are often too afraid to ask for. A lack of supportive naming, however, can create another problem.

We will not name what we are unwilling to grieve. If honest naming dignifies the wound, *collective grief* is a needed salve. Like changing the stigma of depression, corporate acknowledgement helps overturn the profound isolation abuse victims feel. Unfortunately, unwanted experiences translate into unwelcome testimonies. Is there a will to listen to the abused? In spite of our rhetoric there is a form of exploitation that happens "in here" too. This trafficking needs our family care. Such collective grieving for our abused brothers and sisters is an ethic cultivated by shepherds who have faced their own pain. However, leaders who try to live with uninspected pain will not be able to enter into the pain of others. In a needed show of transparency, leaders can learn to speak of abuse, addictions, and depression in their own families—even their abuse—not just cancer, poverty, and racism. Do abused movie actors have a greater reason to speak of their abuse than ministers?

Abuse has an ugly attack factor that can drain the will to help. It's not a rare contracted illness. Abuse is an active plundering of a fellow image bearer. Add to this the power plays, incest (80 percent of sexual abuse victims), spiritual hypocrisy, addictions, and forms of revictimization and you have a complex *relational ecosystem* that no single leader is equipped to address. The body of Christ is needed. Today, too many abused are merely "farmed out" to others. But how many psychologists understand Paul's theology of the new citizenship or the sexual ethics intended to define the church in the latter days (1 Thess 4:3-8)? In the market-driven church, abuse simply doesn't sell. We've forgotten that healing a survivor restores a community.

All this scares even the *non*abused. Victims desperately need their spiritual family. But *theological* healing is the hardest medicine to find. If victims are lost in narratives of anger and an absentee God, faith communities hide behind an aversion to ambiguity and family "cases" they would rather not

---

[11]On the struggle of survivors in marriage, see my "Reclaiming Beauty Amidst Brokenness," in *Marriage: Its Foundation, Theology, and Mission in a Changing World*, ed. Curt Hamner et al. (Chicago: Moody Publishers, 2018), 225-41.

face. But the sacrifice of grieving is necessary for a ministry of presence that is willing to sit in the pain of our abused brothers and sisters. For abuse victims, silence is a deafening answer that is further damaging.

When the church tactfully acknowledges its sexually abused, then healing can be extended beyond the private walls of a therapy office. In the church, collective grief is a nourishing ethic that includes healing services, anointing, prayer circles, biblical stories, specific liturgy, special sermons, biblical laments, testimonies, responsive readings, dramas, healing rituals, and prayers of healing written by survivors.[12]

I've found that most people are willing to enter into the suffering of abuse pain when guided, but they need to be taught how to collectively value this pain within their spiritual family. Let's put it this way: when April is annually acknowledged as the National Sexual Assault Awareness month; when pastoral prayers name sexual abuse; when survivor testimonies admit their on-going struggles; when sermons unpack biblical texts on sexual violence; when survivors declare their desperate allegiance to God; when church policies are updated and volunteers receive training; when abuse support groups are offered for both men and women; then a healing environment has been activated. Wounded lives are now connected with open grief. Such public venues allow survivors to be seen and heard. Victims have endured enough damage in the dark.

Shared empathy addresses the disenfranchised grief of sexual abuse.[13] Disenfranchised grief reflects a searing pain that is not intentionally named, publicly mourned, ritually incorporated, or homiletically engaged. While sexual abuse is seventy-five times more common than pediatric cancer, its lack of address is part of the reason most victims have left the church. Yet there are many biblical passages that leaders could use to validate the experience of sexual violation.[14] Lament is also the language of victims' grief, not just sin's confession. If we are unwilling to lament, then we are unprepared to face the pain that needs it.

---

[12]See the insightful discussion of James B. Gould, "Healing the Wounded Heart Through Ritual and Liturgy," in Schmutzer, *The Long Journey Home*, 293-313.

[13]James B. Gould offers some helpful thoughts on the nature of disenfranchised grief in "Spiritual Healing of Disrupted Childhood," *The Journal of Pastoral Care and Counseling* 60 (2006): 263-71.

[14]Such biblical texts include Gen 34; 39; Deut 22:25-27; 2 Sam 13; Mk 9:42-48; Rom 1:18-32.

We will not grieve what we are unprepared to redeem. When it comes to sexual abuse, what is not transformed risks being transferred. It is a dark reality, but sexual abuse often runs in families for generations. A deep form of redeeming is needed. And for the family of the survivor too, the cost of uninspected pain can be high. By redeeming, I'm referring to *releasing* the survivor from toxic shame, helping them *exchange* some core experiences, and *restoring* their dignity and purpose within the life of the church. Shame is released when the survivor purges the social stereotypes and false messages they've carried. Significantly, the collective faith of the spiritual family can buoy the survivor, renewing healthy patterns of behavior, and restoring trust and relational vulnerability. Observe the restoring impact of "their faith" when Jesus responded with healing for the paralytic (Mk 2:5).

The victim's pain—like the "crime scene"—can defy description: poor prevention measures, betrayed childhood, inadequate policies, transgenerational abuse, colluding family members, complex PTSD, and the rhetoric of a sovereign heavenly Father to whom we owe our "bodies as a living sacrifice" (Rom 12:1). Did you catch any painful ironies here? Taken together, these create a gauntlet of obstacles, some of which survivors will struggle with throughout their lives. Yet the grief and care of brothers and sisters is redeeming. When we grieve, we may cry. However, when we "weep with those who weep" (Rom 12:15 ESV), then we are grieving a *loss*. This shunned grief is spiritual hypocrisy. The unhealed victim actually diminishes us all. Yet with help, a survivor realizes that their violation may have shaped them, but it does not define them.

Society often confuses advocacy for the abused with a vitriolic protest that cares little for the redemptive horizon of faith. With the loss of the transcendent gospel, all that remains is politics. Without redeeming principles, anger easily morphs into hostile ideologies, and spiritual vitality is simply bartered for toxic blogs peddling more empowerment. Like the Hulk, one can remain angry and avoid commitment. Yet healing is more than the art of self-announcement. Whenever the script—inside or outside the church—pushes the victim into center stage and pitches the faith as intolerant, then the redemptive process is paralyzed, and God has to walk! Clearly, there are extreme tensions that survivors of faith must navigate. For some, a notion of divine determinism or disembodied theology is easier to accept. In reality, personal agency and accountability can feel like luxuries for survivors. Obviously, wounded healers are needed in the survivor's healing journey. As Ray S. Anderson observed,

> We begin to trust only a person who can share our pain. The sympathy of those who recognize our hurt and wish to help is not sufficient. Those who are vulnerable at the level of their own pain create access to our pain and thus to the very core of our being, without requiring a commitment or promise. Without the existence of shared pain, those who have had trust shattered cannot find a point of beginning.[15]

We cannot redeem what we prefer to redefine. There is a growing trend to redefine wounds that are "too messy" for refined faith. Healing abuse can be like recouping a battlefield—some ordinances can be repurposed, but none can be ignored. At present, identity politics has metastasized into an era of victim Olympics. Society is far more committed to democratizing suffering than finding healing for the ancient evil of sexual victimization.

Now that anyone can attain victim status, real victims are more than muted, and the ethical compass of responsibility has been pitched for a weaponized PC culture. Moral north no longer exists. Sadly, the church wants to play too, when it redefines incest as a "sad situation," a "family matter" or mentions nothing at all! One must recall Paul's words to the Corinthian church about an incidence of incest "of a kind that even pagans do not tolerate. . . . Shouldn't you rather have gone into *mourning*?" (1 Cor 5:1, 2). The apostle draws on language from Leviticus 18:6-8. Paradoxically, relational wounds actually need relational healing, not professionalized obscurity.

Redefining sexual abuse sabotages healing for the victim, family, and the faith community. The right words are insistent and face reality. The church can bring a healing vocabulary to its abused people, among whom, Paul says, "no one should wrong or take advantage of a brother or sister" (1 Thess 4:6).

The church helps redeem the travesty of sexual abuse when, for example, lament becomes a Christian exhale and believers cry out for their wounded. Because evil is always stronger than isolated individuals, believers are called to remember as a community. Let them cry with their family. These are some practices that healing requires. Redeeming (i.e., sanctifying) a survivor's

---

[15]Anderson, *Shape of Practical Theology*, 306.

experiences is rebuilding their boundaries, helping them not to waste profound suffering, and restoring their true identity in the life of faith. This is the toolshed of the church. The Evangelical Covenant Church hymnal has a gathering song for regular worship—"Each Man and Woman Raise Your Voice"—that intersperses readings between verses. It begins by affirming,

> This is a place where you are welcome. This is a place where you are safe. This is a place where no matter your background, no matter your lot in life, no matter your need or expectations you are welcome here for God is our gracious host.

One of the readings speaks of sexual abuse:

> Her childhood was taken away by her own father. He not only molested her body but raped her soul. It is no wonder that while sitting in this place she shudders at calling God "Heavenly Father." But God will be patient. Trust is something that takes time and the time will come when she will draw close without fear. That's why she's here.[16]

Naming is dignifying and mending, not isolating. But a culture of trauma craves identity without closure and protest without nurture. So the church must declare, in advance of its next victim, that they are ready with the full care of Christ, expressed through his body, in the power of the Holy Spirit. The practice of lament, for example, brings fresh metaphors for the frightened and helps heal an evil that is word shattering.[17] Lament is the language of suffering, and without it, warns Patrick Miller, "Both the lowly and the powerful will be tempted to conclude that the *status is quo*, that possibilities unseen are inauthentic and unlikely, that the world's power to define reality is ultimate and unchallenged."[18]

It is a precious thing to name our most sacred hatreds to God, knowing that our scared Lamb (Rev 5:6) takes wounds seriously. In our time, abuse requires a new mourning. The King who hung naked on a cross is more offended by sexual abuse than we are. Maybe we should lament that, too.

If the language of suffering is going to be reclaimed, there must be a shift from Christianity as a faith of answers to one more willing to find mystery

---

[16]*Covenant Church Hymnal* (Chicago: Covenant, 1996), selections 505 and 867. Surely, we are not in a better place today for abandoning such readings, or sophisticated hymnals, for that matter.

[17]See my "Longing to Lament: Returning to the Language of Suffering," in Schmutzer and Peterman, *Between Pain & Grace*, 103-29.

[18]Patrick D. Miller, "In Praise and Thanksgiving," *Theology Today* 45 (1988): 186-87.

in painful stories and uncomfortable questions.[19] The struggle to shepherd survivors already in our midst will teach us all how to worship in our pain, rather than worship in spite of our pain. Hasn't the ancient Psalter taught us to live in this very tension, to live in theological paradox: that lament and praise, sorrow and joy, actually belong together. Praise makes explicit the context of faith and hope within which the lament is sounded.[20] This is part of what it will take to shepherd the survivors better, who live among us.

Based on her own story of sexual violation, a dear friend of mine has written an example of the laments we need to hear much more in the church:

"To the One Who Also Lay in a Tomb"
(reflecting on Jn 11:5, 6)

Rabbi,
You identify as
the Resurrection and the Life.
Calling you Lord,
we identify as
the ones whom you love.
Yet we are confounded by the order of events:
Now you loved—
So when you heard—
You *stayed* away.
Lord, What?
If you loved,
then *when* you heard,
would not you have come?
Here, they sought you.
Here, they believed in you.
Here, they knew you had the power to save.
But you didn't move to rescue.
You have also heard us,
but you waited just
too many days to save

---

[19]Samuel E. Balentine, *Prayer in the Hebrew Bible: The Drama of Divine-Human Dialogue* (Minneapolis: Fortress, 1993), 292.

[20]Walter Moberly, "Lament," in *The New International Dictionary of Old Testament Theology and Exegesis*, ed. Willem A. VanGemeren (Grand Rapids: Zondervan, 1997), 4:880.

those you say you love.
Lord, if you had been there
when she aborted her child,
Lord, if you had been there
when his innocence was stolen,
Lord, if you had been there
when they were shot on the street,
Lord, if you had been there
when I was raped,
That baby would have lived,
He would have lived,
They would have lived,
I would have still been alive.
We confess that *whatever*
you ask of God,
he will give you.
So why have you not asked for our deliverance
from this illness,
this dying,
this grief?
Now—
You have come to mourn with us,
even to weep with us.
But it is confusing,
this tender-hearted teacher,
so deeply moved.
And yet could not be moved to our aid.
How you love us,
see how greatly troubled by our pain!
And yet the pain was not averted.
We cannot but ask,
You, who has opened the eyes of the blind,
could you not have kept *us* from dying?
In the resurrection,
we will rise again, yes.
But we need resurrection now, O Lord.
We have been dead for too many days.

Our bodies have been made unclean
by this violence;
Our faces have been covered
by great shame;
Our feet and hands have been bound
by our attempts to cope.
We sent word,
but you did not come.
We believed,
but you responded too late.
We knew your power,
but you have let us down.
O, Lord Jesus,
call once again in a loud voice:
"Come forth" to our downcast hearts and tired minds.
Unbind our broken bodies, and let us go
to live once more.
We believe that you are the Christ,
the Son of God.
You have loved,
You have heard,
And *still* you have stayed away.
But stay away no longer.
We don't understand what you mean
that, indeed, you are the Resurrection and the Life,
when our bodies are stone cold in a tomb.
So revive us.
Unbury our belief.
Bring us into the light of you.
If this death is for the glory of God,
If this grief is to reveal your power,
then still, with great effort,
we believe.
Lord, come and see
where we, your children,
have been
aborted, robbed, shot, raped—buried,

where death has become our only companion.
Identify as our dying deity,
even as you are the living God.
If you only had been there . . .
But be here now, instead.
And still, with great effort, we will say,
we believe.
In your name,
the One who also Lay in a Tomb,
we pray to you.

(D. C. W., 2018)

12

Neuropharmacoformation

Christian Formation in an Age of Stupefaction

WILLIAM M. STRUTHERS

Classically, there are three ways in which humans
try to find transcendence—religious meaning—apart from God
as revealed through the cross of Jesus: through the ecstasy of
alcohol and drugs, through the ecstasy of recreational
sex, through the ecstasy of crowds.

EUGENE PETERSON

INTRODUCTION

Psychoactive (mind-altering) drugs such as alcohol, caffeine, nicotine, and marijuana are a part of everyday life for many, and they produce effects ranging from stupefaction (for escape, relief, and release) to increased focus and attention (for productivity).[1] These compounds, often ingested as drinks, smoked, or eaten, can also occupy niches that have medicinal or spiritual cache. Cannabis (marijuana) and its active ingredient tetrahydrocannabinol (THC), is one of the most widely used psychoactive drugs

---

Eugene Peterson, *The Pastor: A Memoir* (New York: HarperOne, 2012), 157.

[1]Greg Wadley, "How Psychoactive Drugs Shape Human Culture: A Multi-Disciplinary Perspective," *Brain Res. Bull.* 126 (2016): 138-51.

in the world. While its recreational use remains controversial in the United States, its complex history of social acceptability runs parallel to its well-known anxiolytic properties.[2] Alcohol is commonly used for recreational purposes, but it is part of Christian communion. While religious attitudes, beliefs, and behaviors can vary widely across cultures (as well as within them), the use of psychoactive compounds to induce mystical/spiritual experiences (MSE) is not uncommon. Interestingly, these pharmacologically induced MSEs can have much in common in their quality and can be significant for both the individual and their religious community. Within a number of religious traditions, plant substances (usually) are ingested as part of sacred rituals. The resulting MSEs involve ecstatic components, and these altered states of consciousness are understood to be tapping into spiritual insights or realms that are framed by the culture's religious tradition. Because of this, the question of the degree to which these variations and commonalities are the result of neurobiological, pharmacological, and genetic factors has become a topic of interest for scientists from several disciplines.

A PSYCHEDELIC GOOD FRIDAY

In the spring of 1962 Walter Pahnke, a theology graduate student at Harvard Divinity School, was working under the supervision of Dr. Timothy Leary. Working with the Harvard Psilocybin Project, Pahnke designed a double-blind study to investigate whether or not psilocybin—the active ingredient in psychedelic "Magic Mushrooms"—could facilitate MSEs in religiously inclined individuals in a familiar religious context. He recruited twenty Protestant students from nearby Andover Newton Theological School to participate in what would become known as the Marsh Chapel Experiment. Prior to the Good Friday service at Boston University's Marsh Chapel, Pahnke provided his twenty participants with either 30 mg of the psychedelic compound psilocybin, or a placebo (a vitamin B3/niacin supplement similar to that found in a 5-Hour Energy drink). He then monitored them during and after the service. While only one of the placebo/niacin subjects reported any significant

---

[2]Simona Pisanti and Maurizio Bifulco, "Modern History of Medical Cannabis: From Widespread Use to Prohibitionism and Back," *Trends Pharmacol. Sci.* 38 (2017): 195-98.

psychoactive effects beyond a flush of warmth that dissipated after an hour, the majority of those who had been given psilocybin reported profound psychological effects.[3]

Pahnke rated these effects across eight different dimensions informed by the American psychologist William James and the Anglo-Catholic mystic scholar/author Evelyn Underhill.[4] William James is one of the first psychologists to scientifically approach altered states of consciousness and the psychological dimension of MSEs, whereas Evelyn Underhill's work is well known among mystics, theologians, and religious scholars. These ratings included scales reporting (1) sense of unity, (2) transcendence of time and space, (3) sacredness, (4) sense of objective reality, (5) deep positive mood, (6) ineffability, (7) paradoxicality, and (8) transiency. Based on these ratings, Pahnke concluded that psilocybin enhanced the religious meaningfulness of the experience. A follow-up of the original study reported that the volunteers who had been given psilocybin still described their experience as overwhelmingly positive twenty-five years after that Good Friday service.[5] Doblin argued that Pankhe's study cast "considerable doubt on the assertion that mystical experiences catalyzed by drugs are in any way inferior to nondrug mystical experiences in both their immediate content and long-term effects."[6] While there have been significant critiques of both the methods and underlying theoretical framework of the study, Pankhe's Marsh Chapel Experiment is regarded by many as a landmark study for those interested in the scientific study of religion, and has more recently been replicated and followed up with similar results.[7]

---

[3]Walter Pahnke, "Drugs and Mysticism: An Analysis of the Relationship Between Psychedelic Drugs and the Mystical Consciousness" (PhD diss., Harvard University, 1963).

[4]William James, *The Varieties of Religious Experience: A Study in Human Nature* (New York: Longmans, Green, and Co., 1902); Evelyn Underhill, *Mysticism: A Study in the Nature and Development of Spiritual Consciousness*, (New York: E. P. Dutton, 1930).

[5]Rick Doblin, "Pahnke's 'Good Friday Experiment': A Long-Term Follow-Up and Methodological Critique," *J. Transpers. Psychol.* 23 (1991): 1-28.

[6]Doblin, "Pahnke's 'Good Friday Experiment,'" 24.

[7]R. R. Griffiths et al., "Psilocybin Can Occasion Mystical-Type Experiences Having Substantial and Sustained Personal Meaning and Spiritual Significance," *Psychopharmacology (Berl.)* 187 (2006): 26883; Griffiths et al., "Psilocybin Occasioned Mystical-Type Experiences," *Psychopharmacology (Berl.)* 218 (2011): 649-65; Felix Hasler et al., "Acute Psychological and Physiological Effects of Psilocybin in Healthy Humans: A Double-Blind, Placebo-Controlled Dose-Effect Study," *Psychopharmacology (Berl.)* 172 (2004): 145-56.

RELIGIOUS CONTEXTS

There are sufficient overlapping neurotransmitter systems (particularly serotonin) to suggest a shared neuropharmacological substrate of MSEs and psychedelic drug effects. Because of the pharmacological and psychological effects of serotonergic hallucinogens, empathogenic drugs, and NMDA antagonists, a pharmacological profile of MSE can be constructed. McNamara details the use of hallucinogenic substances as part of religious rites and rituals.[8] The sacred Aztec "magic mushroom," teonanácatyl, contains the psychoactive compound psilocybin used in the Marsh Chapel Experiment described earlier. The Wixáritari Indians, better known as the Huichol, of the southwest United States and Mexico practice a form of ecstatic religion that relies on the use of the peyote cactus *Lophophora williamsii*. Peyote contains the psychoactive substance mescaline, and its use is overseen in the Huichol community by a shaman.[9] Amazonian Indians in Peru drink ayahuasca, or "yagé," a hallucinogenic brew made from a variety of barks and leaves containing a combination of N,N-dimethyltryptamine (DMT) and monamine oxidase inhibitors.[10] Other plant compounds are also known to induce these altered psychological states and be used for religious, medicinal, or recreational purposes (e.g., opium poppies, mandrake, morning glories, *salvia divinorum*). All of these compounds play a significant role in the spiritual and religious life of the cultures in which they are used.[11] While MSEs, religious, or ecstatic experiences that are induced by drug use may be frowned on in some cultures (particularly modern, industrialized, Western societies) there are some who are more open to their use.[12] Western philosophical and theological traditions have historically focused on the virtues of clear-mindedness, a strong sense of moral agency, self-control, and strength of conscious effort of the will to enact change. Other religious and

---

[8]Patrick McNamara, *The Neuroscience of Religious Experience* (New York: Cambridge University Press, 2009).

[9]A. B. Wolbach, E. J. Miner, and Harris Isbell, "Comparison of Psilocin with Psilocybin, Mescaline and LSD-25," *Psychopharmacologia* 3 (1962): 219-23.

[10]Rick Strassman, *DMT: The Spirit Molecule: A Doctor's Revolutionary Research into the Biology of Near-Death and Mystical Experiences* (Rochester, VT: Park Street Press, 2001).

[11]Andrew B. Newberg, "Transformation of Brain Structure and Spiritual Experience," in *The Oxford Handbook of Psychology and Spirituality*, ed. Lisa J Miller, Oxford Library of Psychology (New York: Oxford University Press, 2012), 489-99.

[12]M. Bolstridge and Ben Sessa, *The Psychedelic Renaissance: Reassessing the Role of Psychedelic Drugs in 21st Century Psychiatry and Society* 202 (Dorset, UK: Muswell Hill Press, 2012).

societal traditions and systems can privilege other forms of consciousness, and this likely plays a role in how these drugs are used, avoided, sanctioned or forbidden across cultures.

CHARACTERISTICS OF DRUG-INDUCED MYSTICAL/SPIRITUAL EXPERIENCES

The challenge of those who wish to understand the role of pharmacologically induced MSEs lies in the ability to discern not just the mechanics of neurotransmitter receptor activation and the role pharmacological compounds within the nervous system, but to frame this understanding with a sensitivity to how these drugs are used across different cultures and religious systems. Each religious system will have its own sense of human flourishing and the manner in which it is best obtained—either through conscious activity, or pharmacological means. "Sober" states enable agency where we maintain control of our actions, whereas many of the substances described in this chapter can compromise agency. A loss of agency may be viewed negatively; unconscious or "intoxicated" states could be interpreted by some as either amoral/areligious experiences, or producing immoral/inauthentic MSEs. They may be viewed as a shortcut to divine insight or a preoccupation with ecstatic states that could distract from other religious doctrine and teachings. The question that remains is whether or not the MSE insights of those who are under the influence of drugs should be considered authentic, valid, or delivering uniquely accessible truth claims. The manner in which these visions are understood is tied to other epistemological issues. For the Christian, however, issues such as syncretism and adherence to biblical teaching related to warnings against drunkenness and sorcery complicate how drugs are discussed, used, and understood within our own faith tradition. What cannot be denied is that wisdom is necessary as we navigate a culture that has come to rely on any number of stupefying agents to deal with all of our problems. From cannabis to antidepressants, and caffeine to ecstasy, the allure of a "pill for every ill" is easy to see.

Altered perception/entheogenic understanding (divine insight). Altered perception is perhaps the most commonly reported experience among drug-induced MSEs and is the hallmark of what it means to be a psychedelic.

This involves vivid hallucinogenic or altered sensory illusory perception: a cinematic, eidetic, or kaleidoscopic experience is coupled with novel and profound insights into divine knowledge about the interconnected nature of reality (entheogenic understanding). Perceptual changes include a modification of visual, auditory, or tactile sensations, as well as altered perception of time and space. Existential or paradoxical insights marked by a profound sense of interconnectedness involving a coherence between concepts otherwise considered logically inconsistent with one another are often accompanied by a sense of harmony, reflective ecological communalism, and an awareness of the divine or sacred.

Psychedelic drugs such as phenthylamines (peyote/mescaline), lysergamides (Lysergic acid/LSD), psilocybin, and ayahuasca/DMT induce this type of effect.[13] These compounds are structurally similar to the neurotransmitter serotonin (5-hydroxytryptaime, 5-HT), which is derived from tryptamine. The differences in effect are due to subtle differences in their chemical structures that may influence the qualitative differences between the drug families' activation of 5-HT receptors. There are a number of 5-HT receptors located throughout the brain, but it is the affinity for the 5-HT2A receptor that appears to be the mechanism of action for these drugs' psychedelic effects.[14] Low doses of serotonergic psychedelics induce visual hallucinations ranging from altered color perception, sensitivity to geometric patterns (i.e., telescopic and kaleidoscopic effects), and surface warping such as contour shifting. Many of these serotonergic psychedelics also have partial affinity for other neurotransmitters such as dopamine receptors and norepinephrine receptors, which likely influences their abuse potential. It should also be noted that serotonergic 5-HT2A receptor antagonism has been considered as a model for schizophrenia and psychoses, complicating the manner in which drug-induced MSE are understood.[15] Over the past two decades there has been an increase in interest in the use of two well-known psychedelic

---

[13]Michael Winkelman, "Psychedelics as Medicines for Substance Abuse Rehabilitation: Evaluating Treatments with LSD, Peyote, Ibogaine and Ayahuasca," *Curr. Drug Abuse Rev.* 7 (2015): 101-16.

[14]Jacqueline Borg et al., "The Serotonin System and Spiritual Experiences," *Am. J. Psychiatry* 160 (2003): 1965-69.

[15]Franz X. Vollenweider, "Brain Mechanisms of Hallucinogens and Entactogens," *Dialogues Clin. Neurosci.* 3 (2001): 15; Franz X. Vollenweider and Michael Kometer, "The Neurobiology of Psychedelic Drugs: Implications for the Treatment of Mood Disorders," *Nat. Rev. Neurosci.* 11 (2010): 642-51.

drugs from this class (psilocybin and ayahuasca/DMT) as treatments for anxiety, addiction, and depression.[16]

Entactogenic affect (intensified affect). Intensified emotional states are common in many drug-induced MSEs. This can be understood not just as a knowledge of, or sense of emotional connectedness, but an affection toward others or with the divine. Knowledge of the divine or connectedness with others is accompanied by positive emotions such as heightened mood, serenity, grandiosity, and the sublime happiness. While these emotional states are often positive in nature, it should be noted that they can also be negative (e.g., "bad trips"). These emotions can be interpreted through a religious lens and have a spiritual dimension to them (e.g., a sense of despair, demonic possession, or damnation in hell). Empathogen-entactogens are structurally similar to stimulant amphetamines that have high abuse potential due to their hedonic value.[17] Empathogens have also been referred to as entactogens due to their ability to induce intense positive emotional states characterized by an increase in prosocial affection and increased empathy alongside the feeling of interpersonal interconnectedness. An overall sense of happiness, euphoria, heightened sense of self-awareness, increased extroversion, and relaxed state are common effects.

In recent years, one exemplar drug of this class has increased in popularity and is commonly used as a recreational entactogen within the rave culture and at clubs and festivals: the designer club drug Ecstasy (3,4-methylenedioxymethamphetamine, MDMA).[18] Recreational doses of MDMA produce euphoria, increased extroversion, modest derealization and depersonalization, and an increase in sociability. Brain imaging studies reveal that in humans MDMA increases cerebral blood flow (CBF) to a number of brain

---

[16]Elisabet Domínguez-Clavé et al., "Ayahuasca: Pharmacology, Neuroscience and Therapeutic Potential," *Brain Res. Bull.* 126 (2016): 89-101; Filip Tylš, Tomáš Páleníček, and Jiří Horáček, "Psilocybin-Summary of Knowledge and New Perspectives," *Eur. Neuropsychopharmacol. J. Eur. Coll. Neuropsychopharmacol.* 24 (2014): 342-56.

[17]Neal M. Goldsmith, *Psychedelic Healing: The Promise of Entheogens for Psychotherapy and Spiritual Development* (Rochester, VT: Healing Arts Press, 2011); Thomas B. Roberts, *The Psychedelic Future of the Mind: How Entheogens Are Enhancing Cognition, Boosting Intelligence, and Raising Values* (Rochester, VT: Inner Traditions / Bear & Co, 2013).

[18]Robert B. Millman and Ann Bordwine Beeder, "The New Psychedelic Culture: LSD, Ecstasy, 'Rave' Parties and the Grateful Dead," *Psychiatr. Ann.* 24 (1994): 148-150; A. R. Green, "The Pharmacology and Clinical Pharmacology of 3,4-Methylenedioxymethamphetamine (MDMA, 'Ecstasy')," *Pharmacol. Rev.* 55.3 (2003): 463-508.

regions, such as the ventromedial prefrontal cortex, the ventral anterior cingulate, the inferior temporal lobe, the medial occipital cortex, and the cerebellum in ways that reduce anxiety and increase this prosocial positive affect. These interconnected brain regions are believed to be involved in the mediation of prosocial behavior and communication, and, as a result, MDMA has recently been used as an adjunctive treatment for psychotherapy resistant posttraumatic stress disorder (PTSD).[19] Known to trigger a transporter-mediated increase in serotonin and 5-HT receptor activation, enhance top-down inhibition of limbic fear-activation by the amygdala, and increase ventromedial prefrontal cortex and orbitofrontal cortical activity to regulate emotional response, MDMA has gained traction as a stabilizing treatment to enable those with PTSD to engage in psychotherapeutic contexts.[20] In the same way that general anesthetics render patients unconscious for surgical procedures, modest doses of MDMA are being used to prepare people to do therapy (because of the avoidance and difficulty dealing with memories that is characteristic of PTSD). The MDMA gives them a neuropharmacological space to facilitate their psychotherapy and deal with their PTSD.

Dissociative dissolution (boundlessness). For many individuals experiencing MSEs there is a profound ego dissolution whereby there is a loss of autonomy and self-control.[21] In MSEs there is an altered perception of embodied nature and time. The individual discovers themselves in an out-of-body experience enabling them to directly commune with the universe, god, or some other spiritual/transcendental reality. This boundlessness involves a separating (dissociation) and dissolution of personal boundaries. There is a lack of boundaries between what is considered to be the self and the other/universe/eternal. Originally referred to as "dissociative anesthetics," there are several drugs that were developed as an anesthetic or sedative that

---

[19]Peter Oehen et al., "A Randomized, Controlled Pilot Study of MDMA (±3,4-Methylenedioxymethamphetamine)-Assisted Psychotherapy for Treatment of Resistant, Chronic Post-Traumatic Stress Disorder (PTSD)," *J. Psychopharmacol. (Oxf.)* 27 (2013): 40-52; Pø Johansen and Ts Krebs, "How Could MDMA (Ecstasy) Help Anxiety Disorders? A Neurobiological Rationale," *J. Psychopharmacol. (Oxf.)* 23 (2009): 389-91.

[20]Oehen et al., "A Randomized, Controlled Pilot Study of MDMA"; Johansen and Krebs, "How Could MDMA (Ecstasy) Help?"

[21]Simon D. Brandt and Torsten Passie, "Research on Psychedelic Substances," *Drug Test. Anal.* 4 (2012): 539-42.

lacked any strong anesthetic effects, which hindered their usefulness for anesthetic purposes. These drugs have been extensively investigated as a target for the pharmacological management of seizures, pain, and other neurological disorders. Drugs such as ketamine and phencyclidine (PCP) are commonly abused dissociatives that are being revisited as potential therapeutics for depression.[22]

Dissociatives broadly alter subjective experience, but their ability to create alterations in the perception of time, self, and environment is widely reported. They can also alter the affective states of both negative (threatening) experiences, as well as pleasant experiences. Derealization (the feeling of being cut off from one's surroundings, trapped in a bubble, or the feeling that surrounding objects are exaggerated) and depersonalization (the feeling of being unreal, inhuman, invisible, foreign, or otherwise being unrecognizable to oneself) are common effects reported by recreational dissociative drug users. Sometimes referred to as disembodiment, these out-of-body perceptions are also common characteristics of near-death experiences and can be a key aspect of MSEs. This sense of dissolution (disintegration of the persona) can be reported as distressing, and as a result increased sensitivity to threatening stimuli can exaggerate negative mood states. In contrast, dissolution can be interpreted as a communion with the universe and a loss of the self. This intense sensation of being disconnected from one's body, as well as a subjective belief that the world around them is unreal (derealization), is sometimes referred to as the "K-hole" by recreational ketamine users.[23]

Dissociative agents appear to exert their influence through antagonism of the glutamate receptor N-methyl-D-aspartate (NMDA) receptor antagonists. The parietal lobe is of interest because it has been implicated for sense of time and space, and personal embodiment. It has also been shown to be connected to MSE brought about by meditation among a variety of religious

[22]K Hirota and D. G. Lambert, "Ketamine: New Uses for an Old Drug?," *Br. J. Anaesth.* 107 (2011): 123-26; Hamilton Morris and Jason Wallach, "From PCP to MXE: A Comprehensive Review of the Non-Medical Use of Dissociative Drugs," *Drug Test. Anal.* 6 (2014): 614-32.
[23]Celia J. A. Morgan and H. Valerie Curran, "Ketamine Use: A Review," *Addict. Abingdon Engl.* 107 (2012): 27-38; Yu Liu et al., "Ketamine Abuse Potential and Use Disorder," *Brain Res. Bull.* 126 (2016): 68-73.

populations.[24] Often referred to as "Angel Dust," nonmedical use of PCP was first reported in the USA around 1967. The bizarre psychomimentic effects were often accompanied by exaggerated accounts of extreme strength, however the psychological effects of PCP are similar to other dissociatives: loss of sense of self, depersonalization, hallucinations, euphoria. Acute paranoia, psychosis, and aggressive behavior are sometimes observed. There is an unpredictability to PCP (as well as other dissociatives) in that some individuals see greater dissociation, others become animated, while others report feelings of strength and invulnerability.

While this is only one model of religious experiences, it is important to remember that not all religious experiences contain elements of ecstasy, visions, divine insight, emotional communion, or out-of-body experiences. The pharmacological substrates that have been described here suggest that psychedelics, empathogens/entactogens, or dissociatives provide a window into understanding the neuropharmacological substrates of altered states of consciousness and, in particular, MSEs. By examining the chemical substances that have been, are being, and will continue to be used for religious and nonreligious purposes, we are able to investigate how nonpharmacologically mediated MSEs (e.g., meditation, spontaneous visions, worship) occur, but will be limited when making claims about subjective authenticity, veracity, or validity; claims beyond the subjective should be closely scrutinized. For example, someone may (during a drug-induced MSE) claim that God has revealed a truth to them that they can engage in an activity that their tradition prohibits. While the experience may have been powerful, significant, and real to them, it would likely be considered heterodox by their faith community and should be carefully handled.

Neuropharmacoformation Terminology and Narratives

Cultural acceptance of marijuana has become so widespread that we are now beginning to see conversations about the effective use of marijuana in combination with yoga, and beverage production combining marijuana with alcohol (e.g., "weed beer"). When we look at how to frame the conversations,

---

[24]Eugene D'Aquili and Andrew Newberg, *The Mystical Mind: Probing the Biology of Religious Experience*, Theology and the Sciences (Minneapolis: Fortress Press, 1999).

it might be beneficial to think carefully about the terminology that we use. For example, it is not uncommon for those in the psychedelic community to ask the questions, "Does it heal? Does it help?" The use of these terms, *healing* and *helping*, invokes a response that Christians can be very sympathetic toward. Unfortunately, the question is rarely followed up with a question such as, "Does it hurt or hinder?" The ability to honestly evaluate the risk and benefit ratio when we use any kind of substance is critically important. Too often we focus only on the things that we want to see, and we ignore the other consequences. Not all healing comes without cost. For example, we might overemphasize a drug's ability to relieve symptoms of medical problems and then find ourselves advocating for its recreational use. We might be ignorant of the negative consequences (side effects) that might hurt or hinder other aspects of that person's life.

It is also helpful to consider a motivational continuum along which the use of drugs can fall. For example, thinking of a drug as a medicine, or a therapeutic drug, adopts this healing narrative. Most of us have no problem with narratives that involve healing; in many ways we will feel an obligation to heal when this narrative is employed. Christians will find themselves (rightfully so) sympathetic to this narrative. Next on the continuum is to move from this one medicinal/therapeutic/healing narrative, to a recreational narrative. While the healing narrative appeals to our desire to alleviate suffering, pain, and dysfunction, the recreational use involves enjoyment, relaxation, and entertainment. This is an appeal that Christians can appreciate because it connects to Sabbath. Who wouldn't like to be relaxed, restored, or enabled to move to a place of recovery? What is wrong with enjoying the good gifts we have been given—especially if they are plants created by God? When we recreate we do things that we enjoy and refresh us. If a drug can refresh us in the absence of any significant disease, dysfunction, or suffering, why should we be denied the opportunity to enjoy it? The obvious danger is that notions of sabbath can easily be corrupted into an indulgent hedonism that distracts from faithful living.

Just beyond the appeal to recreation is the appeal to a narrative of enrichment. Drugs don't just help us enjoy life, they make it better. They enable us to explore the unexplorable, and to escape our finite limitations. Drugs help us explore reality in a way that we cannot otherwise, and we are enabled to escape our current circumstances (which may or may not be unappealing) as we explore that which is beyond our finite reach. Self-described "psychonauts" argue that this is the next step in human evolution and is a pharmacologically enlightened perspective. There are other drugs besides marijuana that we can expect to see moving into the mainstream following the progression that I have outlined here. Drugs such as ecstasy, ayahuasca, psilocybin, and mescaline are all currently being investigated as treatments for any number of mental health disorders. Do not be surprised when the conversation moves away from their medical/therapeutic use into a conversation about recreational availability. Appeals to enrichment, exploration, and transformation will likely soon follow. It will culminate in the final appeal to transformation and self-actualization. Many will claim that they need their [insert your drug of preference here] in order to be the "best version of themselves," or "the me I want to be."

Concluding Thoughts

In light of this, clergy must be aware of the cultural currents and forces involved with these medications. An informed theological understanding of healing, suffering, community, purity, transformation, wisdom, redemption, patience, and the spiritual disciplines is essential. Clarity on the gospel of Christ, what it means to image God, who God is, and how to read Scripture are vital. If I am to be honest with you, as I study the gospel as revealed in the person of Christ, received through the Scriptures, under the direction of the Spirit, and in fellowship with the body of Christ, I am continually amazed at how deep the gospel is, and how complex human beings are. The gospel that I knew as a thirteen-year-old convert has grown, morphed, changed, and matured (I hope) over the last three and a half decades. It is not eschatological fire insurance, nor does it offer an existential escape from this fallen world. I anticipate and hope it will continue to deepen for the rest of my life as my relationship with Christ and my knowledge of the Scriptures increase. In my classes, I teach a *biopsychosocialspiritual* model of human beings, stressing that we are a unity, and we will be resurrected. This is not to say that spirits and body are the same, but that human beings are remarkably complex and that every dimension of this unity influences and is impacted by every other. As I have studied the pharmacology of spiritual experiences, it has deepened this appreciation as well. I anticipate my thoughts on the neuropharmacology of spiritual formation, pharmacotherapy of mental disorders, and cultural attitudes toward new drugs may change in the next decade. Where the thought of medical marijuana was a scandal only twenty years ago, watching the cultural shift toward widespread acceptance of recreational use has been staggering. And while I have no problem with its medical use, I do have concerns about its complete decriminalization with minimal oversight for recreational purposes.

During my time as a psychology and neuroscience faculty member at Wheaton College, I have been asked to consult on a wide array of matters relating to pharmacology and religion by students, colleagues, mental health professionals, clergy, church members, friends, and family. These conversations have ranged from helping pastors understand how to counsel married couples in their congregations who smoke cannabis to enable sexual intimacy to students inquiring whether or not microdosing psilocybin to manage their ADD is a good idea. There are methamphetamine addicts who want to know if they should try ayahuasca to help them in their recovery, and there are seventy-somethings entertaining the use of ecstasy to reconnect with God. There are devout believers afraid that taking Prozac constitutes a lack of faithfulness, religious agnostics willing to give peyote a chance to open their inner eye, and atheists convinced that positive proof that there is no God is found in knowledge of specific neurotransmitter receptors in some brain regions that light up on an fMRI when they are praying. For every college student who has gotten drunk on a Friday night and slept with someone they regret, there is a friend or family member who has lost a loved one due to an opiate overdose. Over the past twenty years, I have attempted to have good faith, honest, and informed conversations with all of these people while striving to remain compassionate, orthodox, and faithful to my own Christian and intellectual convictions; it has not been easy.

These are not small questions that we are asking, nor are they hypothetical situations we are entertaining, but they are questions that demand a response. For example, if someone who is being treated for their PTSD under the care of a psychiatrist is administered Ecstasy as part of their treatment, should "insights" about their trauma that alleviate their symptoms trump doctrinal positions from their religious tradition? If people arrive at personal or universal truth claims incompatible with commonly held interpretations of their religious texts, how should we navigate or evaluate intrapersonal revelations of truth in light of truth claims obtained via other means (such as religious doctrine, sacraments or traditions, or with other individuals' intrapersonal experiences) that appear to be incompatible? While pharmacological investigation and understanding of how hallucinogenic, entheogen, and entactogen drugs work can provide us with insight into psychological consequences and potential religious frameworks, the manner in which these experiences are evaluated in the context of the religious tradition should be left an open question into which philosophers, theologians, and psychologists are not unimportant. Are we pursuing transcendence via stupefaction? Is our hope in pharmacology, or in Christ? When is MDMA a compassion-guided instrument of healing, and when is it worshiped as an idol of ecstasy? The wisdom to discern our motives and the means by which we live a faithful life will not be found at a pharmacologist's bench, or in an fMRI scanner, but it will be informed by them. Consider this a good-faith invitation to collaborate and discern together what faithful living looks like.

13

Spiritual Formation As If Wisdom Mattered

JAMIN GOGGIN

T HE SPIRITUAL FORMATION MOVEMENT within American evangelicalism, forged in recent decades, has been a movement of renewal and retrieval. Pioneered by luminaries such as Dallas Willard and Richard Foster, the spiritual formation movement has renewed a fundamental emphasis of historic evangelicalism—personal relationship with God. It has done so by retrieving spiritual classics and spiritual disciplines with a posture of irenic catholicity. Its impact on contemporary evangelicalism is undeniable, as many churches, seminaries, and Christian publishing houses have wholeheartedly adopted the language of "spiritual formation." However, despite its obvious impact on contemporary evangelicalism, the substance of what has been embraced remains somewhat vague.

What is spiritual formation? This fundamental question exposes rather quickly the plasticity[1] of the phrase *spiritual formation* in contemporary evangelical circles. Perhaps when the words are spoken on stage within the evangelical tent, much of the crowd resounds with a hearty "amen," but what exactly are they affirming? There seems to be an embrace of the movement as such, absent any real grasp on its teleology. It was this concern that Dallas Willard himself voiced to me not long before his death: "The spiritual formation

---

[1]I am borrowing this term from Uwe Poerksen's book *Plastic Words: The Tyranny of a Modular Language* (University Park, PA: Penn State University, 1995).

movement tends to get lost on people who think spiritual formation is about spiritual formation. It isn't about spiritual formation. It's about becoming Christlike. So if you watch some people, they're just doing odd things and they call that spiritual formation."[2]

Spiritual formation has become a kind of hobby within evangelical Christianity. Some people are interested in being gospel centered, some are interested in being missional, and others are interested in spiritual formation. Those interested in spiritual formation commonly embrace certain practices. I suppose these are the "odd things" Willard is referring to. They have a spiritual director. They practice silence and solitude. They talk about things like *lectio divina* and the Ignatian Exercises. They know their Enneagram number by heart. The oddity of such practices in contrast to more traditional evangelical practices like having a "quiet time" is by no means a statement about their validity. However, I would agree with Willard: often those that engage in these unfamiliar practices express their commitment to "spiritual formation," but perhaps struggle to define what it is beyond the doing of said practices.

The depth and durability of spiritual formation's impact on the future of evangelicalism (if there is one) rests on answering our fundamental question: *What is spiritual formation?* Like many renewal movements, the initial adventure of discovering new territory gives way to the demand of building a viable city. The original pioneers of spiritual formation saw something missing in evangelicalism and filled the gap. And yet, the time for bold adventure has passed and infrastructure is needed if the city is going to thrive. Pastors and theologians (or, perhaps pastor-theologians) are needed to build the biblical-theological infrastructure necessary.

The building project will require a lot of time and a large team. My hope is to do some initial identification of where we need to start building, and perhaps do a little bit of initial scaffolding. If Willard is correct, that spiritual formation is ultimately about becoming Christlike, then this is surely a worthy endeavor. In fact, I can hardly imagine a more fitting task for pastor-theologians whose work is fundamentally attached to the local church, filled with real people wondering what it means to "attain to the unity of the faith

---

[2]Taken from transcripts of a conversation I had with Dallas Willard at his home in May of 2012.

and of the knowledge of the Son of God, to mature manhood, to the measure of the stature of the fullness of Christ" (Eph 4:13 ESV).[3]

I will focus my attention in the present chapter on a critical piece of biblical-theological infrastructure—*wisdom*. I will do so with a particular emphasis on Wisdom literature, due to its unique canonical role of defining and describing wisdom—the art of living well. The spiritual formation movement has given little sustained attention to the resources of Wisdom literature. If Ellen Davis is correct that Wisdom literature "is spiritual guidance for ordinary people," then this is surely a glaring omission in a conversation dedicated to the nature of the Christian life.[4] What genre of the canon could be more fertile ground for discussion of the practical realities of being formed in Christ by the Spirit?

The lack of engagement with Wisdom literature in the spiritual formation movement is in many ways the inheritance of its evangelical heritage. For many, Job, Proverbs, Ecclesiastes, and Song of Songs (the traditional Wisdom corpus), are challenging to understand, much less apply. Our historical-grammatical hermeneutic often leads us to places of regressive debate about their original authors and readers. Our historical-redemptive hermeneutic often ignores their canonical contribution all together, finding no place for them in the narrative plotline of redemption. In populist evangelical readings these books offend tender sensibilities. The book of Job refuses to accept our God-protecting, self-soothing explanations for evil, and declares, "Bad things happen to good people." The book of Ecclesiastes upends every form of "prosperity gospel" imaginable with a torrential rejection of "think positive" pop-psychology. Song of Songs, well it doesn't mention "promise rings." The book of Proverbs is perhaps the most embraced, but often for the worst reasons. It is viewed as a tome of moralism that finally gets down to the business of dispensing with all the "saved by grace alone" talk and gives us concrete "*dos*" and "*don'ts*" that we can follow to ensure a life of success and happiness. I must confess it took me nearly fifteen years of pastoral ministry to invest considerable time focusing on Wisdom literature in my preaching and pastoral care because I wasn't quite sure what to do with these

---

[3]The ESV translation will be used throughout unless otherwise specified.
[4]Ellen F. Davis, *Proverbs, Ecclesiastes, and the Song of Songs* (Louisville, KY: Westminster John Knox Press, 2000), 1-2.

inspired texts. In recent years I have discovered Wisdom literature to be immensely "profitable for teaching, for reproof, for correction, and for training in righteousness" (2 Tim 3:16-17).

In this chapter I will initially invest in the development of a brief theology of wisdom, which will in turn fund a direct engagement with Wisdom literature—Job, Psalms, Proverbs, Ecclesiastes, and Song of Songs. As the rich resources of Wisdom literature are brought to the forefront, my hope is to provide a more sturdy biblical-theological foundation on which spiritual formation can stand. An ancillary benefit of grounding our understanding of spiritual formation in the categories of wisdom is its potential inner-church apologetic for the movement. Many within evangelicalism remain wary of entering the house of spiritual formation, but perhaps a letter of invitation sealed with the insignia of wisdom will strike a note of hospitality necessary for those who are cautious or concerned.

Jesus, the Wisdom of God

A proper exploration of Wisdom literature is dependent on first establishing our hermeneutical true north, Jesus Christ. To speak of wisdom is to speak of Jesus, and to speak of Jesus is to speak of his person and work. Jesus is both the fountain and fulfillment of wisdom. As the fountain of wisdom, Jesus, the eternal Logos, pours forth in his work of creation and redemption. As the fulfillment of wisdom, the incarnate Christ collects and completes the wisdom of Wisdom literature. Reading Scripture christologically necessitates both lenses—fountain and fulfillment.

Jesus, the fountain of wisdom. In 1 Corinthians 1 the apostle Paul provides us with a robust christological account of wisdom. According to Paul, Christ doesn't merely possess wisdom. He is "the wisdom of God" (1 Cor 1:24). This identification of Jesus is not rogue theological ingenuity, but faithful apostolic witness in keeping with Jesus' self-identification.[5] Paul goes on to argue that Christ is the wisdom of God *for us*. In the words of Paul, "Christ . . . became to us wisdom from God" (1 Cor 1:30). Christ, the

---

[5]In Mt 23:34 Jesus declares, "Therefore I send you prophets and wise men and scribes, some of whom you will kill and crucify, and some you will flog in your synagogues and persecute from town to town." Interestingly, in the mirror synoptic text, Lk 11:49, Jesus states, "'Therefore also the Wisdom of God said, 'I will send them prophets and apostles, some of whom they will kill and persecute.'" When Jesus speaks, the "Wisdom of God" speaks.

wisdom of God, gives himself to us climactically on the cross. Paul argues that the fountain of wisdom flows in the spilled blood of Jesus, and he recognizes that such a mode of wisdom appears foolish in worldly terms (1 Cor 1:20-25). The cross is a stumbling block to many, but to those with eyes of faith it is the height of wisdom—power in weakness, light in darkness, life in death.

While his cross-centered redemptive work is the climactic revelation of divine wisdom, this does not negate the significance of his work in creation. In Proverbs 8:22-23 Wisdom declares, "The Lord acquired/possessed me by bringing me forth at the beginning of his way . . . before his other earliest works. From everlasting I was woven together, from the very beginning, from the earliest times of the earth."[6] Wisdom continues in Proverbs 8:30, "Then I was beside him [constantly], like a master workman, and I was daily his delight, rejoicing before him always."[7] Who is this eternally begotten (brought forth) "master workman" establishing the created order? He is the one confessed in the Nicene Creed: "The only begotten Son of God . . . by whom all things were made." He is the one spoken of in John 1:1, "In the beginning was the Word, and the Word was with God, and the Word was God" and in Colossians 1:15, "He is the image of the invisible God, the firstborn of all creation." Jesus, the eternal Logos, is the source of all wisdom. His act of creation entailed a pouring forth of wisdom into creation.

Jesus, the fulfillment of wisdom. Jesus is not only the fount of wisdom, but also the fulfillment of wisdom. In Luke 24:44 Jesus himself declares that he is the fulfillment of the law and the prophets, but also of wisdom.[8] In short, Jesus is the fulfillment of Wisdom literature—Job, Psalms, Proverbs,

---

[6]This is the translation provided by Daniel J. Treier in *Proverbs & Ecclesiastes* (Grand Rapids: Brazos Press, 2011), 7. The present chapter does not afford the space to engage Treier's argument for the translation and the broader interpretive decisions he makes regarding the passage. That being said, it is important to signal my agreement with Treier regarding Proverbs 8.

[7]Treier, *Proverbs and Ecclesiastes*, 8. I am following Treier's affirmation of Bruce Waltke's translation here by including the word *constantly* in the ESV translation.

[8]In Lk 24:44 we read, "Then he said to them, 'These are the words that I spoke to you while I was still with you, that everything written about me in the Law of Moses and the Prophets and the Psalms must be fulfilled.'" Commenting on this verse, Marshall states, "It is debatable whether the reference is simply to the Psalms themselves as a primary source of messianic texts . . . or to the 'Writings,' i.e., the third division of the OT canon here named after its principal component. For the latter view. . . the three-fold division of the OT was in existence by this date." I. Howard Marshall, *The Gospel of Luke* (Grand Rapids: Eerdmans, 1978), 905. My argument is based on a "three-fold division of the OT" interpretation of this passage.

Ecclesiastes, and Song of Songs. Jesus, the one who has "knowledge of the Holy One" (Prov 30:3), is the one who "has ascended to heaven and come down" (Prov 30:4). His fulfillment of wisdom is made manifest in the primary features of his redemptive work—life, death, resurrection, and ascension. The incarnate Christ is the one Isaiah spoke of:

> The Spirit of the LORD shall rest upon him,
> > the Spirit of wisdom and understanding,
> > the Spirit of counsel and might,
> > the Spirit of the knowledge and the fear of the LORD.
> And his delight shall be the fear of the LORD. (Is 11:2-3)

Jesus' fulfillment of wisdom is demonstrated through the dual vocation of his incarnational life. Jesus is the ultimate student (or, child) of wisdom, and the ultimate teacher (or, sage) of wisdom. He fulfills both of these vocations embedded in the pedagogical logic of Wisdom literature. In Luke 2:41-52 we are introduced to Jesus as a missing child. His parents, Mary and Joseph, departed Jerusalem following the Feast of the Passover, only to realize Jesus is not with them in the caravan. Jesus remained at the temple. Luke provides us with this detail: "After three days they found him in the temple, sitting among the teachers, listening to them and asking them questions" (Lk 2:46). Here is Jesus, the faithful student of Israel, heeding instruction from the teachers of Israel. Of course, Luke emphasizes that Jesus has remained at the temple not merely to heed the wisdom of the teachers, but ultimately he has remained at the temple to be in his "Father's house" (Lk 2:49). Jesus has obeyed as a true and faithful child. He has heeded the call of Proverbs 1:8: "Hear, my son, your father's instruction." Luke concludes the story by emphasizing the reality of Jesus' maturation in wisdom. We read in Luke 2:52 that "Jesus increased in wisdom and in stature and in favor with God and man."

This scene in Luke 2 not only provides a window into Jesus' vocation as student, but also as teacher. The boy Jesus was not merely listening while in the temple, but he was also speaking. Luke tells us, "All who heard him were amazed at his understanding and his answers" (Lk 2:47). Jesus is the ultimate sage. This hint of his sagely vocation in his developmental years points us forward to the character of his pedagogical vocation throughout his public ministry. In the Gospels we see that Jesus' teaching is distinct in its authority and depth. We read in Matthew 7:28-29, "And when Jesus finished these sayings, the crowds were astonished at his teaching, for he was teaching them as one who had authority, and not as their scribes." As Jesus himself declares in Matthew 5:27-28, "You have heard that it was said . . . but I say to you."

Christ's fulfillment of wisdom culminates once again in his redemptive work on the cross. At the cross the deep things of God (Job 11:7) initially spoken in Job, Psalms, Proverbs, Ecclesiastes, and Song of Songs are ultimately proclaimed in the anguished cry of death. At the cross we discover that Jesus is the divine/human arbiter longed for by Job, one "who might lay his hands on us both" (Job 9:33). And yet, it is not only his death, but also his resurrection and ascension that fulfills this mediating hope of wisdom. Jesus, the one laid "in the dust of death" (Ps 22:15) is not abandoned to Sheol (Ps 16:10), but he, the Redeemer, lives (Job 19:25) and has "ascended to heaven" (Prov 30:4; see also Jn 3:13).

Reading christologically. If Christ is the wisdom of God and Scripture is his Word, then all of Scripture can fittingly be called "Wisdom literature." As the late John Webster reminds us, "Holy Scripture is a *unified* attestation of Jesus Christ, and so in an important sense a single, coherent text."[9] Holy Scripture is a unified word of wisdom precisely because it is a word spoken by the Word who is wisdom. If this is the case, then what is the unique role of Job, Psalms, Proverbs, Ecclesiastes, and Song of Songs in our journey of wisdom in Christ by the Spirit? While all of Scripture is a word of divine wisdom, Wisdom literature is not only a word *of* divine wisdom, but also a word *about* divine wisdom. To state it a bit differently, Wisdom literature provides us with the grammatical rules necessary for identifying "wisdom speak" in the rest of the canon. But, these grammatical rules are of no help if we don't first know the language we are speaking. This is where our christological lens for wisdom is helpful because the language we are speaking is Jesus Christ.

This christological lens of wisdom provides us with two hermeneutical principles for reading Wisdom literature wisely. First, we must read Wisdom literature *in light of Christ.* If Jesus is the fountain and fulfillment of wisdom,

---

[9]John Webster, *The Domain of the Word* (New York: Bloomsbury T&T Clark, 2012), 17.

then he is the Alpha and Omega of Wisdom literature. He is the source and the goal of Job, Psalms, Proverbs, Ecclesiastes, and Song of Songs. Jesus, the wisdom of God, speaks to us in these texts, ultimately about himself. The contours of his redemptive work, his life, death, resurrection, and ascension, shape the nature of wisdom. Second, we must read Wisdom literature *in Christ*. In the words of the apostle Paul, in Christ "are hidden all the treasures of wisdom and knowledge" (Col 2:3). Salvation in Christ is a rich reward indeed. In the words of Proverbs 3:13-14,

> Blessed is the one who finds wisdom,
>   and the one who gets understanding,
> for the gain from her is better than gain from silver
> and her profit better than gold.

To gain Christ and be found in him is to gain wisdom and be found in wisdom (Phil 3:8). Therefore, the cultivation of wisdom depends on union and communion with Christ. In salvation the Spirit unites us with Jesus, the wisdom of God, who is the way, the truth, and the life (Jn 14:6). In our ongoing communion with Christ by the Spirit we learn to walk the way of wisdom and to know the truth that leads to life. In this sense, the art of living well is the art of abiding in Christ. Ultimately, this means that the cultivation of wisdom is a relational endeavor. We must be wary of searching Wisdom literature thinking in it we will find life, all the while missing the One who is life (Jn 5:39).

This christological hermeneutic for reading Wisdom literature is "able to make you wise for salvation through faith in Christ Jesus" (2 Tim 3:15). We come to the text weary and worn out, as those who have not learned wisdom, and if we ask in Christ by the Spirit, wisdom will be given (Jas 1:5). Only those who are in Christ by the Spirit can truly read Wisdom literature in light of Christ by the Spirit. Christ has given us the "Spirit of wisdom," so that we might have "the eyes of [our] hearts enlightened" to know him (Eph 1:17-18). In the words of Christ, "When the Spirit of truth comes, he will guide you into all the truth, for he will not speak on his own authority, but whatever he hears he will speak, and he will declare to you the things that are to come. He will glorify me, for he will take what is mine and declare it to you" (Jn 16:13-14). The Spirit enables us to read *in Christ* and *in light of Christ*, so that we might *know Christ*. In the end, our search for wisdom in

Wisdom literature is an ever deepening of our communion with Christ (1 Jn 5:20). In the words of Gregory of Nyssa, "The true lover of wisdom has as his goal the divine One who is true wisdom."[10] If we desire wisdom, we must come to the "river of . . . delights" poured forth by the "fountain of life" (Ps 36:8-9). If we ask for the living water of wisdom, he is graciously disposed to offer it to us in such abundance that we will overflow with wisdom (Jn 4:10; Jas 1:5).

THE WAY OF WISDOM OR THE WAY OF FOLLY

Many theological motifs could be explored in our investigation of Wisdom literature. In this chapter I will narrow the scope of our investigation to a theological motif fundamental to the entirety of the Wisdom corpus, what is often called the "two ways"—*the way of wisdom* and *the way of folly.* Throughout Wisdom literature we find the way of wisdom paired with the notion of righteousness and the way of folly paired with the notion of wickedness (Ps 1:1). The language of *wisdom-righteousness* and *folly-wickedness* carries with it implications for a life of piety and ethics. The way of wisdom is "like the light of dawn" (Prov 4:18), which "leads to life" (Prov 10:16) and those who walk its path "he [God] loves" (Prov 15:9). The path of folly is "deep darkness" (Prov 4:19) ending in death (Prov 14:12), and it is an "abomination to the LORD" (Prov 15:9). In short, the way of wisdom is marked by the dynamics of fellowship with Yahweh and the way of folly is marked by the dynamics of prideful autonomy.

The heart of the way. Having briefly outlined the distinctions between the "two ways," we do well to invest more energy in contemplating the center of the way of wisdom. Simply put, the center of wisdom is the heart. The fountain of divine wisdom is poured into the heart, which is why the sage instructs us to "Keep your heart with all vigilance, for from it flow the springs of life" (Prov 4:23). If a life of wisdom begins with the heart, then we must contemplate the disposition of the heart required for the journey.

The knowledge of God is the theological first principle of wisdom. A quest for knowledge apart from the knowledge of God is the definition of foolishness. In the words of Gerhard von Rad, "The search for knowledge

---

[10]This quote from Gregory of Nyssa is from *Ancient Christian Commentary on Scripture: Proverbs, Ecclesiastes, Song of Songs*, ed. J. Robert Wright (Downers Grove, IL: InterVarsity Press, 2005), 34.

can go wrong because of one single mistake at the beginning. One becomes competent and expert as far as the orders of life are concerned only if one begins from knowledge about God."[11] The knowledge of God is not theoretical, but personal. As personal knowledge, it is both rational and relational. According to John Calvin, this knowledge of God necessitates knowledge of the self.[12]

A heart that possesses this double knowledge is marked by fear and love. In the book of Deuteronomy the "fear of I am" and the "love of I am" are synonyms.[13] Wisdom literature presents this relation of fear and love in a dialectic that is only resolved in eternity, where the redeemed will be like him, for they shall see him as he is, and where they shall know as they have been known (1 Jn 3:2). In the age of faith, fear and love both belong in the heart that knows God. There is a kind of simplicity of heart proper to those who have come to know God in the truth of his divine simplicity. The unity of these affections (fear and love) is grounded in the unity of God, who is powerful and holy, loving and forgiving. Ultimately, the fear of the Lord is a fear in love and the love of God is a love in fear. The way of wisdom is traced along the *trajectory of fear* and the *trajectory of love* in Wisdom literature. Both the fear of the Lord and the love of God function as foundational beginning points from which the student of wisdom must never depart. A brief mapping of these two trajectories will demonstrate the dialectical relationship at the heart of wisdom.

The fear of the Lord. Throughout the Wisdom corpus we are told the "fear of the Lord" is the beginning of wisdom (Prov 1:7; 9:10; Job 1:1; Eccles 3:14). In the words of John Donne, the fear of the Lord "is the art of arts, the root, the fruit, of all true wisdom."[14] Just as a painter depends on foundational principles such as rhythm, balance, and contrast to create a beautiful work of art, so too must the artist of wise living depend on this foundational posture of heart. But how could the fear of the Lord be the entry point of

---

[11]Quoted in *Discovering the Way of Wisdom* by Edward M. Curtis and John J. Brugalletta (Grand Rapids: Kregel Publications, 2004), 21.

[12]John Calvin, *Institutes of the Christian Religion* (Peabody, MA: Hendrickson Publishers, 2008), 4.

[13]Bruce Waltke notes, "Deuteronomy treats 'love of I am' and 'fear of I am' as synonyms (cp. 5:29 with 6:2, and 6:5 with Josh. 24:14; cf. 10:12, 20; 13:5)" in *An Old Testament Theology* (Grand Rapids: Zondervan, 2007), 161.

[14]This quote from John Donne is cited in the *Reformation Commentary on Scripture: Psalm 1–72*, ed. Herman Selderhuis (Downers Grove, IL: InterVarsity Press, 2015), 274.

true wisdom? While fear may contain notions of awe or respect, we must not lose sight of the emphasis on fear as such, and subtly reduce it down to those notions.[15] We are called to fear the Lord in Wisdom literature, and yet Scripture is full of God's command to have no fear in his presence.

The first time we encounter fear as a posture of heart in response to God's presence it is undeniably negative. In Genesis 3, Adam and Eve's fear of the Lord is a fear of condemnation and death in the presence of a powerful and holy God. Their guilt and shame has resulted in an attempt to hide from the presence of God. This is not the fear of the Lord leading to wisdom, but rather a fear of the Lord resulting from folly. Adam and Eve did not "see fit to acknowledge God" and as a result were given over "to a debased mind to do what ought not be done" (Rom 1:28). They acted as though there is no God (Ps 14:1) and embraced the folly of the devil, who is "wise in his own eyes" (Prov 3:7). Having rejected *wise fear*, Adam and Eve were left with *foolish fear*. They rejected a true fear called for in God's creation and command, and embraced a false fear called for by the serpent's lies.

Throughout Wisdom literature, the fear of the Lord leading to wisdom is tied to an encounter with a powerful and holy God, just as it was in Genesis 3. First, we see the fear of the Lord show up in the face of God's power. Its tone is heard in the voice of Job before the whirlwind:

> I had heard of you by the hearing of the ear,
>   but now my eye sees you;
> therefore I despise myself,
>   and repent in dust and ashes. (Job 42:5-6)

Second, we see the fear of the Lord show up in the face of God's holiness. Throughout Wisdom literature the fear of the Lord is connected to the law. We read in Ecclesiastes 12:13, "Fear God and keep his commandments, for this is the whole duty of man." Thus far, we imagine ourselves in the same position as Adam and Eve in the garden, made aware of our guilt and shame and fearful of condemnation and death. Here we stand, alongside Adam and Eve, before a powerful Creator who is holy and righteous, as those who have sinned and

---

[15]See Tremper Longman III, "Fear of the Lord," in *Dictionary of the Old Testament Wisdom, Poetry, and Writings*, ed. Tremper Longman III and Peter Enns (Downers Grove, IL: InterVarsity Press, 2008), 201.

fallen short of God's glory (Rom 3:23). How is the fear to be known here different from Adam and Eve's fallen fear? What makes this fear distinct?

In Psalm 34 we encounter the transition from one mode of fear to another. On the one hand we are told by the psalmist, "I sought the LORD, and he answered me and delivered me from all my fears" (Ps 34:4). And yet, we are told, "The angel of the LORD encamps around those who fear him" and, "Oh, fear the LORD, you his saints" (Ps 34:7, 9). There is a kind of *transformation of fear* taking place here grounded in the mercy and forgiveness of God. So, we read in Psalm 130:3-4,

> If you, O LORD, should mark iniquities,
> O Lord, who could stand?
> But with you there is forgiveness,
> that you may be feared.

The psalmist has come to "taste and see that the LORD is good!" (Ps 34:8), and unlike Adam and Eve, there is no need to be ashamed in his presence (Ps 34:5). Ultimately, what we discover is the fear of the Lord leading to wisdom is a fear of the Lord forged in love. In this sense, the dialectic of fear and love has a developmental structure. Knowledge of God who is holy and powerful, and loving and forgiving, is what defines *wise fear*.

The love of God. If wise fear is forged in love, and the fear of the Lord is a posture of heart at the beginning of wisdom, then it should be of no surprise to us that Wisdom literature presents the love of God as a companion posture of heart at the beginning of wisdom. In Proverbs 2 and Proverbs 8 we hear the initial call of wisdom. The invitation is not governed by the motif of fear, but rather love. "Lady Wisdom" calls young men to embrace her with the language of marital union, intimacy, affection, and romance. Lady Wisdom's invitation to seek her stands in contrast to Lady Folly's seduction. The imagery is intended to provoke the contrasting realities of the two ways, while appealing to the language of love. While Lady Wisdom offers that which has enduring value and is life giving, Lady Folly offers quick and cheap pleasure, which ultimately leads to death. In this sense, the beginning of wisdom is a wooing of the heart's desires down a path. Once again, Genesis 3 looms in the background. We read in Proverbs 3:18 that Lady Wisdom is "a tree of life to those who lay hold of her; those who hold her fast are called blessed."

This romantic language is not left at the beginning of wisdom's path, but serves as a trajectory of growth in wisdom throughout the book of Proverbs. For example, while Proverbs 7 warns of a literal adulteress, it also speaks theologically of Lady Folly. Likewise, the "excellent wife" in Proverbs 31 is not only a description of a godly spouse, but is also a description of Lady Wisdom in all her glory. One's commitment to Lady Wisdom is a lifelong covenant of love marked by an ever-deepening intimacy and delight.

The allegory of romantic love initiated in Proverbs is further developed in the Song of Songs. I agree here with Robert Jenson, who argues that Song of Songs "is about the love of Israel and the Lord, and to read it by construing theological allegory is to read what we call its canonical plain sense."[16] In Song of Songs the image offered by Proverbs 8 is exhausted with provocative detail. In the Song of Songs the young men of Israel have their burgeoning desires provoked and led down a path of embracing wisdom. Lady Wisdom finds a lead role in the Song of Songs as the bride pursued by the young man. The corresponding imagery is striking as we consider what wisdom offers and how the bride of Song of Songs is described. We read in Proverbs 7:4, "Say to wisdom, 'You are my sister,' and call insight your intimate friend," and in Song of Songs 4:9 we read,

You have captivated my heart, my sister, my bride;
   you have captivated my heart with one glance of your eyes,
with one jewel of your necklace.

We are reminded it is "Lady Wisdom" who is "better than jewels" (Prov 8:11). We read in Proverbs 3:3,

Let not steadfast love and faithfulness forsake you;
   bind them around your neck;
   write them on the tablet of your heart.

In Song of Songs 8:6 we read, "Set me as a seal upon your heart, as a seal upon your arm." What we learn from Song of Songs is that the beginning of wisdom is a union in love marked by desire and affection. What we learn in Proverbs is our love for Lady Wisdom is a response to her loving call. In short, we love wisdom because wisdom first loved us (1 Jn 4:19). Here we see

---

[16]Robert W. Jenson, *Song of Songs* (Louisville, KY: Westminster John Knox Press, 2005), 8.

clearly that knowledge of God is not a cold, cognitive notion, but rather one of radical intimacy and affection of the heart. Wisdom demands genuine experience as befits lovers becoming one flesh. And so, we discover that the love of God and the fear of the Lord function together as a foundational posture of heart guiding one's feet along the path of wisdom. To walk the way of wisdom rather than the way of folly is to embrace this dialectic of heart, as opposed to reducing wisdom to one posture or the other.

THE WAY OF JESUS

Having briefly explored the theology of the two ways presented by Wisdom literature, with a particular focus on the heart of the way of wisdom, we now turn our attention to Jesus. Wisdom can only be known in light of Christ. If Christ is the fountain of wisdom, it follows that the way of wisdom carved out by Wisdom literature is in fact the way of Jesus. The person of Jesus is *the way* (Jn 14:6). In his incarnation, Jesus has come not to forge a new path, but rather to show that he has been the path all along. He has come not as a new rock in the wilderness, but rather to reveal the truth that he is the rock by which the water of divine wisdom has always poured forth (1 Cor 10:4). As such, those who seek to follow Jesus are called to the dialectic of fear and love. Jesus calls his disciples to love God (Mk 12:30), but he also calls them to fear the Lord (Lk 12:5). The cross stands as the climactic moment in the redemptive work of Christ revealing the way of wisdom. Here we are called to see at once the power and holiness of God, and the love and forgiveness of God. At the cross, law and gospel meet. Christ takes on himself the condemnation and death we have feared, and extends to us mercy and grace. At the cross we are invited to know a hidden wisdom marked by loving fear, which seems foolish to the world, but to those who know Christ it is the wisdom of God.

As we observe the life of Christ in the Gospels, we also see clearly that Jesus is the fulfillment of the way of wisdom. As the faithful child of Israel, he never diverges from the path of wisdom marked by loving fear. The words of Isaiah's prophecy are fulfilled in the baptism of Jesus: "the Spirit of the LORD shall rest upon him" (Is 11:2). "The Spirit of counsel and might" (Is 11:2) leads Jesus from the waters of baptism into the wilderness. In the wilderness Jesus recapitulates the story of Adam and Eve in the garden. Faced with the serpent's ancient temptation of prideful autonomy, the true and faithful child, Jesus, delights in the "fear of the LORD" (Is 11:3). His repeated scriptural rebuttals of the devil reveal a heart that has delighted in the law of the Lord day and night (Ps 1:2). Rather than falling prey to Satan's temptation to realize his kingly vocation apart from the Father's will, Jesus declares, "You shall not put the LORD your God to the test" (Mt 4:7). Jesus fulfills the way of wisdom by embracing the path at the very outset of his ministry.

Jesus' fulfillment of wisdom is not only expressed through his vocation as the ultimate child, but also as the ultimate sage. We hear instruction in the way of wisdom all throughout Jesus' teaching ministry. We hear the subversive character of the way of wisdom articulated in his kingdom parables, where grace and judgment form a familiar dialectic. It is Jesus the sage who proclaims, "If anyone would come after me, let him deny himself and take up his cross and follow me. For whoever would save his life will lose it, but whoever loses his life for my sake will find it" (Mt 16:24-25). Jesus makes known a holy, powerful, loving, and forgiving God, calling people to know him.

Wisdom is only known in light of Christ, and as such wisdom is only known in Christ. By grace through faith we are united with Christ by a work of the Holy Spirit. As the apostle John meditates on the atoning work of the cross, which has made this union possible, he reflects on the impact it has on the way we understand fear and love. We read in 1 John 4:18, "There is no fear in love, but perfect love casts out fear. For fear has to do with punishment, and whoever fears has not been perfected in love." John is arguing here that there is an objective work of love accomplished in the cross of Christ, which has cast out *foolish* fear—fear of condemnation and death. And yet, John recognizes the reality of our being formed in this love and purged of this fear experientially in our ongoing communion with Christ. He recognizes it is not until we are ultimately "perfected in love" that we will no longer carry such fear.

And yet, this does not mean no fear remains. Rather, the way of wisdom known in Jesus entails not only the purging of *foolish* fear, but also growth in *wise* fear. The love of Christ made known on the cross, and shed abroad in the hearts of those who have been united with him, is a love that transforms fear of God in the human heart. For while the forgiveness and love we have received invite us to boldly draw near to the throne of grace (Heb 4:16), we are to do so with awe and reverence, recognizing our God is a consuming fire (Heb 12:28-29). If we are in Christ, we are in wisdom, and as such are those who are being transformed by love. As those who are in wisdom, we now begin the long road of coming to know God from the heart in such a manner that foolish fear is not only purged, but wise fear is cultivated. We are on a journey of growing in the dialectic of wisdom—fear and love. We are being formed into the image of Christ Jesus, who embodied in his incarnate life the way of wisdom we have been called into. We are called into an abiding relationship marked by a loving intimacy like that of the husband and wife in the Song of Songs. We are called to an abiding relationship marked by a fear of the Lord, who is sovereign and holy like Job before the whirlwind. Formation in Christ by the Spirit is formation in obedient love. As Jesus declares in John 15:10, "If you keep my commandments, you will abide in my love." The pilgrimage of formation into Christlikeness is a pilgrimage of wisdom, which begins in the heart that has encountered God in Christ in loving fear. It is a pilgrimage oriented by eternity. And so, we read in Psalm 136:1 that God's "steadfast love endures forever," and in Psalm 19:9, "the fear of the LORD is clean, enduring forever."

FORMATION IN WISDOM

If spiritual formation is ultimately about our union and communion with Christ, and if Christ is the wisdom of God, then Christian spiritual formation is a process of maturing in wisdom. It is first and foremost coming to know he who is himself wisdom, and it is consequently being formed in his wisdom by the work of the Holy Spirit. As we have already seen, this journey of wisdom begins in the heart formed in loving fear.

As I stated at the outset of this chapter, there is a great deal of work that remains to be done. A whole team of pastor-theologians is required to identify and develop the biblical-theological infrastructure needed to stabilize spiritual formation in the land of evangelicalism. I have endeavored to present one piece of infrastructure I believe to be necessary—*wisdom*. While I have explored the heart of the way of wisdom, many other elements of the pilgrimage mapped by Wisdom literature have remained unattended. Pastor-theologians must plunder the treasures of Wisdom literature with the questions of spiritual formation in hand, in order that we might present a rich vision of the Christian life centered on Christ to the church. The whole of Wisdom literature provides a vision of *the art of living well in Christ by the Spirit* that is marked by relational intimacy and practical import. In short, Job, Psalms, Proverbs, Ecclesiastes, and Song of Songs offer deep wisdom regarding the nature of abiding in wisdom and bearing the fruit of wisdom.

Contributors

Vincent Bacote (PhD, Drew University) is an associate professor of theology and the director of the Center for Applied Christian Ethics at Wheaton College in Wheaton, Illinois. He is author of *The Political Disciple: A Theology of Public Life* and *The Spirit in Public Theology: Appropriating the Legacy of Abraham Kuyper* along with contributions to other publications.

Daniel J. Brendsel (PhD, Wheaton College) is minister of college and twenties life and corporate worship, and the director of the Mission Training Academy, at Grace Church of DuPage in Warrenville, Illinois. He is coauthor of *An Interpretive Lexicon of New Testament Greek* and author of *"Isaiah Saw His Glory": The Use of Isaiah 52–53 in John 12*.

Marc Cortez (PhD, St. Andrews University) is professor of theology at Wheaton College and Graduate School. He has authored and edited many books including most recently *ReSourcing Theological Anthropology, Come Let Us Eat Together! Sacraments and Christian Unity*, and *Christological Anthropology in Historical Perspective*.

Jamin Goggin (PhD Candidate, University of Aberdeen) is a pastor at Mission Hills Church in San Marcos, California. He is the coauthor or editor of several books, including *The Way of the Dragon or the Way of the Lamb* and *Beloved Dust*.

Gerald Hiestand (PhD, University of Reading) is senior pastor at Calvary Memorial Church in Oak Park, Illinois, and the cofounder and director of the Center for Pastor Theologians. He is the author and editor of numerous articles and books, including *The Pastor Theologian: Resurrecting an Ancient Vision*, and *Beauty, Order, and Mystery: A Christian Vision of Human Sexuality*.

Joel D. Lawrence (PhD, Cambridge University) serves as the senior pastor of Central Baptist Church in St. Paul, Minnesota, and as faculty associate at Bethel Seminary in Arden Hills, Minnesota. Joel is the author of *Bonhoeffer: A Guide for the Perplexed*, as well as of numerous articles and book chapters.

Cherith Fee Nordling (PhD, University of St. Andrews) is associate professor of theology at Northern Seminary in Lisle, Illinois. She is the author of *Knowing God by Name: A Conversation Between Elizabeth A. Johnson and Karl Barth.*

Pamela Baker Powell (DMin, Pittsburgh Theological Seminary) is a retired Presbyterian clergywoman and pastoral theology professor/dean of students (Bethel Seminary-SW; Trinity School for Ministry). She now serves as a parish associate at Glen Ellyn Presbyterian Church and a pastoral counselor at Central DuPage Pastoral Counseling Center. A popular speaker, she is the author of various articles and a forthcoming book on friendship.

Andrew J. Schmutzer (PhD, Trinity International University) is a professor of biblical studies at Moody Bible Institute, and serves on the board of directors for MaleSurvivor. Andrew is the author and editor of numerous books including *Between Pain & Grace: A Biblical Theology of Suffering* (with G. Peterman), *The Long Journey Home: Understanding and Ministering to the Sexually Abused, Naming Our Abuse: God's Pathways to Healing for Male Survivors of Sexual Abuse*, and most recently "Reclaiming Beauty Amidst Brokenness," in *Marriage: Its Foundation, Theology, and Mission in a Changing World*. Andrew and his wife (Ashley) regularly speak on the issue of sexual abuse.

Rachel Stahle (PhD, Boston University) is pastor of the First Presbyterian Church (ECO) of Towanda, Pennsylvania. She is the author of *The Great Work of Providence: Jonathan Edwards for Life Today.*

William M. Struthers (PhD, University of Illinois at Chicago) is a professor of psychology at Wheaton College in Illinois where he coordinates their neuroscience program and teaches courses in neuroscience, psychopharmacology, and core studies. He has written several articles and chapters integrating science and religion/faith, and is author of *Wired for Intimacy: How Pornography Hijacks the Male Brain.*

Siang-Yang Tan (PhD, McGill University) is professor of psychology at Fuller Theological Seminary in Pasadena, California, and senior pastor of First Evangelical Church Glendale. He is an ordained pastor and licensed psychologist, and fellow of the American Psychological Association. He is the author or coauthor of numerous articles and books, including *Counseling and Psychotherapy: A Christian Perspective*, *Lay Counseling*, revised edition, and *Shepherding God's People: A Guide to Faithful and Fruitful Pastoral Ministry*.

Kevin J. Vanhoozer (PhD, Cambridge University) is research professor of systematic theology at Trinity Evangelical Divinity School in Deerfield, Illinois. He is mentor to the Augustine Fellowship of the Center for Pastor Theologians. Kevin is the author or editor of several books, including *Pictures at a Theological Exhibition: Scenes of the Church's Worship, Witness, and Wisdom* and *Hearers and Doers: A Pastor's Guide to Making Disciples Through Scripture and Doctrine*.

Todd Wilson (PhD, Cambridge University) is the president of the Center for Pastor Theologians, in Chicago. Todd is the author or editor of a number of books, including *Real Christian: Bearing the Marks of Authentic Faith* and *Mere Sexuality: Rediscovering the Christian Vision of Sexuality*.

Author Index

Subject Index

Scripture Index

CENTER FOR PASTOR THEOLOGIANS

The Center for Pastor Theologians (CPT) is an evangelical organization dedicated to assisting pastors in the study and written production of biblical and theological scholarship for the ecclesial renewal of theology and the theological renewal of the church. The CPT believes that the contemporary bifurcation between the pastoral calling and theological formation has resulted in the loss of a distinctly ecclesial voice in contemporary theology. It seeks to resurrect this voice. Led by the conviction that pastors can—indeed must—once again serve as the church's most important theologians, it is the aim of the CPT to provide a context of theological engagement for those pastors who desire to make ongoing contributions to the wider theological and scholarly community for the renewal of both theology and the church.

Toward this end, the CPT focuses on three key initiatives: our pastor theologian fellowships, our *Bulletin of Ecclesial Theology*, and our annual conference. For more information, visit pastortheologians.com.

More Titles in this Series

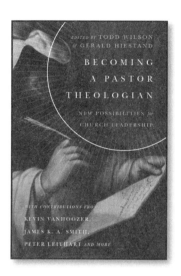

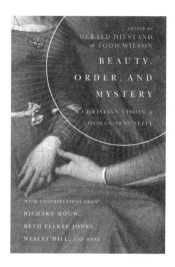

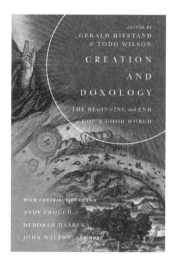

Finding the Textbook You Need

The IVP Academic Textbook Selector
is an online tool for instantly finding the IVP books
suitable for over 250 courses across 24 disciplines.

ivpacademic.com